The WOMAN TRIATHLETE

Christina Gandolfo

EDITOR

HUMAN KINETICS

Library of Congress Cataloging-in-Publication Data

The woman triathlete / Christina Gandolfo, editor.
    p. cm.
  Includes bibliographical references and index.
  ISBN 0-7360-5430-8 (soft cover)
  1. Triathlon--Training. 2. Women athletes. I. Gandolfo, Christina.
  GV1060.73.W66 2005
  796.42'57'082--dc22

                            2004020137

  ISBN-10: 0-7360-5430-8
  ISBN-13: 978-0-7360-5430-0

Acquisitions Editor: Martin Barnard; **Developmental Editor:** Leigh Keylock; **Copyeditor:** Patrick W. Connolly; **Proofreader:** Pamela Johnson; **Indexer:** Betty Frizzéll; **Graphic Designer:** Robert Reuther; **Graphic Artist:** Francine Hamerski; **Photo Manager:** Dan Wendt; **Cover Designer:** Keith Blomberg; **Photographer (cover):** © Brian Bahr/Getty Images; **Photographer (interior):** Dan Wendt, unless otherwise noted; **Printer:** United Graphics

Human Kinetics books are available at special discounts for bulk purchase. Special editions or book excerpts can also be created to specification. For details, contact the Special Sales Manager at Human Kinetics.

Printed in the United States of America   10   9

The paper in this book is certified under a sustainable forestry program.

Human Kinetics
Web site: www.HumanKinetics.com

United States: Human Kinetics
P.O. Box 5076
Champaign, IL 61825-5076
800-747-4457
e-mail: humank@hkusa.com

Canada: Human Kinetics
475 Devonshire Road, Unit 100
Windsor, ON N8Y 2L5
800-465-7301 (in Canada only)
e-mail: info@hkcanada.com

Europe: Human Kinetics
107 Bradford Road
Stanningley
Leeds LS28 6AT, United Kingdom
+44 (0)113 255 5665
e-mail: hk@hkeurope.com

Australia: Human Kinetics
57A Price Avenue
Lower Mitcham, South Australia 5062
08 8372 0999
e-mail: info@hkaustralia.com

New Zealand: Human Kinetics
P.O. Box 80
Torrens Park, South Australia 5062
0800 222 062
e-mail: info@hknewzealand.com

For my mom and sisters, who always cheer the loudest.

CONTENTS

ACKNOWLEDGMENTS

It's with gratitude that I recognize the many people who supported this project. First and foremost, thanks to the many talented women who contributed to this book: Lisa Bentley, Bonnie Berk, Gale Bernhardt, Lori Bowden, Kim Brown, Linda Buchanan, Libby Burrell, Britt Caling, Liz Dobbins, Heather Fuhr, Jackie Gallagher, Siri Lindley, Barb Lindquist, Bettina Younge, and Joanna Zeiger. Thanks also to Martin Barnard, Leigh Keylock, Matt Fitzgerald, John Segesta, Jay Prasuhn, John Yeast, M.D., and Jennifer Yeast.

INTRODUCTION

If you've done an all-women's triathlon, then the number of "testosterone-free" race series that have popped up across the country in recent years probably doesn't surprise you. From the long-standing Danskin Triathlon Series to newer races that invite women of all abilities to test their physical and mental limits, women-only events are wildly popular for good reason: they offer a kind of encouragement and "all-comers-welcome" attitude of the sport's early years. But mostly, all-women's races sell out rapidly because, in a sport where it's one person against the clock, they symbolize a team effort put forth by everyone from age group standouts to first-timers to make hundreds of individual goals and dreams come true.

It's this very idea of women helping women that created *The Woman Triathlete*. In its purest form, it's a shared approach by some of the greatest female triathletes and coaching professionals in the world—from world champions to Olympians—who offer up their wisdom to make every woman's triathlon experience more successful and ultimately more enjoyable.

While women have long participated in triathlon—consider that Lyn Lemaire beat two-thirds of an otherwise all-male roster at the second ever Ironman event in 1979 and that some of the sport's biggest stars continue to be women—when it comes to the amateur ranks, triathlon has long been identified as a cult sport in which lean, Speedo-clad guys on high-priced tri bikes rule the streets.

But recent years have seen a shift in amateur participation, with record gains being made among female participation. Races like those organized by the Danskin Triathlon Series boast some of the greatest participation rates worldwide. Likewise, equipment manufacturers are churning out women-specific bikes, apparel, and other gear at an unprecedented rate, and growth is being further spurred by training groups organized to raise money for charitable causes, all of which are supported in majority by women.

As such, women triathletes are becoming more knowledgeable about endurance training and at the same time becoming hungrier for information. It's no secret women differ from men in terms of both physical and psychological makeup, and a book aimed specifically at female triathletes is long overdue.

When you first glance at the table of contents of *The Woman Triathlete,* it might not look vastly different from other triathlon training books on the market. However, you can be assured that every word in this text is written by a woman with you—the female athlete—in mind.

Because it is a collaborative approach, you'll notice that the methods of some contributors, particularly in the training-specific chapters, may vary slightly. I have preserved these differences in the interest of showing that there is no one-size-fits-all answer to training. They are intended to open your eyes to subtle variations used by highly accomplished women that should ultimately be tested and combined to create a customized training regimen that is right for you.

The larger themes remain consistent: that the most effective training comes from building a strong endurance base that is enriched by both strength and speed, all of which are absorbed and further developed by adequate recovery. Within this scope, you will learn how to use core conditioning to increase your performance, how to eat for optimal endurance, how to train for everything from a sprint-distance race to an Ironman, what equipment you'll need to succeed, how to employ mental strategies that will guarantee your success, how to manage and prevent injuries, and how to maintain your triathlon-specific fitness while pregnant. Additionally, regardless of your strengths and weaknesses in the sport, you will gain insight from key training secrets from the world's best triathletes and coaches.

More than just an instructional manual, *The Woman Triathlete* is to be used as a training companion in your quest for peak performance. Think of it as both a trusted coach and a training partner that will remain at your side and motivate you on even the toughest of days. The text is designed to be used year in and year out—taking on new meaning each time it is read—and to grow worn and tattered with each new breakthrough performance.

Above all, remember that at the heart of this work is a collaboration and sharing of knowledge. As you gain insight with each new chapter make a point to impart what you learn to other women, encouraging them to become the best they can be. It's through this shared approach that you will become not only a more powerful athlete whose own training approaches are reinforced, but part of a movement in which women, every bit as much as men, continue to break through barriers that once existed only as hopes and dreams.

—*Christina Gandolfo*

1

Training in Three Sports, Excelling in One

Linda Buchanan, MS

In the world of single-discipline endurance sports, triathletes are often referred to as "jacks-of-all-trades and masters of none." Successful triathletes know better, however, and will wisely argue that competing in their sport requires a high level of skill that involves mastering three sports in one. And while it's true that many people enter the sport of triathlon having previously specialized in one of its three disciplines, those athletes who view their triathlon training as a cohesive undertaking aimed toward succeeding in *one* sport have the best results.

The ability to approach training in this manner requires strategic thinking and is not always easy, particularly for people who are new to the sport. Whether you are a beginner or a more seasoned triathlete, this chapter will provide you with ways to strategize your training to improve overall performance in swimming, biking, and running.

STRENGTHENING YOUR WEAKEST LINK

As in any sport, the ability to maximize your strengths in a given area can pay off in triathlon. However, a common mistake many people make is relying too heavily on their strengths and ignoring their weaknesses. Although it's not quite as fun to work on your weakness, that is often where the maximum benefit is found. In my own case, I began competing in age-group swimming at age 10 and went on to become a collegiate swimmer. It would have been easy for me to concentrate the majority of my triathlon training in the water, but since I was already a good swimmer, knocking a few seconds off my 100 repeats wasn't going to yield much greater results overall. There was simply much more to be gained from hill workouts on the bike and 400 repeats at the track. In other words, I'd see much faster finishing times by bringing my cycling and running up to speed with my swimming.

© John Segesta

This doesn't mean that you should take your strongest discipline for granted. Rather, you should spend some time investigating how much improvement you can reasonably make in each discipline and divide your training time accordingly. For instance, if you're a slow swimmer, a decent runner, and a strong cyclist, your training should reflect an emphasis on improving your swim, maximizing your run, and maintaining your fitness on the bike. Depending on your strengths, improving your weakest link (e.g., shaving one minute off your swim) will not always yield huge gains in terms of finishing times, but it can go a long way toward improving your overall confidence and enjoyment of the sport.

Maintaining strengths and improving weaknesses produce a unique skill in triathletes — that of mastering three sports in one.

Specific techniques for strengthening your skills in each discipline are discussed in detail in subsequent chapters.

UNDERSTANDING THE PURPOSE OF YOUR PROGRAM

One of the keys to successful training is to understand the whys behind your workouts. Too many people make the mistake of approaching their training from an "all-or-nothing" philosophy—going hard every time they train—or of simply plodding through their workouts, neglecting to push their body and mind to their performance potential.

A proper triathlon training program (as discussed in chapter 2) includes a base period in which you build an aerobic base to handle further training; a strength and endurance phase that increases your aerobic capacity; a speed and intensity period; and the all-important recovery phase, which is the period that allows your body to adapt to the training you have performed.

Failing to follow a structured plan will lead to subpar performance and will put your body at risk for injury. Even athletes who subscribe to a periodized training plan may still be tempted to stray from prescribed workouts. My best advice in this regard is to resist the temptation! You must listen to your body (do not train if you are overly fatigued), but if your program calls for a hard effort, you should give your all to reach your desired training effect. Conversely, if you are scheduled for a long, slow distance workout, any effort to push the pace will be counterproductive to your overall training. No matter which discipline you are training in, balancing endurance workouts with speed- and strength-building workouts is critical to peak performance.

Above all, however, consistency may be the most important factor in your development as a triathlete. You may not perform like a star every day or every time out, but the workouts add up, your body develops muscle memory, and your mind adapts to the challenge of training. Training has a cumulative effect, and while change and development can sometimes be subtle, sticking to both the hard and easy workouts (at the correct times) cannot be overemphasized.

APPROACHING THE SWIM

The swim is the shortest of the disciplines in triathlon, both in time and distance. In spite of that, a good triathlete cannot afford to underemphasize swim training. Whether you are a champion swimmer or a novice, your goal is to get through the first discipline of triathlon having expended the least amount of energy possible. The fresher you come out of the water, the more speed and power you will have for the rest of the event. And the more comfortable you are in the water, the easier you will get through the "thrashfest" known as triathlon swimming.

For swim training, many triathletes like to spend the majority of their time doing distance freestyle because that's what they will do in an event. However, to develop your swimming ability as efficiently as possible, you should include interval training to work on speed and $\dot{V}O_2$max, technique work to improve stroke efficiency and prevent injury, stroke work to prevent muscle fatigue and increase variety, and sprints to increase power and strength. To that end, joining a Masters swim program is highly recommended. Most programs have numerous triathletes on their rosters, and the coaches work to accommodate the triathletes. (More information on Masters programs, as well as swim training, can be found in chapter 3.)

To prepare for the swim in an upcoming race, the best strategy is to familiarize yourself with the swim course and conditions. If possible, you should swim the course (or a portion of it, depending on the distance of your race) before race day.

© Nigel Farrow

Become familiar with the course before the race — you'll have more confidence and can prepare for changes in terrain.

STRATEGIZING FOR THE BIKE

For a strong race, you must control your effort and energy expenditure on the bike segment, and you must know your goal pace based on what you have done in training. This will allow you to work as efficiently as possible while saving precious reserves for the run.

As with the swim, you should familiarize yourself with the bike course before the race. It's easy to think, *I'll just be following everybody, so it doesn't matter,* but you will be more confident and have much less anxiety if you can check out the course prior to the event. If possible, drive or ride the course in the days before the race to learn where the hills are, where you will be able to conserve energy, and where the technical sections exist. When you start the bike segment of a race, keep the distance to be completed in mind and try to settle into your pace as quickly as possible.

The key to pacing is time trialing—riding a set distance by yourself for time; basically, it's you against the clock. To become a good time trialist, you must learn to be smooth on your bike—pedal circles, avoid just pushing on the downstroke, relax your upper body, and concentrate. You can practice this by establishing your own course on roads you are familiar with and timing yourself on this course on a weekly or biweekly basis. To get maximum benefit, enlist a friend to go with you and take turns chasing each other. You will be surprised how hard you will ride to catch someone.

Near the end of the bike leg, use lower gears and try to spin as much as possible to loosen your leg muscles. Stand up on the pedals and move around if you can. Visualize the transition area. Ride slowly into the transition so you can regain your bearings for the bike–run transition. (Transitioning from bike to run will be covered in greater detail in chapter 4.)

SUCCEEDING ON THE RUN

For many, the run can be the most daunting discipline in triathlon because it requires a large volume of aerobic energy after two other aerobic events. As you gain time and distance on your running legs, however, you will begin to increasingly appreciate running—the pure physicality of it, the flight of escape, the release of breathing deeply, the awareness of supporting and working your entire body, and the opportunity to run in beautiful settings such as at the beach or on trails.

The run segment of a triathlon has the added pressure of cumulative fatigue; therefore, this must be incorporated into your training. To become more comfortable with running tired, your training each week should include a couple of runs that are done when you are tired—for example, at the end of your day or after another training session (running off the bike is critical to triathlon run performance and is covered in detail in chapter 5).

The run is also the discipline in which mental toughness must be relied on most heavily. Numerous techniques that can help in this regard are discussed in chapter 11. There are also a few basic things to keep in mind when approaching the run. First, remind yourself that it's easy to keep going when you feel good, but it's a sign of character to keep pushing through when things start to get tough. Remember that this is the challenge you signed up for: This is your moment—your chance to prove you can go the distance or earn that PR you've been training for all season.

Also, keep in mind that the most difficult moments in triathlon—whether they come in the swim, bike, or run—are often the moments when you learn the most about yourself as an athlete, and many times, as a person. View this as an opportunity (free wisdom along with peak fitness!), and use it to improve future performances.

LEARNING FROM THE MASTERS

One thing that I always did as a professional athlete, and still do, is watch and study better athletes. Theirs is a world that is based on fluid, efficient movements, which have typically been learned through countless hours of repetition and coaching. Careful observation of them (you may want to ask a coach to point out specific techniques you should look for) just may provide you with a shortcut in your training.

Break down what you see one step, stroke, or pedal at a time. Study one component at a time—for example, head position, pitch of hand on entry, stride length, or arm swing. What is the first movement of their arm after the catch in freestyle? How much upper-body movement is there when they are on their bike? How does their footfall change at different paces? After studying a technique, you should try it. Does it help? If so, use it, but always keep watching and learning.

By watching other athletes and trying their techniques, you will gain valuable body awareness, which will ultimately translate into faster times, less energy expenditure, and, of course, you will look great too!

FINDING A BALANCED APPROACH

Workouts within each discipline should include a balance of all the elements of training. Be sure to include interval, distance, and technique work. For even better results, you should balance your triathlon activities with complementary activities. Stretching and yoga should not be overlooked as means to increase flexibility and range of motion, leading to more efficient use of muscles and joints as well as injury prevention. Include strength training to help keep muscles balanced and also to prevent injury.

Balance also carries beyond your workouts. The best athletes are able to incorporate the demands of triathlon training into their lives, not vice versa. They are able to resist the temptation of letting training dictate their lives. Balance is key, not only to performance, but also to overall enjoyment. There is no doubt that competing in triathlon requires a level of discipline and sacrifice (if it were easy, everyone would be doing it!). But, be mindful of times when it's appropriate to choose family, friends, holidays, or Little League games over training. I'll bet anything that you will still be the most dedicated athlete on your block—even if you miss a workout.

KEEPING IT FUN

Although you'll never succeed in triathlon without dedicated training, one of the most important tips I can give you is to remember to incorporate some fun into your workouts. Most people get into the sport to have fun while challenging themselves and testing their limits, but triathlon can become all-consuming. You should try to include at least one workout per week (maybe even one per sport) that is just plain fun for you. Whether it's running on the beach, swimming in the ocean, or doing your easy ride with your kids, keeping your training as fun as possible will go a long way toward ensuring long-term success.

Of course, athletes sometimes have different definitions of fun. For instance, my favorite ride was also one of my hardest—a 30-mile ride on a hilly route. I worked the hills and rode easy when not on a hill. Even though this was ultimately one of my harder workouts, it was scenic, invigorating, and fun, and I looked forward to it every week.

Whatever is "fun" for you, if you indulge yourself, the results will come more easily, and the journey will be much more enjoyable!

Setting Your Triathlon Goals and Planning Your Training

Libby Burrell, MS

Your objective may be to finish the distance, achieve a PR, or win your age group, but the first challenge of triathlon is transforming the broad goal of "doing your best" into something tangible that will get you where you want to go. Doing this involves laying out clearly defined objectives that build on one another, as well as organizing your training in a step-by-step fashion that leads to increases in speed and endurance and, ultimately, peak performance.

All of the training plans in this book follow a periodized design that accounts for a gradual build in endurance, speed, and distance with the proper recovery time. This chapter will help you understand the philosophy behind the plans and help you modify your training to meet individual needs.

DEFINING YOUR OBJECTIVES

Triathlon is like a puzzle. To master it, you must break the larger "problem" into smaller challenges that will lead to your desired outcome. The first step is determining your objective. Do you want to finish your first sprint race? Become competitive at the Olympic distance? Work your way up to an Ironman? Earn a PR in your favorite distance? While each person's answer will vary and may include a combination of possibilities, the important thing is to know where you want to go before you plot a course to get there.

Once you define your objectives, you must break them into short-term goals that will build toward your ultimate objective. For instance, if you're hoping to crack the top 10 at an Olympic-distance race, you might set a short-term goal of shaving five seconds off your 400 repeats at the track to improve your 10K. Or, if you're a new triathlete, you may set a short-term goal of learning to do flip turns to improve the efficiency of your swim training.

I strongly urge anyone interested in measurable improvement to join a triathlon club, seek experienced training partners, or hire a coach (many affordable online options now exist). Regardless of your ultimate objective, these resources can help you to be effective in your goal setting. They will not only put you on the right course but will keep you motivated to get to that ultimate finish.

SETTING A TIME LINE FOR YOUR TRAINING

Planning your training schedule starts with deciding which race, or races, you will target in a given season. If you're an experienced triathlete, you will likely participate in a few different triathlons and select one event as your "goal race." Failing to single out a specific race to peak for will lead to performances that fall below your athletic potential. If you are a beginner, your goal race will likely be the first one you participate in during the season.

In selecting your goal race, make sure to include a minimum of 8 to 12 weeks for triathlon-specific training (for experienced triathletes who have a good aerobic base). If you do not have an aerobic base, you will need to add an additional 6 to 8 weeks of low-intensity training time in the three sports. This base phase of training is designed to condition the body to complete the training program and to ensure that you can go the distance without injury. Essentially, the base phase increases endurance as well as your ability to recover from workouts, but it does little to increase racing speed (building speed is addressed in the specific training plan itself).

Once you have determined your race schedule, it's time to make it all happen. Doing this means carefully planning your program to suit your needs and lifestyle in order to ensure compliance. Using a calendar, mark the race day for your goal race. Work backward from that date, and mark an 8- to 12-week training period commencing on the first Monday of week 1 of the program. If you have the time, consider using a longer training period to allow for some "practice races" in your overall plan. Using practice races as a training technique will be addressed later in this chapter.

The details of your plan will depend on your background in the sport. If you're training for your first triathlon, the focus will be on building a foundation that includes distance at a specific pace and working on skill and technique development. Beginners will spend most of their time on neuromuscular development to enable them to "go the distance" without the risk of injury to muscles, tendons, or joints (i.e., emphasis is not on speed development). Recreational triathletes will spend the endurance development phase focusing on form and duration of workouts at a heart rate that keeps them in the endurance heart rate zone with the occasional session being done at tempo pace. Athletes with a solid training base will focus on

Carefully executed long- and short-term goals will lead to breakthrough performances.

fine-tuning pace to reach a goal pace. For the most part, these athletes need to include a variety of work in the endurance, tempo, lactate threshold, and $\dot{V}O_2$max training zones to develop and manipulate their fitness in the direction of their projected goal pace.

As previously mentioned, the time line that you'll use in the development of your training plan is dependent on your background and objectives. If your objective is to merely cover the distance with no time or placing goals, then 8 to 12 weeks may be adequate time to prepare. On the opposite end of the spectrum, if an elite athlete is setting up a training plan for an extremely important event—Olympic trials, for example—she may follow a four-year plan that is carefully structured into training blocks that include second- or third-level priority races. Over this period, performance limiters are addressed and fine-tuned to elicit the required results; performance is also tested by means of low-priority and then high-priority races. A training period of 8 to 12 weeks will not suffice for this kind of plan.

Schedule workouts according to your own needs and the time you have available to train. If you decide to do a single workout session per day, you will need to fit in six sessions per week (two sessions per week in each of the three disciplines). If your schedule affords more time, you can be more creative in your planning and add multiple sessions per day. Keep in mind that in certain periods of the plan you will need to include transition (or brick) workouts that involve swimming immediately followed by biking, and even more important, biking followed by running. These types of workouts will be discussed in greater detail in subsequent chapters.

TRAINING WITH A PURPOSE

Training with a purpose is the key to a long and healthy triathlon career. A step-by-step progression in training that includes goals for both training and racing must be well thought out and adhered to. This plan needs to be adapted periodically based on the evaluation of short-term training and racing goals. Such planning should start with a list of your strengths and weaknesses. Each of these strengths and weaknesses must then be analyzed in terms of long-term goals you have set for yourself. Technique, endurance, speed, power, strength, and range of motion in each of the three disciplines should all be considered when determining your training profile. As mentioned, transition workouts should be included in any triathlon training program. Races can be won or lost here (particularly in shorter distance racing), and these workouts greatly improve your efficiency.

Everything in your program must exist for a specific reason. These reasons can include the development or training of endurance, speed, power, strength, recovery, skills, strategy, or tactics. Whether you are planning a macrocycle (annual or seasonal plan), a mesocycle (a training block that could be two, three, or four weeks in duration depending on the athlete and her response to training), or a microcycle (a weekly plan that includes the daily details of each session), all of these factors must be considered to provide purpose to your training.

Your 8- to 12-week training plan may include one long controlled pace session per week in each of the three disciplines and one session that is more specific—such as a tempo, interval, medium, or race pace session—depending on the phase of training you are in (base, intensity, or race phase). If you have developed your training program to include four-week training blocks, weeks 1 to 4 will focus on distance at a controlled pace (base phase). For weeks 5 to 8, you will shift to more specific sessions (tempo, intensity, or race pace sessions) while still maintaining a distance focus (intensity phase). The last two to four weeks of the program will concentrate on more specific racing aspects (race phase).

An athlete with a clearly defined plan needs to identify the exact purpose and objective of each session within the plan. This determines how the workout is executed and what the required performance outcomes should

Sample Training Summary Based on 12-Week Training Plan

Phase	Purpose	Workout type	Length of cycle
Base or general endurance phase	Build endurance and prepare the body for distance (at pace); work on technique refinement	Slow and medium endurance workouts that gradually build in duration and focus on form	Weeks 1-4
Specific or build phase	Build strength and speed while maintaining endurance	Endurance maintenance workouts mixed with hill training, tempo training, intervals, and race pace sessions	Weeks 5-8
Competition phase—Peak phase	Taper using reduced volume, pace manipulation, and competition preparation (distance at goal pace) with adequate recovery	Pace sessions or lower-priority races, tempo training, intervals, and specific race preparation sessions followed by strict bouts of recovery	Weeks 9-10
Competition phase—Race phase	Maintenance of strengths and participation in key races	Perform in key or high-priority races	Weeks 11-12

be. She can then determine pace, rest or recovery interval, and the maximum or threshold heart rates for the session. Athletes need to hit paces on the track or in the pool at a specific time of the season, and on many of these occasions, heart rates or perceived exertion scales are of lesser importance. Traditionally, these are the key track sessions in the specific phase of training. Other times, such as for the weekly long rides or runs, heart rate and training within a specific zone are of paramount importance. Thus, with a shift in required outcome for each of the workouts mentioned, there is a completely different set of training and feedback requirements.

If your main goal is to merely "go the distance," the emphasis of your training should be a steady progression of volume (volume could also be related in terms of hours instead of distance covered) to the point where the total race volume can be managed comfortably at a consistent pace. If your goal is a PR, a careful manipulation of frequency, duration (time), volume (distance), and intensity (speed or effort) is in order. It is the manipulation of these variables into a sensible and effective plan that determines a successful program.

Again, the key is doing enough to provide a training effect but not so much that it breaks you down. In fact, some coaches even advocate structuring training to be "recovery based" as opposed to "work based." Recovery-based training (Goldsmith 2002) involves planning training cycles based on an athlete's recovery abilities as opposed to the volume and intensity of workloads she can endure in a specific time. The theory is that recovery-based training allows for individualization based on the ability to adapt to the stresses and strains of training. It takes into consideration the genetic variation (such as muscle fiber type distribution) of an athlete by allowing her recovery ability to determine training loads. When an athlete is unable to recover between sessions due to personal life issues, this type of training also allows the coach to prescribe training loads appropriate to the athlete at each point in time. Furthermore, training can be modified to meet an athlete's situation on a session-by-session basis.

STRUCTURING WORKOUTS TOWARD ACHIEVING A PEAK

As mentioned, the key to a successful training program is a careful mix of work (with a specific purpose) and planned periods of recovery. Many plans have a great mix of tempo work, quality sessions, hill repeats, long runs or rides, and drill and technique sessions but fall seriously short on recovery periods in the daily, weekly, monthly, or season plans. It cannot be emphasized enough that without the careful injection of rest and recovery into the program, all this good work can be in vain. It is during the recovery or rest periods that major gains or improvements are made. Schedule one rest day per week, and you will be surprised at how much of a difference it will make in your performance.

With this in mind, structure a plan that allows you to first build a solid base or foundation, where the focus is on volume and technique. As previously mentioned, this is referred to as the base phase or general endurance phase of training. Then, focus your attention on building strength and working on strength endurance (strength/strength endurance phase). Once you have built a solid endurance and strength base, your attention should shift to specific speed and intensity work based on the distance you will be racing. This is often referred to as the build phase or the specific phase. You must make sure that you enter this phase with a solid grounding in endurance and specific strength endurance training in order to get the most out of the speed phase and then the racing phase. Keep in mind that strength, especially sport-specific strength, eventually translates to speed.

Endurance work and strength training must be maintained through all the subsequent training phases (while the emphasis may shift to more specific speed and pace work). Races, key workouts, or time trials that are carefully scheduled throughout the plan will give you a good indicator of the success achieved throughout each of these phases.

DETERMINING WEEKLY TRAINING TIME

The most effective way to determine training volume is in terms of hours. This includes the hours spent swimming, biking, and running and any form of cross-training you include as part of your program. Training hours are based on the time available in your daily schedule and will vary depending on whether you have major time restrictions or are a competitive athlete looking to move up to the pro ranks. Setting lofty goals for the number of training hours can result in overtraining or feelings of failure (not being able to meet the goal), while not doing enough can leave you short on general fitness and with disappointing results.

If you're a novice, concentrate on total weekly hours. This can also be expressed as training time per session per day for each component of the program. Once you set long-term goals over an extended period (for a year or more), it's time to calculate annual training hours. If you have done all this before and want to start working on training hours for the upcoming season, you may want to consider a 10 to 15 percent increase in hourly volume if you are working toward longer distance events. If, on the other hand, you are sticking to shorter distances and have been performing well on current volume, there is no need to increase the hours. In fact, in some cases you may want to look at reducing the annual hours and varying the volume of intensity work. This may lead to better performances both in training and racing.

If you are a more experienced triathlete, once your annual training hours have been determined, you can plan the number of hours per week that you will devote to training (keeping in mind that you need to gradually build through each training block and allow sufficient time to recover and reap the benefits from your hard work). If your training is organized in three-week training blocks, week 3 will include reduced volume or hours compared to weeks 1 and 2. The same applies to the fourth week if you have designed training blocks of four weeks in duration. The idea is to increase the volume at the beginning of a block and reduce it at the end. So, in a four-week block, the volume is increased from week 1 through 3 and then reduced in week 4.

Although this is the generally accepted model of progression, many athletes have experienced success with a training block that alternates one week of higher volume or intensity work followed by a week of lower volume and lower-intensity work. For athletes who struggle to recover from the progressive loading, this alternate approach may prove successful. The general rule is not to increase the volume (hours) or intensity by more than 10 percent per week. Many coaches only use this 10-percent rule when determining the volume of intensity work in their key swim, bike, and run workouts. By sticking to the 10-percent rule per week for these sessions, you can safeguard against injury and overtraining. For other sessions where endurance is the focus, the volume may be increased by as much as 15 to 25 percent. For example, a two-hour bike ride in the endurance training zone in week 1 may be increased to a two-and-a-half-hour ride the following week. This is a 25-percent increase in volume (hours). As long as the workout is kept in the same training zone, this approach is acceptable;

Log It!

Keeping a training log provides an invaluable resource in pinpointing what works for you and what does not. Note specific information about training days, recovery days, and race days, including the following details:

- Workout or race specifics (type, distance, intensity)
- Pace or cadence maintained
- Time of day
- Weather conditions
- Nutrition information (before, during, and after the effort)
- Heart rates
- Sleep patterns
- Stress level of the day
- Summary of how you feel before and after the workout or race

---

if the session moves more toward a lactate threshold effort (which is performed at high intensity), it is better to keep the volume increase at a safe 10 percent. In other words, you may increase volume or intensity, but not both simultaneously (unless you venture into "crash type" training that requires very careful monitoring and a careful balance of recovery periods included in the mix).

SELECTING TRAINING RACES

Training races carefully positioned within your plan can be vital "dress rehearsals" that give you critical information regarding your training progress. Coaches and athletes often interject training races (B or C category races) into the overall plan in preparation for the key race (A category). These races should be planned for the "down" or recovery week of each training block to ensure that you have rested adequately to perform at the level for which you are aiming. Depending on whether you regard the race as a lower (B or C) category training race, the length of taper will vary. For some races, you may want to "train through" them (no taper), and for others you'll want to back off volume or intensity for three to five days or even longer. If your focus is on sprint events, you might add single-discipline racing events to your training plan. Events such as a 10K run, a 1500-meter or open-water swimming event, or a criterium or road bike race are invaluable in determining how your training is progressing. Athletes training for the longer events can do the same but need to ensure that they do not plan too many distance events in their prerace training phase. Duathlon (run/bike/run) or aquathlon (run/swim/run) events are great for fine-tuning speed endurance and also for practicing transitions.

Like other areas of your training, all forms of racing that are planned prior to your main event must serve a distinct purpose. They can be planned to determine training progress, or they can be regarded as tune-up events for a high-priority race. In many cases, athletes and coaches plan such events to replace the week's quality combination workout and train right through the race without backing off any more than they would before a weekly track workout. This is a mistake if you have planned the race as a tune-up race. It is important to back off, if only slightly, to ensure that the race brings out the quality you are looking for. You want it to meet both the speed and the speed endurance requirements of the given workout while also providing a motivational boost for your goal race.

Preparation races must not dominate the plan but rather should be carefully positioned to complement the program. A common approach is to have a practice race planned in each training block of your program and also two weeks out from your main event. The key to preparation races is sticking to your objective for the race—whether it is to go the distance at a specific pace, to focus on one of the disciplines (e.g., shave two minutes off your 10K), or to improve your transitions. Race frequently (but not so often that it inhibits your recovery) and race smart and with a purpose, saving your best performance for your key race.

SETTING LONG-TERM TRAINING AND RACING GOALS

Although it's easy to get caught up planning for the short term, your plans must ultimately be directed toward long-term training and racing goals. Many elite athletes plan in terms of four-year cycles to peak during the Olympic year. This affords coaches and athletes the liberty to adopt a long-term approach to the development of the athlete. Within the four-year plan, each year is approached with a specific focus, and the training and racing goals are specific to each cycle. This approach allows specific strengths and weaknesses to be addressed in a more comprehensive way that leads to greater adaptation.

This type of long-term approach to racing and training can be used successfully for any level of athlete. You may not be training to make the Olympic team, but you can adopt a similar tactic to meet your own long-term goals—for example, qualifying for the Hawaii Ironman with an age-group win. Too often, athletes want to achieve everything in their first season only to walk away injured or disappointed. Instead, you should plan races and training over a two- to four-year period and leave yourself room (and time) to develop new strengths and to become better adapted in your fitness. This will add a new dimension to your racing and will ensure long-term enjoyment of the sport.

Nine Steps Toward Planning Your Training

- Outline clearly defined objectives for your training and racing that are challenging yet realistic, precise, and measurable.
- Select a goal race.
- Ensure that your time line is in accordance with your background and your specific objectives for your goal race.
- Avoid setting lofty goals in terms of training hours; this can result in overtraining or injury.
- Assess your strengths and weaknesses.
- Include a careful mix of training that has a specific purpose as well as planned periods of recovery.
- Make certain everything in your program has a specific purpose.
- Include training races that are carefully positioned within the training plan to provide feedback about training progress.
- Ensure that your short-term goals lead to a bigger, long-term objective.

Streamlining Your Swim

Barb Lindquist

Because the swim is the shortest of triathlon's three disciplines—both in time and distance—it's commonly underemphasized in training and racing. Triathletes who are not strong swimmers may see it as the "necessary evil" before the bike and run, while others merely overlook it as a warm-up before the real race begins. In reality, the swim is critical to a strong race in which both energy and time are maximized. A poor swim can instill self-doubt, fear, and frustration, while a strong effort in the water encourages confidence and feelings of power—and also puts you in a competitive position among the field.

As a swimmer since age eight, I consider the water my home. And although I have had some great successes in swimming and triathlon, I work hard every day on evolving my technique and transferring my pool ability to open-water racing. In swimming, there are always improvements to be made. Triathletes with a swimming background may not always swim as fast as they once did in the pool, but they can certainly become more efficient and race savvy, saving energy for the rest of the race. Likewise, beginning swimmers can make huge improvements with structured training and technique work.

This chapter will address technique in three parts—body position, how to use the arms and core as one powerful unit, and drills to improve both of these aspects of swimming. The benefits of participating in Masters workouts, and how to transfer your pool knowledge to racing in the open water, will also be discussed.

BODY POSITION

When you think about body position, remember this one simple fact: It's a drag to have drag. If you think being aerodynamic is important on the bike, being hydrodynamic is even more important during the swim. This is because water is a denser medium than air. An easy way to visualize the concept of reducing drag is to pretend there is a camera just beneath the surface of the water filming you from the front. The goal is for your cross section to look as small as possible. Ideally, the camera sees the top of your head and shoulders, with the rest of your body (belly, chest, hips, and feet) tucked into the same profile created by your head and shoulders. In other words, your head and shoulders are breaking the water, and the rest of your body is tucked into their draft. This sounds easy enough, but it's tougher when you actually start to pull, breathe, and kick—all important elements of swimming!

The idea of reducing drag through body position has driven the evolution of swimming technique in the 25 years since I began swimming. When I learned to swim, perhaps like many of you, I was taught to have the water line halfway between my hairline and my goggles. Basically, I was looking forward, and I remember coming home from workouts with a stiff neck. Today, swimmers are taught to keep the head in a more neutral position, looking somewhere between the bottom of the pool and just slightly ahead. The water line hits more at the top of your head instead of your forehead.

Think of your body as a teeter-totter with the pivot point somewhere in your midsection. If you are looking forward and your head is held high in the water (as swimmers used to be taught), your hips would be forced lower in the water. The frontal cross section that a camera would see would show more than just your head and shoulders. The camera would also capture a bit of your chest, hips, and feet. But if you look down, lightly pressing the front of your teeter-totter (i.e., your chest and head) down, then your hips and feet will rise. You will actually feel your butt on the surface of the water. New swimmers generally struggle with sinking hips and legs because their head is held too high in the water. For the teeter-totter idea to work, you must have a strong midsection. Your teeter-totter can't be broken in the middle; otherwise, you might be pressing your chest down and sticking your butt high in the water with your legs still dragging on the bottom of the pool.

Swimming down the pool with your head looking down and your body in line is not difficult. The tough part comes when you need to breathe. For every action of the head, there is a reaction of the body. Keeping your head still while not breathing requires concentration, but keeping your head streamlined while breathing is a challenge for even the best swimmers. Two common mistakes when breathing are lifting the head and tilting the tip of the head either left or right. Remember, for every action there is a reaction. If you lift your head, your hips will sink. If you turn your crown left, your hips will move right to balance your body in the water. Both increase the frontal drag profile. It is easy for a friend to stand at the end of the pool to see if you are guilty of either. If you are lifting your head, think about pressing the crown of your head down, almost lifting the chin when breathing. Another trick is to keep one eye in the water. If you are breathing right, close your right eye, then try to see just above the surface with your left eye. You can gradually progress to seeing only water. If your head is turned left or right when breathing, you might be looking back toward your feet or under your armpit. Think of looking more directly to the edge of the pool.

The second major element of body position involves rolling side to side. You have less drag in the water when you are on your side. Imagine there is a skewer running from the tip of your head down through your hips (like a shish kebab!). Your body is "in-line." You can't break that skewer as you are being rotated left to right.

When you breathe, your head can't move independently from your body. To breathe, you must roll your body so that you are on your side. When you are done breathing, you roll your head and body together so that you are looking down again. Since you don't breathe every stroke, on those where you don't breathe, you still want to roll your body, but your head is left looking downward. When it is time to breathe again, the head picks up the rhythm of the roll, joining the body.

I will talk more about the importance of this roll when I discuss the arm pull and timing, but as far as hydrodynamics are concerned, your body is faster in the water when it is on its side.

Think of perfect body position as free speed. By reducing drag, you go faster without working harder. It requires concentration and attention to detail in workouts, but physically you will have more energy for the bike and run because you aren't fighting the water.

The swim should maximize time and energy, setting you up for a strong bike and run.

© Nigel Farrow

CREATING OPTIMAL PROPULSION

Of course, having perfect body position while just floating in the water won't win you any races; in fact, it won't move you forward. You need to use your arms and legs for propulsion. A number of techniques should be considered when attempting to move yourself through the water as quickly as possible, including the catch position, snapping and rolling (coordinating the snapping of your hips with the roll of your body), and kicking.

The Catch Position

Your arm is a huge paddle, and you want as much surface area for that paddle as possible to "pull" water. Stretch your arm in front of you and bend your elbow so that your hand is under the elbow. This is the "catch position." You are pressing the outside of your elbow forward, slightly shrugging your shoulder and lifting your shoulder blade up and off your back. Notice all the paddle surface area you have in the forearm and upper arm. When you pull, you try to maximize that surface area as long as possible. Now, if you "drop the elbow" when you pull, you are basically leading back with your elbow, and the only surface area you get is the skinny part of your upper arm. In the water, this is called "slipping" through the water. Obviously, the more surface area you pull, the harder it is on your muscles. That's why people take the easy route and slip, because they don't have the strength to pull all that water.

So you know catch position—that high elbow with the fingers pointing down on the front of your pull—but what do you do once you achieve that high elbow position? Start thinking of your arms as extensions of your body core, not as independent appendages pulling you through the water. If you can start to use your core to help you pull your arms, you are on your way to mastering a major swimming concept.

Let's combine the principle of the high elbow with the idea of the arm as an extension of the core. When you enter your hand in the water, you want to get to that catch position as quickly as possible. The old school used to teach entering the hand halfway between the head and full extension, gliding the hand forward under water to full extension, then starting the pull. The problem is that at full extension, most people drop their elbow and push their hand forward to create drag. The new theory is to enter the hand close to full extension with the elbow already in a high elbow position. Your hand enters at a 45-degree angle to allow air bubbles to slip off. Your fingers point toward the bottom of the pool while you roll to your side and get your hand and body into the catch position quickly.

Once in the catch position, think of your arm, shoulder, and lats as one unit. They are your anchor. While on your side, to pull your arm you must snap your hips to the other side, and your arm will automatically pull in a proper **S** pattern under your body. Try it on land right now. Bend over at the waist, with your right arm in catch position and your left hip pointed behind you. Rotate your hips and shoulders so your left hip is down and your right hip is behind you. The arm naturally pulls.

Snapping and Rolling

As your hand pulls through the water, you should always have your fingertips pointed toward the bottom of the pool. This will help keep your hand deeper in the water and away from your chest, ensuring that your hand catches still water instead of moving water. Many beginners make the mistake of having their fingers parallel to the bottom. My coach in Australia always says to have your hip "open the door" for your hand. This means that before the hand clears the hip, the hip should roll up toward the surface of the water. If you are aggressive with the hand entry (without slapping), you are aiding the hip snap. It's almost as if you are quickly rolling to your side.

The movement of your arm above the water (during the recovery phase) can affect your body position and catch. If the upper arm is low and parallel to the surface of the water, it is very difficult to roll the shoulder. Plus, as you enter the hand, the hand might tend to cross over your center line. You want that upper arm and elbow to be above your body, either with a high elbow and the hand dangling below it or with a straighter arm recovery (high elbow with hand above the elbow). Remember, you want to look as "skinny" as possible from the end of the pool, and this high elbow recovery will ensure both that and an efficient shoulder roll.

Speed is created by the dynamic of how quickly you can snap the hips and pull the arms while keeping the elbow high and the body position efficient. Speed is part arm speed, part strength, and *all* technique. All swimmers have experienced a 25 where they have spun their wheels while working hard but swimming sloppy. For "clean" speed, you need a quick arm cadence that is aided by your core. This will allow your hand to move faster as it pulls from the entry to exit. The more strength you have, the faster you can do this. But it is specific high elbow strength that is needed. To achieve this, every upper-body exercise you do in the gym should be done with a high elbow.

I've seen beginners experience moments of brilliance with this hand–hip connection and speed. But it might only last a 25 before those little muscles that keep the elbow up, the head in line, and the hips snapping get tired and lose coordination. Be patient and you'll be able to increase it from a 25 to much longer.

The Kick

Not much is said about the kick when it comes to technique. Here are three concepts to keep in mind: First, you want to have a "tight" kick, meaning you keep the feet within that cross section of the head and shoulders (no wide, floppy kicks). Second, be conscious of what your feet do when you breathe. Many people will stop the kick or float the legs very wide when they breathe. Practice keeping the feet tight and kicking while breathing. Third, ankle flexibility is important. Flexible ankles will help keep your feet parallel (as opposed to perpendicular) to the bottom of the pool, allowing for increased propulsion. Kicking while wearing fins can increase ankle flexibility, as can sitting on your ankles and rocking back gently. Increasing ankle flexibility should be a gradual process and should be done carefully because the ankles are a delicate joint.

For those of you who are poor kickers, there is good news. If you maintain proper body position, your legs should float to the surface. It's ideal to use them for propulsion, but don't worry if they are just dragging along in the draft as long as they don't negatively affect your body position.

Some people believe that since triathlon involves cycling and running after the swim, you should kick as little as possible while swimming. But I believe that if you naturally swim with a strong kick in workouts, your legs will be able to handle that same effort in a race. I use a strong six-beat kick throughout my training and racing, and I've always considered it a benefit to my swimming. If you find that your legs tire in the swim because of overkicking, you may need to learn to swim a main set with an intense upper-body effort while relaxing the legs.

IMPROVING TECHNIQUE WITH DRILLS

Drill work is key to reinforcing proper technique, strengthening the small muscles that tire easily, and teaching neuromuscular memory. Drills should never be rushed. You should feel playful and ready to experiment as your body moves through the water. Drills are great to do as part of your warm-up. They can reinforce good technique before you start a main set. They are also great in a cool-down. If your technique was sacrificed in a hard set, you can use drill work to remind yourself of proper form.

Following are seven of my favorite drills and information on how and when I like to use them.

SCULLING

The sculling drill concentrates primarily on the feeling of the high elbow in the catch of the stroke. In this drill, you are on your belly, your head is looking down, and you are kicking. Your elbows are on the surface of the water, and you are pushing them in front of your shoulders. You should feel like you are shrugging your shoulders. When you look left or right underwater, you see your elbows. Your hands are pointed at the bottom of the pool and are sculling slowly back and forth (like windshield wipers) a few inches in front of your elbows (see figure 3.1). Your palms point out as you scull out, and your palms point toward each other as you scull in. You should feel like you are pressing the outside of your elbows forward. This is a flexibility issue, so it might feel a bit uncomfortable, especially if you normally swim with a dropped elbow. To breathe, lift your head up, just like sighting for a buoy; then put it down and rebalance your body. This drill focuses on using the high elbow catch, feeling the water with the sculling hands, rebalancing the body after sighting, and kicking. A 25 at a time is enough for this drill, but you can do multiple 25s throughout your workout. When swimming after sculling a 25, you should feel like you are catching more water with the high elbow. You should feel really smooth. At the start, you may only hold this awesome feeling for 20 yards, but eventually, as you get stronger and teach those elbows to stay high, you'll be able to hold it for the whole workout.

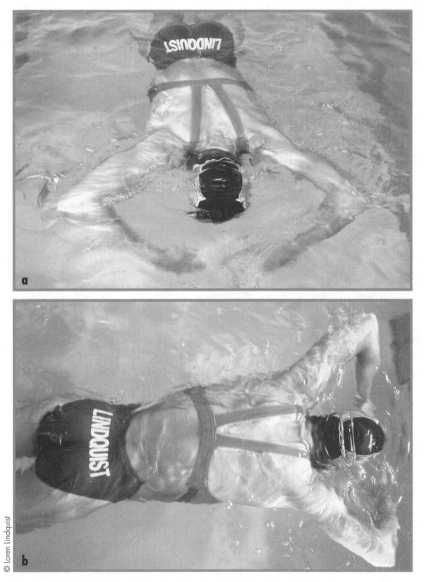

© Loren Lindquist

Figure 3.1 Sculling: *(a)* **front view and** *(b)* **overhead view.**

CATCH AND SNAP

A high elbow underwater timed with a dynamic hip snap is the key to swimming efficiency. The catch and snap drill slows everything down so that you can really feel the timing involved in swimming. You enter your hand, pointing your fingers toward the bottom of the pool while pressing the outside of your elbow forward (see figure 3.2). This gets you to the coveted catch position. While on your side, hold your position for a second to really feel the high elbow. Then initiate the rest of the arm pull with an aggressively fast hip snap, accelerating the hand past the hip. You will find that you spend a few more seconds than normal on your side as you feel that high elbow, but then you quickly roll to the other side because of your quick hips. I love doing this drill in warm-up because it gets me to slow down, feel the catch, and be dynamic with an aggressive pull. It's not a physically demanding drill, so feel free to test it at longer distances.

© Loren Lindquist

Figure 3.2   Catch and snap drill.

LEFT ARM/RIGHT ARM ONLY

If you're able to master this drill, you have all the components of the perfect stroke. In this drill, you have one arm down at your side while the other is pulling. You must roll the shoulder of the arm that is not pulling. That shoulder clears the water when it rolls up. Then, while the pulling arm is recovering above water, you force it to point toward the bottom of the pool (see figure 3.3). This drill works on body alignment (you will zigzag down the lane if your head is out of alignment when breathing), kicking (it's critical to maintain a steady kick since there's a lull in forward momentum when you recover the arm), body position (if you lift your head to breathe, your hips will sink), body roll, and arm strength. If you build up to doing 300 straight for each arm without feeling like you are wiggling, you have arrived at the destination called *perfect stroke*. This is a power drill, creating strength because you are pulling with just one arm. I like to do this drill either in conjunction with other strength components, such as pulling or IM work, or at the end of the workout for that little extra effort to work my shoulders.

Figure 3.3   Left arm/right arm only drill.

FIST DRILL

The fist drill is an excellent means of getting a "feel" for the water. Swimmers use the term *feel* to describe the feeling of getting a handful of water. The fist drill involves simply swimming with your hands closed in a fist to initially take away that "feel." When doing the fist drill, you will feel like you aren't going as fast down the pool. But then, when you open your hands up, you'll feel like you are pulling a great volume of water. I use this drill on sets where I am alternating between really fast swims and easy recovery swims. I do the fist drill on the easy recovery, and I open my hands up for the fast swims. My hands feel twice their normal size. Note: If you have a tough time keeping your hands closed during this drill, look for fist gloves at your local swim store—they confine your hands in the fist position as you perform the drill.

FINGERTIP DRAG/ZIPPER

If you are a "swinger" who struggles with shoulder roll, this drill is for you. A swinger is someone whose arms are wide from her body on the recovery. Unfortunately, it is impossible to get a good shoulder roll if you have a low arm recovery. Remember, if your coach is watching you from the end of the pool, you want to look as "skinny" as possible, keeping the recovering arm close to your body. The fingertip drag drill involves simply dragging your fingertips along the surface of the water when they are in the recovery phase (see figure 3.4). This forces a high elbow recovery. You can still cheat on this drill by dragging your fingertips on the surface of the water wide from your body. To eliminate this temptation, use the zipper drill. This drill has the same purpose as the fingertip drag drill, but on the recovery you rub your thumb up your side to the armpit—"zipping up" your side (see figure 3.5). On both drills, you will notice that you are getting a fantastic body roll because of the high elbow created.

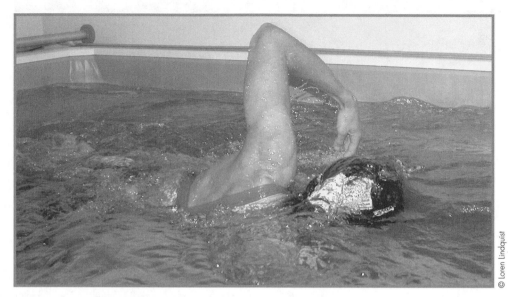

Figure 3.4   Fingertip drag drill.

Figure 3.5   Zipper drill.

SIGHTING

Swimming head down in a pool works fine, but it's not very realistic for open-water swimming. During a race, you'll need to lift your head to see through traffic in front of you and to locate buoys. Since I'm usually leading the swim, I sight every sixth stroke. For me, when my left hand enters the water, I press down on it to lift my body and head out of the water only as far as necessary (see figure 3.6). Then I turn my head to the right to finish the breath and rhythm. In fact, in a flat lake swim, I will lift my head only to under my goggles. In an ocean swim, I wait until I feel on the top of a swell, and I might need to lift my head higher. I like to use a sighting drill in swimming repeats, lifting my head to look at the end of the pool every sixth stroke, or maybe three times a lap. You can put an orange cone at the end of the lane to train yourself to focus on the color that most buoys are, but sighting on a swim bag or coach can be good as well. Concentrate on rebalancing quickly after each sighting, pressing down to get the hips up within one stroke.

© Loren Lindquist

Figure 3.6 Sighting.

STROKE COUNT

Counting the number of strokes it takes to do one length of your pool can help you become more efficient. There is an ideal balance between the number of strokes it takes and your time. For example, I can cross a 25-yard pool in 11 strokes if I really slow my stroke down and glide more, but my time would be 18 seconds. I can also cross the pool in 16 strokes in 13 seconds. Which is better? Well, if I'm swimming a sprint race, then I'd go with the 16 strokes, but I would work on decreasing that number (through strength work and drill work for efficiency). But I'm a triathlete who concentrates on 1500-meter swims in open water. And since I can't hold that 16 stroke/13-second speed for the whole race (yet!), and the 11 stroke/18 seconds is too slow, I find a balance between the two for my race pace. I can do this by doing a set of 100 repeats at race pace. I count my strokes per length and throughout the set. I then find the average number for that set. For example, for me it might be 14 strokes. Knowing this, when I am in the middle of a main set and I'm getting tired, I can count my strokes to make sure I am staying efficient. If my number is higher than 14, that may mean that I am dropping my elbow and slipping through the water, or it may mean that my kick is tiring or even that I'm not rolling enough on my side to allow a good hip snap.

Just by counting the number of strokes and by knowing what I usually do, I can tell whether I'm efficient. I can also use this drill when I am experimenting with a new technique principle. The goal is to work on my technique so that I can decrease the number of strokes per length while keeping the same time, or keep the same number of strokes per length but in a faster time.

MASTERS SWIMMING

Racing all over the country and the world has given me an opportunity to swim with many different Masters programs. One thing I've learned is that the types of swimmers and the coach have a huge influence over the program. The swimmers might be focused on racing at meets or merely on getting in some social time with a bit of exercise. Or, they might be triathletes who are desperately trying to strengthen their weak link and move up to the next lane.

Masters swimming can be a great way to learn structured swim training and efficiency drills, providing you find a coach and group that will complement your goals. Make sure to discuss your swim and triathlon goals with the coach before joining a program. If the program is a good fit, swim with a Masters group for at least two workouts a week. Swimming by yourself on easy days is fine, but swimming with others who are faster than you can be a great motivator to improve your own swimming. Plus, swimming with a group adds a social element to your training and is a lot more fun.

Choose your workouts. Many big swim programs have set workouts on certain days. For instance, Monday is long aerobic sets, Tuesday is sprint day, Wednesday is stroke work, and so forth. If you have the flexibility in your work and personal schedule, I suggest balancing three types of workouts: short speed work, anaerobic threshold (race pace) work, and technique or IM work. All workouts will have a component of each of these, but the main emphasis will vary.

Talk with the coach. As mentioned, when you join a swim program, you should arrange to talk with the coach. First tell her that you are interested in technique tips, not just hammering out meters. The coach may then be more open to stopping you during a set to provide personal instruction. Secondly, give a copy of your race schedule and swim goals to the coach. She may not look at it again, or she may really help you peak for your races. Either way, you will make her feel like a part of your journey and "team."

Learn the lingo. "Descending, fast average, negative split, rotating IM . . ." The lingo of swim workouts can sound like a foreign language at first. Don't be afraid of the unknown, however. Don't spend the entire workout swimming freestyle at the same pace and effort just because you don't understand what the coach is saying. Without holding up the group, ask the coach or a fellow swimmer to explain the workouts. If the workout is rolling along too quickly to inquire during the workout, do so after the workout or in the locker room. Be encouraged by the fact that within two weeks you will most likely absorb all the language you need. See also the sidebar on page 32.

Learn to swim other strokes. Too many triathletes fall into the trap of thinking they only need to practice freestyle since that's what they will swim in a race. Big mistake! I am a huge believer in the benefits of doing IM training. And, no, IM does not stand for Ironman. IM is *individual medley,* which involves swimming equal distances of butterfly, backstroke, breaststroke, and freestyle in that order. Some triathletes think that IM stands for grab your pull buoy and paddles to swim free. There are many benefits to IM training. First, by using different muscle groups, you are building a more well-rounded musculature. Second, it is easier to get your heart rate up in IM training and ultimately increase your lactate threshold levels. Third, it adds variety to your workouts.

Richard Quick, my swim coach at Stanford, used to say that if you are a freestyler and you swim only free in practice, you are "dulling your sword." Specifically, each stroke can help your freestyle. Butterfly strengthens your core, creates coordination, and can build upper-body strength; backstroke stretches your pecs; and breaststroke pull has the same high elbow scull as the freestyle catch. As a swimmer for more than 25 years, I still love doing IM work and regard it as key to strength development and mental sanity in the pool.

Learn to read the pace clock. It's difficult to know if you are getting faster if you don't know how fast you are going. In a big program, it's easy to just follow the leader without looking at the clock. Learning to do fast "time

Common Training Terms

Build: To increase in effort and/or speed over a specified distance.

Interval: The time given to complete a distance, plus rest. For example, if the interval is 50 meters in 1 minute 45 seconds, and it takes you 1 minute 30 seconds, you have 15 seconds rest before beginning the next interval.

Rest interval: The time between completing one distance and beginning another.

Descend: To swim each repeat in an interval at a faster pace. In doing so, your actual swim time for each interval decreases, or "descends."

Set: A number of repeated swims at specified distances with a rest interval between each effort. For example, doing six sets of 50s means swimming two lengths (or one lap) without stopping, and then resting for a stated period. To complete the full workout, you would repeat this six times.

Fast average: Within a set, each given distance is fast (in time). The goal is to maintain each distance consistently fast.

On the top/on the bottom: An expression used to signal when a group will start a distance or set. Starting on the top means at the 60-second mark on the pace clock; starting on the bottom means at the 30-second mark.

Circle swim: Done when there are more than two swimmers in a lane. Swimmers swim up on the right side and return on the left. As a matter of lane etiquette, each swimmer starts five seconds after the swimmer in front of her to allow space between each person in the lane.

Stroke: Optional stroke workout, usually any stroke other than freestyle (the crawl).

Qual/dist: The first half of the workout is swum distance freestyle; the second half is sprints.

IM: Individual medley—all four competitive strokes in the order of butterfly, backstroke, breaststroke, and freestyle. Each stroke is swum one fourth of the total distance.

Negative split: The second half of the swim is swum faster than the first half. For example, in a 500-meter swim, if the first half is swum in 5 minutes, the second half must be done faster, with a final result under 10 minutes.

Warm-up: The beginning period of a workout in which the body prepares for the impending effort. This is a critical portion of any swim workout to maximize effort and reduce the risk of injury.

Cool-down: The final period of a workout in which intensity is decreased while the body's cardiovascular and muscular systems recover.

math" makes swimming fun. For instance, try choosing one technique aspect to change on a repeat to see if you go consistently faster or slower. The only thing that drives a swim coach crazier than a kid not knowing when to leave on a repeat is an *adult* who doesn't know how fast she is swimming.

Take a peek at the fast lane. Without being a distraction, find a spot to hang out underwater in the fast lane. You can use the lane line to keep you submerged. Look at what the faster swimmers are doing with their body position, arm pull, and kick. You can watch them from above water to see how steady their head position is and how they aren't wiggling down the pool. As a caution, keep in mind that even the fastest swimmers don't have perfect technique. They may be doing something contrary to what you've learned while still swimming faster than you even hope to. If you see something questionable, consult your coach before making any changes to your technique.

Videotape your technique. The best way to improve your technique is to watch it. My husband told me repeatedly that I was not rolling far enough on a nonbreathing stroke. No matter how many times he told me this, I thought I was doing it correctly. It wasn't until I saw myself on video that I believed him. Underwater taping is ideal, but you can learn quite a lot from above-water taping. Here is what I suggest: Grab a couple of tri-friends or Masters swimming buddies. After a good warm-up, tape each other in three speeds—easy, 1500-meter pace, and sprint pace—from both the front view and by walking alongside the pool. Then have a potluck party and be sure to invite your coach and spouses for extra ribbing. If you each offer to pay the coach $20 for his time, the investment would be well worth it. You can learn so much from watching what others do both right and wrong. Remember, for every action in swimming, there is a reaction. Even a novice eye can pick up some basic mistakes.

Here's what to look for: From the frontal view, is your hand crossing over the center line created by your spine, or are you rolling your body onto that center line? Are your hips wiggling left to right instead of rolling as a unit with your shoulders and body? When you breathe, is your head moving left or right or lifting up, or is it staying in-line with your spine? Are your arms recovering wide and flat, or are they close to your body helping you roll? From a side view, when you breathe, are you lifting your head or do you keep one eye in the water? At the catch of the stroke, do you drop your elbow or does it stay high? Is your hand slowing or accelerating at the hip exit? Do you have a dynamic hip snap? And what about those beautiful legs that triathletes just love to use so much? Does your kick drift wide and stop when you breathe, or is it steady with small kicks throughout the stroke? I can't stress enough how quickly you can change your stroke when you see yourself swim.

MASTERING OPEN-WATER SWIMMING

There are very few triathlons that feature a pool swim. However, every other body of water is fair game—rivers (with or without currents), lakes, canals, and oceans. Each body of water presents its own set of challenges, but that's the joy of triathlon—overcoming challenges! Transferring your pool swimming to the open water can sometimes seem like changing to a different sport. However, by arming yourself with a few tips for race day you can calm your nerves and make yourself a better overall swimmer. It is one thing to read the following tips, but the more times you race, the easier the swim will get. As good a swimmer as I was when I started triathlon, it took me at least a year of racing to start coming out of the water first and to maximize all my years in the pool.

Where to Line Up

Do you remember the Pythagorean theorem from geometry? It says that the square of the long side of a triangle is equal to the sum of the squares of the other two sides. When applying this theorem to triathlon swimming, it tells you that if you line up on either the far left or the far right (where there aren't that many people), you will not have to swim many more meters to the first buoy than if you line up at the shortest line in the middle (where everyone seems to congregate). What Pythagoras didn't know is that lining up on the outside saves you wasted energy and possible elbows to the nose. Whether to line up far right or left depends on a few things. First, if you are swimming a clockwise course, the first turn will be to the right. In this case, I like to line up on the far left so that if everyone merges at the first buoy, I will be on the outside of the merging mess. That gives me the option to swim wider around the first buoy instead of being merged into. Second, there may be a current or wind that could push you left or right. If possible, watch earlier waves to see if the group generally drifts one way or the other. Or, you can do a float test: While floating, focus on a point on the shore and see if you drift one way or another. Once you know whether there is a drift, you can decide where to line up.

Deciding whether to line up in the front, middle, or back of the wave depends on what your goals and strengths are for the race. Decide which type of triathlete you are. If you're a newbie who hasn't raced much and feels finishing is the primary goal, line up at the back of the wave. When the gun goes off, count to at least five before you start swimming. This will allow the masses to go and will give you a bit of clean water. Plus, you get to actually see all the women in front of you going for it. Very inspirational! If you have a few triathlons under your belt, and you are confident in your swim and not afraid of people swimming around you, try to find someone who is faster than you and line up next to her. That way you can get on her feet and draft her in the swim. If swimming is your strength, then you want to line up in the front, sprint out fast, and try to get no one on your feet. If someone is on your feet, she is actually slowing you down, so drop her!

Sighting During a Race

Going back to geometry, remember that the shortest distance between two points is a straight line. You can use this in your swimming, but you must choose two stationary points—your body moving through the water is not a stationary point, but the turn buoy is. While standing on shore, look toward the turn buoy to see if there is anything on the other side of the water to align it with. In a lake or river, there may be a building or a hill with trees on top. The buoy and the other visual point behind it are your two stationary points. While you are swimming, keep those two points lined up to help you know you are swimming a straight line. Staying on course is a lot easier after you've made the last turn and can keep sighting toward the swim finish.

As mentioned in the drills section, you must find a rhythm within your stroke to lift your head to sight. I find that the more often I sight, the easier it is to find the buoy when I lift my head. When in a calm body of water, you only have to lift your head to right below the goggle line. While in the ocean, it is ideal to sight when you feel a swell carrying you up high. Don't always trust the feet in front of you to be swimming a straight line!

© Nigel Farrow

The start of an open-water swim can be fast. To prepare, practice it in training or start at the back of the pack where you'll be less likely to be in the mix.

Pacing

In a pool, you need only to count the lengths to know how far you've swum. In the open water, it is more difficult to know how far you've swum. If possible, inquire about the approximate distances between the turn buoys. Is it a square course of 500 meters to the first buoy, 500 meters across, and 500 meters back to shore? Is it a rectangular course of 300, 900, and 300 meters? Are there other buoys between the turning buoys that are equally spaced along the longer sections? By finding out the distances to the major turn buoys, you can divide your energy expenditure, pace yourself better, and stay focused.

If you were swimming 1500 meters in a pool, ideally you would start out the first 200 comfortably and build from there so that you have even 100 splits. An open-water swim is a different story. The start of an open-water swim is fast. Blame it on nerves, wanting to get clean water, or the competitor in all of us, but the pace is usually faster than what you'd do in the pool. Knowing this, you can either train for it or you can be very aware and try to avoid it.

Warm-Up

Because the swim is first, your swim warm-up is more critical than the bike or run warm-up. Before the race, have a goal time of when you want to be in the water warming up. Depending on the number of waves and the individual venue, you may or may not get to warm up on the course. If you can warm up on the course, practice both the swim entry and exit. You should practice these the day before the race if possible. If it's a beach start, count the number of steps you'll take in the water before it gets too deep to run. Then when the gun goes off, all you need to do is count that number and do a shallow, flat dive.

Besides practicing the entry and exit, you must warm up the body. Think about how long it takes in a pool workout to feel good in the water. This may be 10 to 15 minutes. Once you have swum a bit, do three or four surges of 20 strokes, starting the first one at race pace then building to your starting pace.

If the water is really cold, you have a decision to make regarding whether to get in at all. I think it is important to get in the water before the race, but only if you know you will be able to warm up outside the water before the race starts. Under no circumstances do you want to start the race cold.

TRANSITIONING FROM SWIM TO BIKE

Preparation for the "fourth leg" of triathlon, as transitions are sometimes called, begins long before the gun goes off. Some transition skills are specific to the racing venue, and others can be practiced in training. First and foremost, you should show up at the transition area on race day with plenty of time before the race begins. Fifteen more minutes of sleep is less critical than 15 more minutes spent familiarizing yourself with the transition area and taking time to relax. During your prerace preparation, either the day before the race or race morning, you should run the flow of the transition area—what I call your *ins and outs*. Run from the swim exit to your bike, then push the bike to the mount line. Continue this for the bike in and run out, then the finish line chute. When you are running out of the water to your bike, notice any changes in terrain. Are there steps, dirt, rocks? While finding your bike, how many racks did you pass? Does your rack have a sign? How far down the rack is your bike? On the left or right? I put my red-and-white-striped Stanford towel under my bike so that while I run down the rack, I need only to focus on the ground for the towel instead of looking at all the bikes. If you practice running to your bike while in a calm frame of mind, you will have a much easier time finding your bike during the middle of battle.

During the race, be methodical about your exit. Don't try to multitask. First, get out of the water and run 5 to 10 steps with high elbows to help get your knees up. I can't tell you how many beginners I have seen try to get out of their wet suit while still walking out of the water. It's hard enough to run out of the water without having your arms behind you pulling on a strap. Second, put your goggles up on your forehead so you can see well. Third, if you are wearing a wet suit, grab the pull strap with one hand, and with the other one, release the Velcro neck strap. While running up to your bike, pull the wet suit down to your waist. Fourth, when your wet suit is down to your waist, take off your goggles and cap. If you do this too early, your hands will be too full to remove your wet suit. This sounds logical, but in the heat of the battle simple things can be forgotten. Lastly, if there is a water station on the way to the bike, splash some water on your face to rid yourself of salt or lake water.

Try to simplify your transition. Unless there is cold weather, you only need to put on your cycling shoes (unless you have them attached to the bike already), glasses, and helmet. Since you have already practiced your bike exit, you know where to push your bike with a light jog. After you cross the mount line, get on your bike and enjoy the ride!

Building Power on the Bike

Bettina Younge, PhD

As the longest of triathlon's three disciplines, the bike arguably offers the most opportunity for achieving a strong finish. A strong, well-executed bike segment can make up for weaknesses on the swim and set you up for a quick and powerful run. The key is to build efficiency during your bike training and become accustomed to riding at a consistent pace that ultimately leaves just enough fuel in the tank for a strong finish.

In this chapter, you'll learn about aerodynamics and bike fit that affect your performance, drills to improve technique and efficiency, strength and endurance workouts, and tips for transitioning from the bike to the run.

AERODYNAMICS AND BIKE FIT

How fast you finish the cycling portion of a race depends on the power you're able to produce during the ride. Ultimately, power output depends on just two variables: force and speed. Very simply, it depends on how hard you push and how fast you pedal. The three forces you need to overcome to move forward are air resistance, rolling resistance, and, on climbs, gravity. Because gravity and rolling resistance depend on weight, most cyclists try to minimize weight. This is most easily achieved by using a lighter bike and componentry, but these come at a high cost. Rolling resistance also depends on the road surface, as well as the make, thickness, and pressure of your tires. The biggest resistive force, however, is air resistance, which is dependent on your speed and frontal surface area. At 20 miles per hour on a flat road (gravity is zero), rolling resistance makes up less than 25 percent of the total resistance, while air resistance makes up more than 75 percent. The most effective way to reduce air resistance is to draft behind (or even next to) another rider. For a triathlete without the option to draft (drafting is not permitted in most amateur triathlon racing), reducing frontal area has the greatest effect on performance. Aerodynamic equipment—such as bike frames with tear-shaped tubes, deep-dish wheels and discs, narrow water bottles, tight skin suits, and streamlined helmets—can reduce some of the frontal area. However, a rider's body is by far the biggest obstacle. Bike fit for a triathlete is therefore optimized with biomechanical fit and aerodynamic positioning; many triathletes even choose to ride a less comfortable setup in favor of better aerodynamics. Keep in mind, though, that a comfortable setup that incorporates aerodynamics will usually result in increased power output. Because road cyclists are allowed to draft, they tend to place greater importance on biomechanical fit, comfort, and handling of the bike than triathletes do, but triathletes would be well served in finding a comfortable setup.

It is relatively easy to adjust a traditional bike fit to a more aerodynamic fit. The most cost-effective investment is a set of aerobars. Better yet, using an ergo-stem along with your aerobars will allow you to more completely adjust the position of your handlebars. A second seat post and saddle combination will allow you to quickly move back and forth between a road position and a time trial position with just one bike frame. Because a traditional road bike fit often results in better (i.e., easier) handling of the bike, it is useful to be able to switch back and forth between setups. You can convert your bike to match your workout—aerodynamic position for solo efforts and time trials or a traditional bike fit for group rides and hilly routes. Before you adjust your bike fit to a more aerodynamic position, measure (and mark with tape) how your bike is set up. It is always a good idea to have the option of going back to a position that already works for you. Once you have the necessary measurements, move your saddle forward one or two centimeters. Because this reduces the distance from your saddle to the bottom bracket, you may also need to move the saddle up (usually about half the distance that you moved it forward). Now check your reach by leaning forward into the aerobars. The front of your shoulders should be aligned vertically with the back of your elbows. This position allows you to rely on the skeletal rather than muscular support of your upper arms for the weight of the upper body. Your comfort and flexibility should determine the height of the handlebars relative to the saddle. For example, if your hamstrings feel tight, your handlebars need to be moved higher. Most likely, your cleat position and your saddle tilt can remain in the same position as they were in before.

No matter how aerodynamic you want to be, injury prevention and comfort should be your main concerns with regard to fit. Your knee rotates through many cycles on a ride—in just one hour of racing at 90 revolutions per minute, you are completing 5,400 rotations per leg! If your bike is not properly fit to your biomechanics, you will be at high risk for injury. Also, if you are uncomfortable on the bike, you may become distracted by repetitive twinges instead of being able to focus on your effort. Because a proper bike fit is critical, you should be fit at a reputable triathlon or cycling shop, by a certified fit specialist, or by a coach or physical therapist who has experience in bike fit. A proper bike fit should always include setting up your cleats (on the bottom of your shoes) in the proper position: If your knee is restricted to the wrong range through each pedal cycle, you're almost guaranteed injury. Athletes looking to be very competitive in triathlon should consider being fit by a professional fit specialist who will take into account every aspect of their biomechanics when adjusting their position. Look for someone who specializes in triathlon-specific fitting, and expect to pay $50 to $100 for the service (and anywhere from $200 to $1,000 for services that include power output measurement or wind tunnel testing).

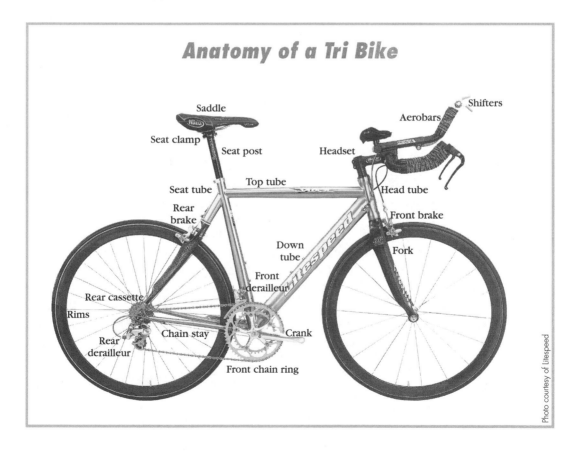

Anatomy of a Tri Bike

Saddle — Shifters — Aerobars — Seat clamp — Seat post — Headset — Seat tube — Top tube — Head tube — Rear brake — Front brake — Down tube — Fork — Front derailleur — Rear cassette — Rims — Chain stay — Crank — Rear derailleur — Front chain ring

Photo courtesy of Litespeed

Even with a good bike fit, you may find that you are uncomfortable on your saddle at times. If you experience this, consider the following:

- Never wear anything under your cycling shorts. The shorts are designed so that there are no seams in sensitive areas. Wearing undergarments adds those seams back between you and your saddle. Also, make sure you buy women's shorts to ensure a proper fit.
- Wash your shorts after each ride to avoid infections.
- Use a chamois cream or ointment to prevent saddle sores and chafing. Apply it to both your body and the shorts for maximum protection.
- Use a women-specific saddle. They are designed to support the wider sit bones of a woman's body and provide increased comfort.

USING DRILLS TO IMPROVE TECHNIQUE AND PERFORMANCE

Without a doubt, confidence on the bike will greatly affect your performance. For most athletes, the more familiar they are with their bike, the more willing they are to ride at higher speeds, corner more aggressively, and push themselves harder. To feel more control on your bike, proficiency in the following is a must: shifting and braking, steering, pedaling, cornering, riding in a group, and bike maintenance (covered on page 47).

To promote proficiency in these areas, a variety of drills can be employed.

Shifting and Braking

Proper shifting and braking are critical for many reasons: They allow for a smooth ride at an efficient cadence; decreased energy loss from acceleration and deceleration; fewer mechanical problems (such as a dropped or broken chain, a worn chain ring, or broken derailleur cables); reduced risk of crashing; and less wear and tear on your bike (drivetrain, brake pads). You should practice shifting (seated and standing) to achieve proper cadence. Learn to look at the grade of road in front of you and predict the gear that you may need. In most cases, you will find that it is best to shift the rear derailleur to a central cog first before moving the front derailleur to the large or small chain ring. Shifting with the front derailleur first and then adjusting the rear derailleur can cause "cross-chaining" and increases the likelihood of a dropped chain.

While shifting can be critical in a race, you should hardly need to use your brakes when racing. Yet, braking is a vital skill, and knowing how to do it properly can save you from trouble in both training and racing. You may have been told to use the front brake cautiously to avoid flying over the handlebars when used incorrectly. But if you really need to brake, the front brake can provide about 150 percent more stopping power than the rear brake. Testing the limits of my brakes over the years has saved me from many accidents. When an abrupt stop is necessary, use a combination of your front and rear brake. Practice this in training to get a sense of how hard you need to squeeze each brake without "fishtailing." As with a car, you'll want to begin stopping early and avoid "slamming" the brakes as much as possible. If you need to stop quickly, apply an increasing amount of force until you stop. If you need to brake over an extended distance, such as a long downhill, alternate your brakes to avoid overheating the rims of your wheels. Also, if you need to slow down slightly, try changing your position on the bike—if you make yourself bigger or move out of the draft of another rider, you can use the wind to brake. You will use most of these skills in your everyday riding—be aware of what you are doing and vary your approach periodically to make conscious and practiced choices when shifting and braking.

Steering

Skilled steering and, in particular, learning to ride a straight line depend mostly on an athlete's ability to relax on the bike. Steering drills are easy to incorporate into any session of a weekly training routine. The easiest drill is to simply ride on the white line along the shoulder of the road (choose a road with little road traffic). You will be most successful if you focus on the line well ahead of you and simply relax. When you find yourself riding a straight line without focusing on it, practice riding with one hand as you would when you are drinking or looking back. The most stable position for your hand is close to the stem; the farther out your hand is on the handlebars, the more your hand movement affects your steering.

Another great steering exercise is riding indoors on rollers because you only have one or two feet (depending on the rollers) of width for your ride (imagine riding on a treadmill).

© John Segesta

Cycling drills that emphasize techniques like steering and cornering increase confidence and performance.

After a bit of practice (and usually a collection of chairs, doorways, and other supporting surfaces to help keep you upright), it gets easier to relax on the bike and naturally ride in a straight line. Also consider taking out some of your friends to practice bumping and leaning on each other—test just how much weight you can transfer onto another person while still riding. You may even want to practice overlapping wheels to see what best helps you "recover" from such an incident. Note that bumping and leaning exercises are best practiced on a soft, grassy field. If you do fall, keep your hands on your handlebars to protect your wrists (this requires practice). The more confident and relaxed you are on the bike, the more efficient you will be.

Pedaling

A rider's power output is determined by the torque on the crank arm and the rider's cadence. To increase power output, a cyclist must be able to apply greater force on the pedal and must be able to pedal at a higher cadence. The ability to ride at varying cadences is a skill that is easy to practice. Likewise, a cyclist's ability to apply greater force on the pedal depends on conditioning as well as skill training.

Different cyclists prefer to ride at different cadences. One athlete may prefer to "mash" the gears at a lower cadence, while another may prefer to spin faster using easier gears. Nevertheless, both athletes can be moving at the same speed. For triathletes, choosing cadence is an important decision because it can directly affect run performance. Studies have suggested that riding at a higher cadence near the end of the bike leg may notably improve running speed. A good rule is that the transition from bike to run will be easier if the cycling cadence closely matches the running stride rate. For both disciplines, a typical range is 85 to 95 revolutions per minute or strides per minute. For triathletes, the bulk of cycling training should take place at these cadences. Yet, it is important to train at various cadences to become more comfortable and efficient, to improve pedal stroke, to work on bike-handling skills, and to improve strength at any given cadence.

Here are some examples of recovery workouts using cadence drills:

- 6 to 10 × 1 minute at 120+ rpm with 1+ minute at 90 rpm, all easy.
- 6 to 10 × 15- to 30-second "spin-ups" (possibly some standing) with a minute or more of recovery. To begin the spin-up, shift into a small gear and start pedaling while continuously increasing cadence to as high a cadence as possible.
- Easy ride with spin-ups in an easy gear on several downhill sections of the ride. Possibly lengthen the duration of the spin-up and hold the high cadence as long as you can.
- Easy ride with 4 to 10 × 30 to 60 seconds of one-leg pedaling with easy pedaling between drills.

Consider incorporating these active recovery workouts on any of your recovery days.

Examples of tempo workouts using cadence drills (these could be done on climbs) include the following:

- 2 to 5 × 10-minute tempo effort at 60 rpm with 5 to 10 minutes easy at 90 rpm.
- 2 or 3 × 30-minute tempo effort at varying cadence, such as 5-minute intervals at 60 and 100 rpm with 10 minutes easy at 90 rpm.

Tempo workouts are designed to stress your body and should not be performed on recovery days; incorporate them as moderate strength work into your weekly cycling training.

Other workouts of even higher intensity should also incorporate varying cadence. All workouts can be done outside, on a trainer, or on rollers. Rollers are particularly useful for high-cadence drills on recovery days. Group rides, during which speed varies frequently, also improve an athlete's ability to ride at different cadences. Three additional tools for cadence training are motor pacing behind a motorcycle (properly equipped with a roller or stayer's bar), including accelerations around the motorcycle, fixed-gear riding on rolling terrain, and mountain biking. Mix up your cadence drills creatively and make them fun!

Cornering

Although most races have fairly straight, nontechnical courses, there are plenty of events where cornering will make a big difference, and you need to be ready for them when the time comes. There are different ways to practice cornering. A good way to begin is to find an experienced rider and follow her through a corner. Ask her to be conservative so you know that you can trust her wheel and stay relaxed. After several loops through a technical course, gradually pick up speed. When cornering, try to keep most of your weight on the outside pedal while leaning into the turn—for most corners, remember to keep the inside pedal up unless you're sure you can pedal without hitting the ground. If the inside of the corner is always lower than the outside of the corner, as is the case on a car-racing track or velodrome, you can almost be certain that you can pedal through a turn. In the opposite case, when the corner is "off-camber," keep your inside pedal up until you are through the main part of the turn. Most likely, you'll find yourself on a road that is fairly flat, and your ability to pedal through a corner will depend on your speed, comfort, and how you corner. Some athletes quickly improve their cornering ability by pushing their limits; others do better by gradually getting more aggressive and faster while staying within their comfort zones.

Most athletes corner by "turning"—that is, they use their handlebars to steer through the corner while also leaning. In unstable conditions, such as on a wet or gravel road, this is not advised. Instead, try to keep the bike as upright as possible and move only the handlebars (no leaning) to turn through the corner. This type of cornering can be tricky to learn at first, but it greatly reduces the risk of sliding out in unstable conditions. Your bike may still slip a bit, but because your position is mostly upright, you'll avoid sliding out.

Countersteering is one of the fastest and most stable ways to corner with your bike, particularly at high speeds. Many cyclists intuitively countersteer on fast descents, but it generally takes practice to become skilled at countersteering on technical courses. To countersteer, push with the inside arm (the arm that is closest to the inside corner) against the handlebars, almost locking the elbow, while pulling with the outside arm on the handlebars. This causes the bike to lean toward the center of the corner. The upper body should stay fairly vertical during countersteering. This is difficult at really slow speeds, so countersteering is best practiced on slight downhills, where you can gain speed easily and focus on the cornering technique.

Group Riding

One of the best ways to become more relaxed and comfortable with your bike is riding with a group. At first, these rides may seem taxing, but most athletes feel comfortable after a few rides. Long rides usually go by quickly when riding with friends; also, group rides naturally require the rider to incorporate most of the drills previously outlined. In addition, these rides can improve your speed because you may be forced to ride at a slightly faster pace than you're accustomed to going on your own.

STRENGTH AND ENDURANCE WORKOUTS

Cycling in a nondrafting triathlon primarily requires endurance, strength, and muscular endurance. These abilities are developed through endurance, tempo, and lactate threshold workouts, which will be discussed in detail below. $\dot{V}O_2$max training through long, high-intensity intervals increases anaerobic endurance and develops an athlete's ability to tolerate exercise fatigue. Such training will especially benefit well-trained triathletes and those competing in shorter events, but it is less important for triathletes competing in long-distance events. Short, very high intensity $\dot{V}O_2$max efforts improve explosive strength but are hard on the body and are of limited importance for a nondrafting triathlete. Any of the drills previously discussed can be incorporated into almost any of the following workouts to further improve efficiency on the bike. For a detailed explanation of these training zones, see table 7.1 on page 91. Also see the "Training Zones" sidebar in this chapter.

Know How to Maintain Your Bike

Most athletes find themselves more comfortable and more willing to push their training to a new level when they know they can handle the most common problems encountered on a ride. Easy recovery days and rest days present a perfect opportunity to practice changing tubes, pedaling back on a dropped chain, adjusting gearing, and so forth. If you know how to shift and pedal to get your chain back onto the ring (see explanation below), you should lose no more than two seconds in a race because of a dropped chain. Stopping, getting off your bike, pulling the chain back on, and starting back up will cause unnecessary delay. Also, it should become second nature to check your bike at the beginning of each ride to make sure that your skewers are tight, the headset works properly, and the brakes are adjusted.

Fixing a Dropped Chain

If you drop your chain off one of your front chain rings during a race or training ride, follow these steps: Allow yourself to coast and quickly determine if the chain dropped to the inside of the small chain ring or if it dropped to the outside of the big chain ring. If you find the chain to the inside of the little chain ring, shift your front derailleur as far to the outside as possible (as if you were shifting into the big chain ring). Then, carefully and slowly begin to pedal—it may take a couple of seconds, but in most cases, your chain will catch one of the teeth of the big chain ring and, after one rotation of the chain ring, will be back in place.

If your chain drops to the outside of the big chain ring, quickly shift your front derailleur as far to the inside as possible and start pedaling slowly. The chain usually catches one of the teeth of the little chain ring. Keep pedaling until the chain is back on. This works in almost all cases, and you can use the same trick when you are working on your bike (simply use your hands to move the pedals).

Periodically, the chain ends up stuck. If this happens, backpedaling one quarter of a rotation may get it unstuck. If that doesn't help, you'll need to resort to getting off your bike and manually placing the chain on the chain ring.

If you drop your chain frequently, check the adjustment of your front derailleur—it may be a problem that can easily be avoided by a small turn of a screw.

If you are unsure about any of these basic skills, ask your local bike shop to help, or attend a bike maintenance clinic in your area. If you trust your bike, you will be willing to push it closer to its limits.

Endurance

Endurance training is the crucial first step in preparing for a triathlon. It stimulates metabolic, cardiovascular, and pulmonary adaptations in your body and further prepares your musculoskeletal structure for more strenuous (and more injury-free) training. Endurance workouts can be done alone or with a group. In the beginning, your heart rate should mostly be in the lower zones; as you become more fit, it is acceptable to be on an endurance ride that at times pushes you up to, and even above, lactate threshold (LT). If you have the option to choose the terrain for your endurance rides, vary your rides between flats, rolling hills, longer hills, and even the trainer or rollers; any are suitable for these workouts. Remember that easy recovery rides can be part of endurance work as well. Sprint-distance triathletes should incorporate at least a few endurance rides of up to 1.5 to 2 hours; Olympic-distance triathletes up to 2.5 to 3.5 hours; half Ironman athletes up to 4.5 to 6 hours; and Ironman athletes up to 6 to 8 hours. These rides also offer great opportunities for drill work!

Tempo

When you feel prepared for slightly harder efforts, increase the intensity of your endurance rides. This could happen simply because you are riding in a group and are trying to keep up, because you push yourself harder for a given period, or because you push your pace up a climb. Prolonged tempo efforts will help build your muscular endurance; tempo workouts at lower cadences of 50 to 75 revolutions per minute (harder gears) will help develop your strength. Take caution, however, because grinding gears will increase your injury risk (pay close attention to any aches or pains). Typical tempo efforts are 10 to 60 minutes long (or sometimes longer for triathletes competing in long-distance events) and can be repeated several times. These are key workouts for Ironman-distance training because they will match race effort. For suggested tempo workouts, see the workouts listed under cadence drills earlier in this chapter, and don't be afraid to mix them up.

Lactate Threshold

Lactate threshold is defined as the point at which the body's clearance of lactate cannot keep up with its production. Lactic acid is produced in muscle during the anaerobic breakdown of glucose (the body's primary fuel for anaerobic exercise) and diffuses into the blood where it is buffered to lactate (an ion). The presence of the ion and the change in acidity (through the buffering) affect the body's ability to do work. The goal of lactate threshold (LT) training is to increase the occurrence of the lactate threshold to a higher percentage of an athlete's aerobic capacity, maximizing the time an athlete can perform at high intensities without the diminishing effects of lactate buildup.

Your power output at your lactate threshold is a good predictor for expected performance. It indicates what your workload ability will be at high levels of intensity while staying aerobic. For most athletes, it is easiest to bring their heart rate up to LT during efforts done on hilly terrain. Once you can get your heart rate up to LT successfully on such a workout, include LT workouts on the trainer, and eventually, on flat or rolling terrain. Similar to the tempo workouts, you should vary the terrain and cadence you choose. Most sprint- and Olympic-distance triathletes race at heart rates near their lactate threshold. A PowerTap device can help you measure power output (see figure 4.1).

Here are some examples of LT workouts:

- **Long timed workouts.** 1 to 3 × 20 to 30 minutes at a heart rate at or just below your LT with 10 minutes of recovery between efforts.

- **Distance intervals.** 1 to 3 × 5 to 10 miles at a heart rate at or just below your LT with 5 to 15 minutes of recovery between efforts. Try to match time (or ride for a given time and try to match the distance) on the repeat efforts.

- **Fartlek.** Here's your chance to get creative! Fartlek, or "speed play," workouts are a great way to incorporate unstructured efforts into your training and break up a week of training that may otherwise be very deliberate. You can simply go for a ride and pick some landmarks (from here to the turn at Lefthand Canyon, between hills, and so on) or a random duration (four minutes) to pick up your speed and then recover.

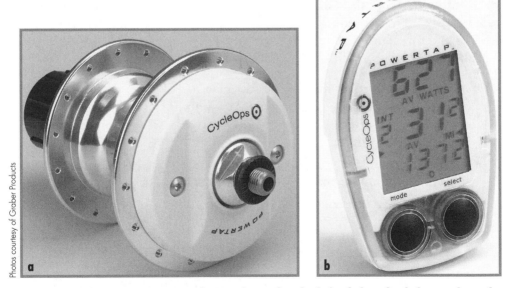

Photos courtesy of Graber Products

Figure 4.1 PowerTap consists of *(a)* a device for the hub of the wheel that gathers the data, and *(b)* a CPU that attaches to the handlebars and displays the data.

- *Lactate crisscross.* 2 or 3 × 15 to 30 minutes at a heart rate that alternates every 2 to 10 minutes between slightly above LT (up to LT plus 5 bpm) and slightly below LT (LT minus 8 bpm to LT minus 3 bpm), with 10 minutes of recovery between efforts. These are great workouts for race preparation. Because it's difficult to stay at your LT in a race, you may at times ride above LT and then have to back off to recover just below LT. Similarly, you may need to ride up a small hill during which your heart rate surpasses your LT heart rate and then recover on the downhill while still pushing the pace.

- *Team time trial or pacelining.* Group riding sessions can be great fartlek-style LT workouts. Team time trial or pacelining sessions can also mimic the crisscross workouts. You will be just above LT during the time that you are pulling into the wind, and then you recover just below LT when you are drafting. You don't have to match too closely in abilities with your riding partners: The strongest person will ultimately do more work by spending more time pulling into the wind than a weaker rider, but by the end of the ride, all of you should have had a successful LT workout.

$\dot{V}O_2max$

$\dot{V}O_2max$ workouts develop your aerobic and anaerobic capacity and your ability to tolerate higher lactate levels. These workouts prepare riders for situations when anaerobic endurance becomes important; thus, $\dot{V}O_2max$ workouts are more important for road racers and triathletes who race in draft-legal events or events with steep, short hills. For beginning triathletes, the greatest benefits will be derived from training in the zones below $\dot{V}O_2max$ (endurance, tempo, and lactate threshold).

Here are some examples of $\dot{V}O_2max$ workouts:

- *Long intense intervals.* 1 or 2 sets of 4 to 8 × 2 to 6 minutes at all-out (barely sustainable) effort with 2 to 4 minutes of recovery between intervals; 10 minutes of recovery between sets. The efforts start when you begin to pedal harder.

- *Group rides.* Hard group rides in which everyone takes a turn pulling provide a good informal means of $\dot{V}O_2max$ training.

- *Short intense intervals.* 4 to 10 × 15- to 20-second efforts with plenty of recovery.

Recovery

Ranking at the top of the list of important workouts are recovery rides. Recovery days allow you to become a faster athlete; hard workouts without recovery will only make you slower in the long run. A quality recovery day may simply involve an easy one-hour spin. Be smart about picking your riding partners for recovery days. Don't ride with someone unless she is scheduled to do a recovery spin also, and don't ride with someone who is a much stronger cyclist. You may even find that going alone gives you the best recovery workout.

Bricks

As discussed in previous chapters, you should combine cycling and running workouts in the form of brick or transition workouts. You can combine short bike rides with longer runs or longer bike rides with shorter runs; also consider multiple sets of bike and run combos in one workout. Similarly, simulate the swim-to-bike transition in a few workouts, and you will have your bases covered for the next event.

Training Zones

For purposes of this book, I define the training zones as follows:

Zone 1—Recovery
Zone 2—Endurance
Zone 3—Tempo
Zone 4 and 5a—Lactate threshold
Zone 5b and 5c—$\dot{V}O_2$max

You can find more information on training zones in table 7.1. You should note that the training zones used by many coaches, including myself, vary from these definitions. The revised zones are defined as follows: zone 1—recovery and endurance; zone 2—tempo; zone 3—lactate threshold; zone 4—long and short intensive repetitions; zone 5—sprinting. By simply referring to the definitions of these two training zone guidelines, it's easy to make conversions when needed.

TRANSITION TIPS

Efficiently moving from one discipline to the next is a critical element of training that's often overlooked. Because the bike falls in the middle of the race, you must consider how both the swim and the run will affect your bike performance. By having a game plan in place, and practicing both swim-to-bike and bike-to-run transitions, you'll not only head into race day with added confidence, you'll be one step ahead of many of your competitors.

Biking After the Swim

Simply practicing setting up your bike in transition will go a long way toward making your transition between swim and bike as seamless as possible. There are many decisions to make: Are you comfortable mounting the bike so that you can leave the shoes on the pedals? Are you using rubber bands to hold the shoes upright as you run with the bike? Where is the best place for your helmet, glasses, and food? Can you run holding the bike by the seat or do you have difficulty guiding it? Are you comfortable riding with your feet on top of your shoes so you can get up to speed before putting your feet into the shoes? Or should you put your bike shoes on before unracking your bike?

Make these decisions before your race and then practice your routine until you feel comfortable with each step. You can even simulate coming out of the water by doing some sit-ups and push-ups and turning around in place for a bit before running over to your bike and practicing the transition. It becomes much more difficult to simply snap your helmet buckle when you are disoriented and under pressure. A few tips for T1:

- Start kicking a little harder toward the end of the swim to warm up your leg muscles for the upcoming transition.
- Always snap your helmet before taking your bike off the rack (this is race regulation at most events).
- Run with your bike on your right so you are away from the chain ring.
- Hold your bike by the seat when you run. This allows you to run upright and faster than if you were holding it by the handlebars (master this before trying it in a race).
- Get up to speed on your bike before putting your feet into your shoes—you'll lose much less time.
- Whenever possible, observe the pros in a race to pick up additional tips. Watch how effortlessly they move from one discipline to the next.

Moving From Bike to Run

A few tips for T2:

- Near the end of the bike leg, be sure to shift to an easier gear and increase your cadence to improve leg speed for the run. Also, get out of the saddle a few times to stretch your legs (ideally while continuing to pedal) and get them ready to support your body weight.

- Dismount on the left side of your bike, away from the chain ring.

- After swinging your right leg over your saddle for the dismount, step through with your right leg between bike and left leg. This way, you don't cross your legs and risk tripping when you land on the ground.

- Never unbuckle your helmet until you have racked your bike; in many races, you can end up with a penalty or disqualification for doing so.

By ensuring comfort and proper fit on your bike, by incorporating technique drills into your training, and by adding specific strength and endurance workouts, you'll not only have a lot more fun than simply hammering out the miles, but you'll be amazed at how quickly the minutes will fall away from your splits. Remember, the fresher you finish the bike, the greater your chance of finishing strong!

Running Strong to the Finish

Heather Fuhr

For many athletes, the run is one of the biggest mysteries in triathlon. It can be the icing on the cake of an already great day; it can punctuate a difficult race with a happy ending; and, when not carefully executed, it can darken what began as a bright and promising effort, leaving you feeling depleted and disappointed by your result.

Whether you're a naturally gifted runner or a self-proclaimed plodder doesn't matter. Either way, you'll benefit from run-specific training that's implemented with triathlon racing in mind. A good run program includes a gradual build in endurance, an emphasis on form and technique, a steady build in speed, and a proper recovery strategy to allow your body to adapt to increased run fitness. For triathlon run training, all of this must be done with an eye on performing well following a swim and bike.

BUILDING RUN ENDURANCE

As with any type of training, you must lay a foundation before adding speed and distance to your run program. Without the ability to withstand the physiological (both aerobic and muscular) demands of running, all hopes of running fast are quickly dashed. As discussed in chapter 2, building endurance is referred to as the base phase of training. During this phase, you are building your aerobic base through consistent training, and you are strengthening the muscles, tendons, and joints associated with running so they will be ready to handle future workloads. All runs during this phase should be kept aerobic in nature (adding in some accelerations and drills once a week is acceptable), meaning they should be performed at 70 to 80 percent of your maximum heart rate (or 80 to 90 percent of your lactate threshold heart rate) and no more.

The base phase should be a minimum of 6 weeks and up to 12 weeks in length, depending on the amount of time before your first race. If you already have a first race selected, mark it on the calendar and count backward to the present. Take at least 30 percent of the total time for base training.

After an aerobic base has been built, endurance can be increased by adding "key run" workouts to your training. These key workouts may include hill training, fartlek, road intervals, or track workouts. (Descriptions of key run workouts are provided later in this chapter.)

In any run training program, there are three main workouts that should be performed on a weekly basis: the long run, the key run (intervals), and the transition run. By including these workouts in your training regimen and by being consistent, you will see dramatic improvements in your overall endurance and running potential.

To build your endurance efficiently and with a reduced risk of injury, follow these basic guidelines:

- ***Never make increases across the board.*** Build the length of your long run and your key run simultaneously while leaving the distance of your "easy" runs the same.

- ***Build gradually.*** When building on the long run and key run, add no more than 10 percent duration and distance each week. Remember, you'll benefit from a cumulative effect, and bumping up your mileage and intensity quickly will not allow your body time to adapt. Remind yourself that more is never better until you are *ready* for more!

- ***Don't make the fatal mistake of neglecting recovery.*** As with many types of training, you'll benefit most from a gradual build in duration and intensity followed by a recovery period that allows your body time to absorb fitness. For example, build for two weeks followed by one week of recovery. During your recovery week, cut your long runs by 20 to 30 percent, and replace your key run (which should also be cut in duration by 20 to 30 percent) with an easy run that may include optional drills and accelerations.

KEY RUNS

Key runs, which are incorporated following the aerobic build phase, are designed to add both specificity and speed to your run workouts. Without them, your running will eventually plateau, and you'll never reach your true potential as a runner. Use these workouts to "spice up" your training, to increase your speed, and to push through performance barriers. Following are descriptions of the different key runs you may incorporate.

Perfecting Your Form

It's true—some people are naturally gifted with near perfect running form that's beautiful to watch. The rest of us have to work at it, fighting against genetics to move forward quickly and efficiently. If you fall into this second category, take heart knowing there are many techniques you can use to improve your form and, ultimately, your running. Following are seven keys to improving your run form:

- *Strike the ground at a point that is just beneath your body.* Striking in front of the body (a common tendency) actually acts as a braking force to your run stride.

- *Look ahead.* Think of centering your head on your shoulders and avoid the tendency to look down. Leaning forward causes a strain on your lower back and leads to lost energy.

- *Run tall.* Keep your shoulders back and relaxed, and run proud!

- *Tuck your elbows.* Any side-to-side movement of the arms translates to wasted energy. Keep your elbows tucked in and keep your arms moving in a straight line.

- *Keep your hands relaxed.* Your hands should be loosely cupped; running with clenched fists requires excess energy.

- *Think "fleet feet."* Concentrate on a quick turnover of your feet as opposed to powering your whole body toward a faster finish. A quick run cadence will lead to both efficiency and speed.

- *Don't forget your hips.* Your hips act as your center of gravity. Concentrate on keeping them faced forward to lead you in a straight line.

Hill Runs

Hill workouts build strength and speed, and they are an excellent first approach to speed training. By learning to run fast uphill, you train your fast-twitch muscles to respond quickly and to provide the explosive power that fast running requires.

If you can't stomach the idea of performing hill repeats, keep in mind that actual repeats are not necessary if you have access to a hilly route. In my opinion, incorporating a hilly route is ultimately more effective at improving your running because you learn not only to run strong going uphill, but also to continue a strong pace over the crest of the hill and down the other side. Many people work so hard getting up a hill that they are forced to pull back and recover when they reach the top. If you teach your body to maintain a strong pace throughout, you'll create a much more even effort that is easier to maintain both physically and mentally.

Of course, if you don't have access to a hilly route, performing simple hill repeats will do the trick. Just make sure to use the approach outlined above: Maintain a strong pace up the hill and over the crest, and then turn around and recover down the hill before repeating.

Technique Tip for Hill Running

Use your arms to generate increased power (your legs will naturally follow the cadence set by your arms) and take smaller steps, landing on your forefoot to provide a more explosive "toe off."

Speed-Building Techniques

There are a number of workouts that can be performed to build speed: drills and accelerations, fartlek, track workouts, and road or trail intervals. A mix of these speed-building techniques should be included in your training program after a proper base has been built.

Accelerations

The simplest means of increasing your speed is through accelerations (strides) and drills. The purpose of these techniques is to teach the body to run efficiently at a pace faster than normal. Throughout normal training workouts, the body becomes accustomed to a specific pace and stride length, making it increasingly difficult to "change gears." By adding drills and accelerations, you teach the motor neurons associated with running to fire at a faster rate, facilitating faster running.

Accelerations are short (80 to 120 meters) strides that involve building your speed throughout. Pick a flat stretch of grass, road, or track and accelerate your pace while avoiding an all-out sprint. Then, jog or walk back to your starting point and repeat four to eight times. Perform accelerations once per week at the end of an easy run. Make sure you are fully recovered between each repetition before starting the next. Because the length of the acceleration is short, you are building speed without the fatigue and muscle breakdown is minimized. For this reason, accelerations can be performed year-round.

Drills

Both of the following drills are used to exaggerate a certain aspect of the run stride, leading to greater running adaptation. The drills should be incorporated into your training along with accelerations once per week at the end of an easy run. For each of these, the goal is not to cover a lot of ground; rather, they should be performed with minimal forward movement.

HIGH KNEES

This drill exaggerates the knee lift action of the running stride. Keeping a normal upright posture, and going up on the forefoot, bring the knee up to (but not beyond) the height of your hips (see figure 5.1). Keep the arms bent at 90 degrees or slightly less and synchronize them with your legs (opposite arm, opposite leg). The rate of this drill should be as fast as possible (significantly faster than your running stride) while maintaining correct form. Try not to bend forward to watch your feet or lean back like a drum majorette. Start with 4 sets of 30 steps and build up to 8 to 10 sets, keeping the repetitions at 30 steps.

Figure 5.1   High knees.

Figure 5.2   Butt kicks.

BUTT KICKS

This drill exaggerates the heel lift action of the running stride. Keeping a normal upright posture, and going up on the forefoot, simply kick the heel up to your butt (see figure 5.2). Again, don't forget about synchronizing your arms, and try not to lean forward. Start with 4 sets of 30 butt kicks and build up to 8 to 10 sets, with the repetitions remaining at 30.

Fartlek

Fartlek is a Swedish word meaning "speed play." This type of workout is considered an unstructured speed workout. Fartlek workouts are ideal to include during some of your first interval workouts for the year (as an introduction to speed training), and they can be incorporated whenever you feel like "playing" with your speed.

During your key workout for the week, warm up for at least 15 minutes and include any number of pick-ups of whatever length you choose, and then cool down for 10 to 15 minutes. For example, you may choose to pick up the pace for two light poles and then run easy for three; you might decide to run fast over a favorite stretch of road and then ease off for a couple of blocks; you might go fast for three minutes and then easy for five. This approach forces your body to handle whatever you throw at it while also keeping your workouts fun and challenging.

Road Intervals

Road intervals are a more structured workout performed on trails or roads. The intervals are performed for a specific length of time with a specific recovery. After warming up for a minimum of 15 minutes, perform a set number of intervals of a specific length of time. The length and duration will depend on the length of the race you're training for and the amount of time until your race. The shorter the distance of the race, the shorter the intervals should be. The closer you get to your race, the higher the intensity should be.

Here are some examples of interval workouts:

Sprint distance: Do a 10- to 15-minute warm-up and a 10-minute cool-down with one of the following main sets in between:

1. 4 minutes fast, 2 minutes of recovery; 2 minutes fast, 1 minute of recovery; 2 minutes fast, 1 minute of recovery; 1 minute fast, 1 minute of recovery. Descend your effort throughout.
2. 4 to 6 × 2 minutes fast and 1 minute 30 seconds easy (building throughout).
3. 1 minute, 2 minutes, 3 minutes, 3 minutes, 2 minutes, 1 minute fast with 2 minutes easy between each; descend throughout.

Olympic distance: Do a 15-minute warm-up and a 15-minute cool-down with one of the following main sets in between:

1. 6 minutes fast, 3 minutes of recovery; 4 minutes fast, 2 minutes of recovery; 2 minutes fast, 1 minute of recovery; 1 minute fast, 1 minute of recovery. Descend your effort throughout.
2. 4 to 6 × 3 minutes fast and 2 minutes easy (building throughout).
3. 1 minute, 2 minutes, 3 minutes, 4 minutes, 3 minutes, 2 minutes, 1 minute fast with 2 minutes easy between each; descend throughout.

Half Ironman: Do a 15- to 20-minute warm-up and 15-minute cool-down with one of the following main sets in between:

1. 8 minutes fast, 3 minutes of recovery; 6 minutes fast, 2 minutes of recovery; 4 minutes fast, 2 minutes of recovery; 2 minutes fast, 1 minute of recovery. Descend your effort throughout.

2. 4 to 6 × 4 minutes fast and 2 minutes easy (building throughout).

3. 1 minute, 2 minutes, 3 minutes, 4 minutes, 4 minutes, 3 minutes, 2 minutes, 1 minute fast with 2 minutes easy between each; remain steady on the way up and then descend on the way down.

Ironman: Do a 15- to 20-minute warm-up and a 15- to 20-minute cool-down with one of the following main sets in between:

1. 10 minutes fast, 4 minutes of recovery; 8 minutes fast, 3 minutes of recovery; 6 minutes fast, 3 minutes of recovery; 4 minutes fast, 2 minutes of recovery; 2 minutes fast, 1 minute of recovery. Descend your effort throughout.

2. 4 to 6 × 5 minutes fast and 3 minutes easy (building throughout).

3. 1 minute, 2 minutes, 3 minutes, 4 minutes, 5 minutes, 4 minutes, 3 minutes, 2 minutes, 1 minute fast with 2 minutes easy between each on the way up and 3 minutes easy between each on the way down (because there is more recovery, you should be able to go faster on the last 4, 3, 2, 1 minutes).

Track Workouts

Track workouts are a great way to gauge improvements in performance because they take place in a controlled environment. An athlete can compare similar workouts over a period of time to note improvements. As with the road intervals, the length of the track intervals and the intensity of these intervals will depend on the length of the race and the amount of time until your race. The shorter the distance of the race, the shorter the intervals should be. The closer you get to your race, the higher the intensity should be.

Here are some examples of track workouts:

Sprint distance: Do a 10- to 15-minute warm-up and 4 to 6 repetitions of accelerations before—and a 10-minute cool-down after—you perform track intervals using one of the following main sets:

1. 2 or 3 × 800 meters hard with a 400-meter jog recovery (steady throughout).

2. 3 × 400 meters hard (200-meter jog recovery), 4 × 200 meters hard (200-meter jog recovery). The 200s should be faster than the 400s.

3. 4 × 200 meters hard (with 200-meter recovery), 2 × 400 meters hard (200-meter recovery), 2 × 200 meters hard (200-meter recovery).

4. 8 to 10 × 200 meters with a 200-meter jog recovery; make the second 4 or 5 faster than the first 4 or 5.

Olympic distance: Do a 15-minute warm-up and 4 to 6 repetitions of accelerations before—and a 15-minute cool-down after—you perform track intervals using one of the following main sets:

1. 3 or 4 × 1000 meters hard with a 400-meter recovery (steady throughout).

2. 2 × 800 meters hard (400-meter recovery), 4 × 400 meters hard (200-meter recovery).

3. 4 × 200 meters, 4 × 400 meters, 4 × 200 meters (all with a 200-meter recovery); try to make your last 4 × 200 meters faster than your first 4 × 200 meters.

4. 8 × 400 meters fast with a 200-meter jog recovery; make the second 4 faster than the first 4.

Half Ironman: Do a 15- to 20-minute warm-up and 4 to 6 repetitions of accelerations before—and a 15-minute cool-down after—you perform track intervals using one of the following main sets:

1. 3 or 4 × 1200 meters with a 400-meter jog recovery (steady throughout).

2. 2 × 800 meters (with 400-meter jog recovery), 4 × 400 meters (with 200-meter jog recovery), 4 × 200 meters (with 200-meter jog recovery); descend your speed throughout, performing the 4 × 200s the fastest.

3. 4 × 400 meters hard (200-meter recovery), 1 × 1000 meters hard (400-meter recovery), 4 × 400 meters hard (200-meter recovery); steady on the first set of 400s, maintain for the 1000, then faster on the last set of 400s.

4. 8 to 10 × 400 meters fast with a 200-meter jog recovery; second 4 or 5 faster than first 4 or 5. This is one of the most basic track workouts and one of my favorites. Don't neglect the shorter, faster intervals even for half Ironman racing.

Ironman: Do a 15- to 20-minute warm-up and 4 to 6 repetitions of accelerations before—and a 15- to 20-minute cool-down after—you perform track intervals using one of the following main sets:

1. 3 or 4 × 1 mile hard with a 400-meter recovery; descend 1 through 4.

2. 2 × 1000 meters (with 400-meter jog recovery), 4 × 800 meters (with 400-meter jog recovery); maintain steady pace throughout.

3. 4 × 400 meters (with 200-meter jog recovery), 1 × 1600 meters (400-meter jog recovery), 4 × 400 meters (with 400-meter jog recovery); try to make your last 4 × 400 meters faster than your first 4 × 400 meters.

4. 10 to 12 × 400 meters fast with a 200-meter jog recovery; second 5 or 6 faster than first 5 or 6.

RUNNING OFF THE BIKE

The transition run is what sets triathlon run training apart from traditional run training. Because the run leg of a triathlon is performed immediately after a bike ride, you must teach your legs to transition quickly from the relatively fluid motion of cycling to the explosive movements required for running.

Doing so simply requires practice. Including transition runs in your weekly training schedule gets your muscles accustomed to switching gears quickly, negating the effects of those "wobbly legs" that mark the first few run steps off the bike. To be most effective, transition runs should be performed at least once a week following longer or harder bike workouts. Within 10 minutes of finishing your bike ride (it's a good idea to simulate the amount of time T2 is likely to take you in a race), slip on your running shoes and find your stride.

The length of this run can vary from 15 minutes to an hour, depending on the distance for which you're training. Keep in mind that even for Ironman-distance training, incorporating a transition run that is more than an hour in length is unnecessary, because the goal is merely to adapt your muscles to a change in movement (this usually occurs within 10 minutes) and to get accustomed to running on tired legs. Running longer than an hour following a tough bike workout will simply lead to fatigue that will require greater recovery time.

When properly executed, transition runs lead to both physical adaptation and increased confidence, allowing the run portion of a triathlon to be a welcome challenge as opposed to a dreaded march to the finish.

See table 5.1 for specific guidelines on transition runs based on the length of your goal race.

TABLE 5.1 Length of Workouts

Once a proper base has been built, you can use the following as general guidelines for the length of your workouts.

Type of run	Sprint	Olympic	Half Ironman	Ironman
Transition run*	15-20 min.	20-30 min.	30-45 min.	45 min.-1 hr.
Long run**	1:00	1:10-1:20	1:30-1:45	1:45-2:30
Key run***	45 min.	1:00	1:10-1:20	1:20-1:30

*Ease into your transition run, and if you feel good, get rolling through the middle section.
**The long run is for maintaining your aerobic base, so keep it aerobic (70 to 80 percent of maximum heart rate).
***Key runs should be accompanied by a warm-up and cool-down of 10 to 20 minutes.

DETERMINING TRAINING PACE

Pacing is critical to your overall run success, but unfortunately there's no easy answer to the question, How fast should I run? The best answer I can give is to run at all different speeds!

Too often, people get caught in the rut of doing all their workouts at the same pace—what is known as "the gray zone." This gray zone is generally a pace that is too fast for recovery workouts and too slow for key runs. People generally settle on a pace because they feel it gives them a "good workout." However, falling into this trap will not allow you to reap the benefits of a structured run training program and will lead to performance stagnation.

Following is a guide to determining pace for the various run workouts you will incorporate into your program.

In training, key runs will help you increase the pace you run during racing.

Recovery Workout

Quite simply, recovery workouts should be slow and easy (below 70 percent max heart rate or 80 percent of LT heart rate). If you can't hold a conversation during a recovery run, you're going too fast. The purpose of this workout is to provide "active recovery," meaning easy time on your legs while your body absorbs the harder workouts you've already performed. Too often, people make the mistake of going too hard during recovery runs, jeopardizing the effect of their quality workouts. Here's a simple truth: If you can't trust yourself to go slow during recovery workouts, you're far better off skipping the workout than going too hard.

The duration of your recovery runs should remain constant throughout your training schedule. For instance, if you're training for an Olympic-distance race, shoot for a recovery run of about 30 minutes and stick to it for the duration of your training program.

Key Run

As discussed, key runs are included in your training program to get your body used to running at a faster pace, with the ultimate goal of increasing the pace you can maintain during a race. The idea is to "trick" your body so that when race day comes, the pace you want to run will not seem as hard. To do this, the pace of your key run workouts should include segments slightly faster than race pace. With this in mind, be realistic: If your goal pace is 8 minutes per mile, there's no use in trying to run quarter-mile repeats at 80 seconds, which would equate to a 5-minute 20-second mile. Instead, shoot for repeats in the 1 minute and 50 second to 2 minute range, which would be 7 minutes and 40 seconds to 8 minutes per mile.

Always warm up for 10 to 20 minutes before starting any intervals and cool down for at least 10 to 20 minutes afterward.

Transition Run

The transition run should also be "race pace" specific. Be honest and realistic when determining this pace; it should be run at a pace up to your goal race pace. However, the pace of your transition runs should also be based on how you are feeling on a given day. Allow yourself to ease into your goal pace throughout the run, and if it isn't there on that day, don't worry. Simply slow your pace and allow your body to get used to the concept of maintaining proper run form off the bike.

Long Run

The long run is the main aerobic base run for the week. Its purpose is to maintain or increase your aerobic endurance. For this reason, the run should be kept aerobic, meaning 70 to 80 percent of your max heart rate (or 80 to 90 percent of LT heart rate). Remember, steer clear of the "gray zone"! Long runs should be done at a pace that allows you to maintain a conversation. As your training progresses and your aerobic fitness increases, you can start to build your long run to the upper limit of your aerobic capacity (up to 80 percent of max heart rate or 90 percent of LT heart rate).

INTEGRATING RUN WORKOUTS

As discussed in chapter 1, successful triathlon training involves viewing three disciplines as one distinct sport. As such, training modifications must be made to traditional single-sport models.

The basic purpose of triathlon run training is to teach your body to be able to run fast in a fatigued state.

Following is an example of how to integrate the run workouts described in this chapter into a full triathlon training schedule:

Mon	Tue	Wed	Thu	Fri	Sat	Sun
Swim		Key swim		Swim (optional)	Easy swim	
	Key bike	Easy bike		Easy bike (optional)	Long bike	Easy bike (optional)
	Transition run or easy run		Key run	Easy run with drills and accelerations (optional) Or day off	Transition run	Long run

Here are a few additional points on scheduling:

- Remember, for the Friday workouts, if you can't go easy so that you are getting some active recovery, take a day off!

- Early in the season, you should do just one of the transition runs per week; the other run should be an easy run either before your bike ride or later in the day. As the season progresses, you can include up to two transition runs per week in your schedule; this is purely optional. If doing two transition runs per week, make sure that you vary the pacing of them—one should be faster (race pace specific) and one should be purely aerobic.

- Your "key workout" for the day should take precedence over the others. Focus your energy on this workout and try to keep all other workouts on that day easy.

Whether the run is your strength or your least favorite discipline in triathlon, you can continually improve your times by adhering to run-specific training and by fine-tuning your program. Using the strategies outlined in this chapter, see how quickly you can improve your splits with just six weeks of dedicated run training; and then, if desired, make slight tweaks to determine how much more time you can erase. Doing so not only will ensure a happy finishing photo, it will also boost your overall racing confidence and put you on track for many more strong and happy finishes in the future.

Balancing Training and Recovery

Jackie Gallagher, MS

Triathlon is a sport that epitomizes the concept of *balance*. To be successful, you must balance swim, bike, and run workouts; balance intensities to reach peak performance; and balance triathlon with everyday life. One aspect many people neglect to consider, however, is the importance of balancing work levels with rest and recovery to optimize physiological adaptation. The tendency for many people who want to reach peak performance is to train hard, and when they want to improve even further, to train even harder.

I have found that most women involved in triathlon, whether elite athletes or age-group competitors, are very serious about their performances. They are all out there trying to be the best they can possibly be, and they are very hard on themselves in the process. Many women triathletes have so much going on in their lives—work, taking care of families, training—that they invariably burn the candle at both ends and still expect to perform very well.

So where is the time for rest and recovery? How much do you really need? How do you optimize it within your lifestyle? And what are the implications if you don't get enough? This chapter will help you answer these questions.

MAXIMIZING PERFORMANCE THROUGH RECOVERY

Triathletes are well known for adhering to the adage "more is better." Triathlon is an endurance sport, and whether you compete in sprint (Ha! Still more than an hour of racing), Olympic, or Ironman distance, there is no substitute for long, hard work.

It is a physiological fact that women are better suited to pure endurance sports than men are, due to women's superior fat-burning ability. Believe it or not, it is actually a lot harder for women to "bonk" (i.e., run out of muscle glycogen) than it is for men. A woman's fat-burning metabolism is just much more efficient (plus, as we all know, women have much higher pain tolerance!). This, coupled with a woman's need to juggle so many other activities in her life in addition to triathlon—work, managing her family, and generally doing things for everyone else—leaves little time for rest and recovery.

© John Segesta

The best performances come from capitalizing on properly executed rest periods within your training schedule.

However, rest and recovery are just as important as those long and hard workouts in reaching peak performance. In fact, the gains you make in fitness are actually realized *during* recovery. Training is all about *stimulus, response,* and *adaptation.* You stimulate (challenge) your body with training, and then it responds and adapts. But you must give it the time and opportunity to respond and adapt. Without adequate and appropriate rest, your body does not recover from training, and even with more training, your fitness and performances actually begin to deteriorate.

TRAINING THE BODY TO RESIST FATIGUE

Training in simple terms is about being "resistant to fatigue." In triathlon racing, you want to be able to swim, bike, and run, moving forward as fast as possible for the entire distance of the event. If you can teach your body to move forward at a target speed without getting tired, then you will complete the distance optimally (in PR time).

If during training you run five miles every day at a pace of nine minutes per mile (or a "comfortable aerobic" pace), then you are teaching your body to run five miles at a pace of nine minutes per mile. In other words, the body adapts to what you give it. If, however, you vary your distance and pace in your workouts (some speed work, some work pushing faster than your comfortable aerobic pace, and some slow, easy, efficiency work), you are more likely to teach your body to handle anything you throw at it. If the body never quite knows what it's going to be asked to do, it is more likely to adapt to be ready for anything.

The human body is designed to cope with a whole range of stresses. To adapt to these stresses, however, it needs adequate recovery time. Back to the stimulus/response/adapt concept: If you do a hard threshold training session, and then make sure you recover adequately (cool down, refuel, rest, and so forth), you give your body a chance to say, *Hey, that was a hard threshold session; now I am going to recover, rebuild, and adapt so I can cope better the next time she makes me do that.* In this way, your threshold (the maximum pace you can maintain for longer periods without fatigue) will increase. Similarly, if you do a long endurance ride and come home wiped out from a four-hour effort, but then you go through the appropriate recovery strategies, the next time you go out for a long ride, your body will handle it more easily.

DETERMINING APPROPRIATE RECOVERY AFTER TRAINING

Recovery strategies for elite athletes are becoming more widely researched and maximized. After all, for elites, the more work they can do and still recover and adapt, the better they become. Marathon runner Paula Radcliffe (women's world record holder at 2:15:25) runs 230 kilometers (145 miles) per week. She has a team to help her optimize recovery between sessions and in her overall training, so she can keep up her incredible training schedule. Paula receives a massage every day, adheres to peak nutrition, uses hot and cold baths, and uses the latest research and technology to plan her recovery and, thus, her ability to handle more training.

We mere mortals don't have the time or resources to do all this, but we can do most of the basics. Following are key recovery strategies:

- Consume an adequate amount of fluid during training sessions (at least 600 milliliters or one large water bottle per hour).

- Consume an adequate amount of carbohydrates during training sessions. (Recovery is greatly enhanced if the body does not become too depleted and dehydrated during training.)

- Perform a good cool-down after hard sessions—at least 10 to 15 minutes to keep the blood flowing and to clear lactate and metabolites from the working muscles.

- Refuel immediately after completing sessions. Fuel is absorbed and used in the most appropriate ways immediately after training. For each 30 minutes after exercise, the ability of the working muscles to absorb the fuel is decreased by half.

- Maintain good nutrition *and* hydration at all times to give the body its best chance to function optimally.

- Use hot and cold therapy. There has been much anecdotal evidence to show that hot and cold therapy is excellent for flushing lactate and metabolites from the working muscles and assisting in recovery. Hot and cold baths are the best, but changing the shower alternately from hot to cold can work pretty well, too.

- Elevate the legs; this is particularly useful after hard bike rides (as soon as you get home, lie down and put your legs up against the wall for 5 to 10 minutes).

- Stretch—again, right after sessions if possible. Stretching maintains optimal muscle length and flexibility and also releases muscles (fibers) that are tense from repeated contractions.

- Get adequate sleep. The amount needed is different for everyone, but no one ever seems to get enough! For most people, the standard eight hours is a good goal.

- Get massage. I believe that for anyone training seriously, a massage once a week is a necessity, not a luxury! Regular massage has certainly helped keep me in one piece over the years.

- Finally, use the optimal combination of training: Balancing your sessions is essential in optimizing recovery and allowing you to get the most out of the training you do.

COMBINING TRAINING TO MAXIMIZE RECOVERY

Every triathlete is different in how she copes with different types of work. The key elements of training are endurance, speed, speed endurance (or threshold), and strength-oriented sessions (the latter can be done in different ways within any of the other three). Different people respond differently to training and even respond differently across the three disciplines of triathlon.

It is part of the challenge and enjoyment of triathlon training to pinpoint what works best for you. Pro triathlete Wendy "Wingnut" Ingraham and I spent a lot of time living and training together. But we are very different athletes. I came from a run background, and Wing came from a swim background. She is a strength- and endurance-oriented athlete, and I respond very well to higher intensity speed endurance work. Because I am a natural runner, easy runs were both recovery and background fitness for me. Running was hard work for Wing. Conversely, swimming was hard work for me but could be good recovery from hard sessions for Wing. Even speed-oriented swim sets were almost recovery for Wing, but they'd kill me! On the bike, I liked to get out there for 90 minutes and go hard for 60 of them, which would be too intense for Wing. But she would do four- or five-hour rides and recover very well from them; the same ride would leave me flat for days. So we had to structure our training very differently to work optimally on our weaknesses (running and speed in the bike and run for Wing; swimming and strength work for me) and to use our strengths as recovery while still getting in worthwhile training.

Everyone has limited time and energy for training, so use these tips when combining sessions:

- Don't follow a session in one discipline with the same type of session in another (e.g., don't do a threshold session in the pool in the morning and then a threshold run session in the afternoon).
- In most cases, try to avoid performing two consecutive sessions in one discipline.
- Follow the type of session that is hardest for you with the type that is easiest for you (e.g., follow a hard threshold run session with an easy bike session with high cadence emphasis).
- If you are not naturally strong, leave your major strength session for the last session in a block of work. Then take a rest!
- For most people, a rest (24 hours or more) is best after long endurance sessions.
- Aim to do speed work when you are fresh and will have good technique.

- In any session, if your technique really starts to fall away, and you can't get on top of it even if you really focus on it, STOP and take a rest. Poor technique equals fatigue and is a great sign that you need rest. It doesn't do any good to practice poor technique and bad habits—plus they can lead to injury!

REST, RECOVERY, AND THE BIG PICTURE

Rest and recovery not only are a part of training, but also must be taken into consideration within the context of your everyday life. As mentioned at the beginning of this chapter, many women in triathlon are combining a lot of things in their lives, and training is often fit in where there is time. Sessions might be performed back-to-back in the morning because that is when there is time. It is very difficult to find time to actually "rest" given the lifestyles that most women lead. Doing a hard session in the morning and then buzzing around all day is hardly optimal recovery and does not allow your body to make the most of the session.

A great friend of mine is competitive in the 45 to 49 age group. My nickname for her is "Cyclone Cindy" because she just never stops. She whizzes around doing everything for everyone. She wonders why she trains well for a few days and then gets really "fried" and feels like she can't cope with as much training as she'd like to do. I've had to work hard to convince her to program in some time off where she literally stops and puts her feet up.

Triathlon is certainly something that Cyclone loves to be part of, and she has high expectations of herself, but it is not her first priority; her family is. So we've come up with ways that she can do all the things she needs to in her day. She now has plenty of flexibility and latitude in her training schedule, while also having strategies for maximizing the training she is able to fit in.

I have also convinced her to get regular massage as part of her training (and to take time to cool down and stretch). Cyclone has also found ways to work on some stretching—at her desk while catching up on paperwork, at night in front of the TV, or while standing on the sideline watching her son's lacrosse match.

DETERMINING HOW MUCH REST YOU NEED

Like my friend Cyclone, the amount of training you can cope with and the amount of rest and recovery you need are largely dependent on what else you have going on in your life.

Similar to individual differences within training, different people can cope with different workloads. Professional triathlete Karen Smyers is well known for being a light trainer. But Karen has achieved some amazing results, including a world championship at both Olympic and Ironman distances in the same year (and she is the only woman ever to do so).

I am also a relatively light trainer, and it used to frustrate me that I couldn't train as much as others. Interestingly, however, I didn't *need* to train as much as others to get the results I wanted. Some people can cope with a lot of work, but they also need it to perform at the highest level. Others can't do as much, but once they accept their bodies and how they work, they often find that their bodies dictate what is best for them.

I am a big believer in "listening to your body." I think it will tell you when it needs rest, when it's ready to go hard, and when it needs water, carbohydrate, or protein. Learning how your body functions, and what it can and can't cope with, will help you optimize your potential.

Sometimes people need help listening to their body instead of their mind. My triathlon coach certainly challenged me to do things I didn't *think* I could do. He taught me that there were times to push through my mentally imposed limitations and times when my body was at the point of diminishing returns (and more work would push it over the edge). A good coach knows when to push an athlete through and when to hold her back.

CONSEQUENCES OF INADEQUATE REST

In early 2000, I was so hell-bent on going to the Olympics and doing well that I drove myself into the ground. I thought I needed to train harder than ever before and totally went beyond what was reasonable and what I *knew* worked for my body. I also made the mistake of not listening to knowledgeable and trusted supporters and their objective opinions. I fell into a chronic overtraining state—textbook "chronic overtraining syndrome"—and was unable to realize my Olympic ambitions.

Tiredness

Being tired is part of training. My coach always used to say, "Unless you wake up tired and go to bed tireder, you are not training hard enough!" In a hard block of training, tiredness is part of the process. For the most part, however, you should experience a positive, healthy tiredness—one in which you know you are training but can still perform your sessions well and are still challenging and stimulating your body leading up to recovery and adaptation.

Overreaching

Overreaching is a state of training sometimes used to take an athlete to the next level of fitness. It is a point where an athlete pushes hard (beyond tiredness) and gets every last bit out of her body; for example, a few days of hard training at the end of a training block. After this, the athlete then has a few rest days or very light days to allow her body to completely recover and adapt to a higher level of fitness.

Overreaching can also occur without being planned. Often, if you have been training hard and also have a lot happening in other areas of your life, you will become run-down and find yourself in an overreaching state (which can involve injury or illness). This can signify the edge of overtraining, but recovery is often achieved in a few days with rest, good nutrition, and generally taking care of yourself. The trick is to stay on the right side of the fence!

Overtraining

Overtraining is caused by excessive training loads coupled with inadequate rest, recovery, and nutrition. Symptoms include everything from performance decrements and persistent fatigue to increased resting heart rate, lack of motivation, and increased susceptibility to illness. My experience in this area involved training too hard and too frequently, not taking time off, allowing myself to become stressed, not eating well enough, not sleeping well, and pushing through hard sessions because I felt I *had* to get them done. I didn't heed the warning signs: I was losing weight, sleeping fitfully, and feeling down; my training performances were dropping; and I was feeling weak and sore a lot of the time.

© Nigel Farrow

A week before the first Olympic triathlon trial, I ran 25 × 400 meters and felt tired, running slower than usual. The next morning I did the state cycling 20K time trial championship race. I just couldn't go! Girls who usually rode nowhere near as fast as I did were going past me. I had only one week until trials, so I tried to stay positive. I adhered to my tapering strategy, but I had nothing all week. I went to the Olympic trials and went as hard as I could, but I was way below my usual standard. In my whole career, I had never placed worse than 7th in any event at any level (except for 14th at my first Elite World Champs). On this day, I placed something like 24th. And that finished me off. For several weeks after that, I would walk the 200 meters from my house to the beach and would need to

Overreaching, in which an athlete pushes herself beyond fatigue after a hard training block, is combined with recovery to reach higher fitness.

rest before I walked back home. So much for being a super-fit athlete! It took me many months to recover.

THE FATIGUED ATHLETE

The symptoms of fatigue may vary from decreased performance and general tiredness to an elevated temperature and an increase in resting heart rate. There is no hard-and-fast reason for feeling wiped out during endurance training, but following are some common reasons athletes may experience fatigue.

• **Viral illness.** A lot of research has been conducted on depressed immune systems in athletes. People are generally more susceptible to viral illnesses after periods of stress—hard training, exam periods, a busy work schedule, and so on. More serious forms of viral illness are certainly a reason to *stop* training. In fact, it can be very dangerous to your health to train hard while suffering from a virus (postviral fatigue syndrome and myocarditis are two debilitating subsequent illnesses). Symptoms indicating the need for complete rest include muscle aches and pains, swollen glands, and elevated temperature. With milder illnesses such as head colds, light training is permissible and may even have a positive effect.

• **Iron deficiency.** Iron deficiency is a very common cause of tiredness in female athletes and is often the problem in seemingly unexplainable fatigue. Potential causes include too little iron in the diet, poor absorption of iron by the body, and loss of blood (including from heavy menstrual bleeding). A blood test can easily detect low iron. With increased dietary iron intake or short-term iron supplementation, this is usually easily corrected.

• **Inadequate diet.** Failure to replenish glycogen (carbohydrate) stores after training can lead to fatigue. If you start the day with a "full tank of fuel" but don't replenish your stores, your performance will start to be impaired. You will be "running on empty." Inadequate protein intake can also leave athletes feeling persistently tired. Fueling for optimal performance is discussed in chapter 13.

• **Dehydration.** Dehydration is a common factor in decreased performance during racing or training. Performance decrements can be caused by as little as 2 percent dehydration, and the effects are progressive; by 3 to 5 percent, it can be very serious. It is wise to weigh yourself before and after training as a means of monitoring fluid loss. Chronic dehydration is less documented but is also quite common—it is simply an accumulation of dehydration over several days. The need for avoiding dehydration cannot be overemphasized in all aspects of training and racing.

• **Psychological stress.** Psychological stresses come in many forms and definitely affect athletic performance. These can relate directly to sport or to other aspects of life, and again, they should be taken seriously and taken into consideration with regard to training, rest, and life balance.

- **Exercise-induced asthma.** Exercise-induced asthma (EIA) is just one potential medical problem that can impair performance and present itself in the form of persistent tiredness. Presence of a cough, wheezing, shortness of breath, or a lingering chest infection could indicate EIA. Any symptoms that persist for more than a week or two require a visit to your physician for further investigation.

- **Overtraining syndrome.** Overtraining syndrome is characterized by the following: performance decrements, persistent fatigue, "heavy" muscles, disturbed or restless sleep, changes in appetite, increased resting heart rate, persistent muscle soreness, weight loss, apathy and lack of motivation, feelings of stress, moodiness, depression, and increased susceptibility to illness. It is caused by excessive training loads coupled with inadequate rest, recovery, and nutrition. Recovery from overtraining syndrome usually takes months.

- **Chronic fatigue syndrome.** Chronic fatigue syndrome is defined as follows (adapted from Holmes et al. 1988, in Derman et al. 1997):

  1. New onset of persistent or relapsing debilitating fatigue, of at least six months duration, that does not resolve with bed rest and is severe enough to impair daily activity below 50 percent of normal.

  2. Exclusion of other clinical conditions that may produce similar symptoms.

Chronic fatigue syndrome is similar to chronic overtraining syndrome in many of its symptoms. It is not entirely clear what causes it, and in athletes it may be an extension of overtraining syndrome. Chronic fatigue syndrome can also result from other illnesses and stresses. It is just as common in nonathletes as in athletes, however, so overtraining may not be the main cause.

- **Epstein-Barr virus and glandular fever.** Viruses such as Epstein-Barr and glandular fever are serious viral infections. They do not result from overtraining per se, but they can result from increased susceptibility due to underresting. Some people think that pushing through training and work while suffering from a bad flu can lead to glandular fever. These are the worst kinds of viral infections and can be debilitating, requiring months of rest for full recovery.

The best prevention for most of these conditions is good nutrition and sensible training, interspersed with adequate rest and "down time."

PRIORITIZING AND MANAGING EXPECTATIONS

In my opinion, balancing work and rest levels comes down to three things:

1. Knowing yourself—physically, physiologically, and psychologically

2. Knowing the role triathlon plays in your life
3. Planning ahead to optimize your performance in daily life

Triathlon is only one part of your life. It is the first priority for a very small percentage of people. It is okay that it is not the number one priority for the rest of us! Unless you are a full-time athlete—with time, support, expertise, and financial backing to do everything necessary to optimize performance and recovery—you will never do a *perfect* job of balancing work and rest levels (and optimizing training, recovery, and performance). Your goal, however, should be to do the best you can possibly do.

I hope you compete in triathlon because you love it, it challenges you, and it makes you feel good about yourself. Keep it in perspective and use the knowledge and tips in this chapter to maximize your training within the context of the rest of your life. A very wise person once said to me, "At the end of the day, if you can look at yourself in the mirror and say, 'I did the very best I could do today with what I had,' then you can't do any better than that. You are a champion."

Strengthening and Testing Your Performance

Lisa Bentley

A common pitfall of endurance training is becoming so consumed with covering the miles that the finer points of training are overlooked. In truth, "putting in the miles" is just a small component of structured endurance training. In addition to aerobic conditioning, a well-rounded endurance program includes strengthening the muscles and systems of the body, as well as implementing measures to test your performance.

In this chapter, you'll learn about a variety of performance-strengthening strategies—from core conditioning and strength-building techniques for swimming, biking, and running to methods for testing your performance such as heart rate monitoring and lactate threshold testing. Although the benefits of these techniques may not be seen immediately, over time they will make you a more fit, balanced, and stronger athlete on your way to peak performance.

PRINCIPLES OF CORE CONDITIONING

I've been a triathlete for almost 15 years, but it wasn't until I injured my knee in 1996 that I learned about the value of core strength and how it could elevate my performance. Lucky for me, my physiotherapist not only identified the patella femoral injury that was causing the debilitating pain on the side of my kneecap, but in the process of creating my rehabilitation program, he discovered I had very little core strength. Although I did hundreds of sit-ups and crunches daily, I had scarcely any abdominal stability. My argument at the time was that I didn't race triathlons with my abs. How wrong I was!

Core stability is critical in all aspects of triathlon. A weak core cannot help you grab water in front of your head and pull it through to the hip during a swim stroke. It cannot properly support a body perched on a narrow bike seat, arms stretched out on aerobars and legs pedaling furiously. And a weak core cannot effectively support a body striking the ground on one leg at a time and provide the push-off needed for running. Even if you can manage to do all of these things fairly well without core strengthening, I guarantee you will be a more powerful triathlete with decreased risk of injury if you devote a portion of your training time to core conditioning.

When I am swimming well, I can feel my abs generating power as I move through the water. When cycling, I can only keep my body still when pedaling aerodynamically if I hold my core solid. And when I am running, I can activate my gluteus muscles in the push-off phase as long as my core is tight and holding my hips. If my abdominal muscles are weak, I must rely on my back to get extension through my hip for push-off. That compensation caused me to tear cartilage in my hip a few years back, and as a result, I was sidelined from the 2001 Hawaii Ironman. The conventional remedy for torn hip cartilage is surgery. Even my physiotherapist believed I would ultimately need surgery, but before going that route, he designed a program to work on core strength in my abdominal and oblique muscles. Within a few months, I was running pain free and ultimately avoided surgery. Now I regard work on core strength to be as important as any swim, bike, or run workouts in my training regimen.

Following are key core strength exercises that I incorporate into my training and that you should also consider adopting. All of these exercises should be done while breathing deeply and evenly.

PLANKING ON A SWISS BALL

Mimic the push-up position but instead of having your hands on the ground, place your hands on a physio ball shoulder-width apart with arms almost straight (see figure 7.1a). Your gluteus and abdominal muscles are tight, and your body looks like a plank. Again, try to minimize the distance from your belly button to your back. Hold this position for 15 to 20 seconds. As this becomes easier, add some variation: Lift one leg by using your gluteus muscles only (don't use your back) and keep your abs active (see figure 7.1b). Continue to raise and lower that leg. Another variation is to trace the alphabet with the ball using your hands while balancing. Simply move the ball as if you are drawing each letter with a pen attached to the bottom of the ball. Another variation is to raise and lower your heels as you hold your body balanced on the ball. The key to any variation is that you hold your gluteus muscles tight and keep your belly button contracted toward your back.

Figure 7.1 **Planking on a Swiss ball:** *(a)* standard execution and *(b)* advanced variation, raising one leg.

STANDING AT ATTENTION

Whenever you are standing, use the opportunity to work on your posture. Stand with a slight pelvic tilt and avoid an arched back. Try to minimize the distance from your belly button to your back (drawing your abdominal muscles inward). Many people naturally do the opposite and stand with an arched back with their tummy extended. This shortens the hip flexors, which inhibits the necessary extension when kicking in the pool or pushing off during a run.

MEDICINE BALL POCKET TOSS

Standing on the ground with your feet shoulder-width apart, move the medicine ball from one hip to another as if you are trying to put the ball in your pocket (see figure 7.2), keeping your arms straight. Keep your hips still and core strong.

Figure 7.2   Medicine ball pocket toss.

MEDICINE BALL KARATE CHOP

Slowly raise the ball above your head and lower it to your belly button (similar to the motion of a karate chop). Again, the key is to keep your core motionless and strong. Move the weight of your body to your forefoot to simulate the weight bearing that occurs during running. See figure 7.3.

Figure 7.3   Medicine ball karate chop.

HIP FLEXOR STRETCH

Stretch your hip flexors and strengthen your abs by lying on a weight bench and rolling a basketball on the floor with your foot. Lie down with your butt close to the edge and your legs dangling off the side. Flatten your back by doing a pelvic tilt and by trying to minimize the distance from your belly button to your back. To accomplish this, grab one knee, bring it to your chest, and hold it in your arms. That should flatten your back. If your back still isn't flat, fold a towel and place it under the small of your back. Once you achieve this position, you will have a flat back on the bench, one knee drawn to your chest, and the other leg dangling off the bench. Now, put the basketball under the dangling leg and roll it around from heel to toe (see figure 7.4). This will activate the abdominal muscles and will lengthen and stretch the hip flexors.

Figure 7.4   Hip flexor stretch.

STRENGTHENING FOR SWIMMING, BIKING, AND RUNNING

By incorporating strength work directly into your swim, bike, and run sessions, you can make your strength program more functional as well as more sport specific. Why do hamstring curls lying on a bench when you will not be in that position when running or cycling? In my experience, it is far better to work the hamstrings at angles similar to biking and running and through a similar range of motion. While strength drills are provided in the swim, bike, and run training chapters (chapters 3, 4, and 5), the concept of strength is addressed here to serve as a review and also to introduce additional strengthening strategies.

Swim Strengthening

Swim strength work can be accomplished by integrating pull buoys and paddles into your swim sets. A pull buoy is a Styrofoam floatation device that is placed between your legs to keep them afloat. This is an easy position to maintain for inexperienced swimmers because it effectively takes your legs out of the swimming equation and reduces drag through the water. The training effect of using pull buoys is twofold: It puts the swimmer in a more hydrodynamic position, allowing her to "feel" the proper body position required for fast swimming, and it forces the swimmer to rely on her arms to move through the water. An example of a swim strength set is doing 12 × 200-meter repeats and doing the last 6 repeats with pull buoys. Essentially, when you start to fatigue, you use the pull buoys, which require an even greater muscular effort and cause greater strengthening.

Once you become stronger, add paddles. Hand paddles have a larger surface area and offer greater resistance as you pull your hand through the water. In terms of muscular development, paddles offer the best strength workout for swimming because you are adding a strength component to the proper range of motion while still in the pool. The danger with hand paddles is that improper use can lead to shoulder injury. Make sure you have built up the necessary strength to use them and avoid using them if you have imperfections in your stroke.

If you seek out coaching for any aspect of triathlon, I strongly suggest hiring a swim coach. It is impossible to give yourself feedback in the pool, and inexperienced swimmers have very little body awareness in the water. My swim coach is constantly telling me that I drop my elbow. I never believed him until he filmed me swimming. Yes, I *do* drop my elbow and do a whole host of other things imperfectly. Moreover, a swim coach can recommend the proper time to integrate paddles into your workouts and can help you set parameters to avoid overuse.

Bike Strengthening

Bike strengthening can be accomplished by adding big-gear work and hill repeats to your workouts. Once you develop a cycling base of riding routinely at 90 to 100 revolutions per minute, shift your bike into a hard enough gear that it's difficult to maintain 60 to 65 revolutions per minute. This will force you to push and pull a bigger weight through the range of motion specific to cycling. Start with 2 × 10 minutes of big-gear work with 5 minutes of easy spinning in between. Over time you can work up to 60 minutes of big-gear work. Pay special attention to your knees during this phase, keeping them aligned like pistons moving up and down. Often, when pushing too heavy a gear, the knees wobble and trace a figure eight through the pedal stroke. This can lead to injury since the knee is recruiting additional muscles, tendons, and ligaments (not accustomed to that movement) to do the work.

Hill intervals also build strength on the bike. There are a variety of hill repeats that will accomplish a degree of strength training: You can climb a hill in a big gear with a low cadence; you can climb a hill and force yourself to stay seated the entire time; you can climb a hill and stand for the duration; or you can simply try to get up the hill as fast as possible. The first two methods develop strength, whereas the last two develop threshold, power, and endurance.

Run Strengthening

Strength work for running, like cycling, can be accomplished by running hill intervals or training on hilly routes. One of my favorite hill workouts is tackling a 2-minute hill continuously for 30 minutes. I run hard up the hill and cruise down. This gives me a great strength and endurance workout.

Surprisingly, many of the best strengthening exercises for running may seem mundane and easy. Try the following:

747 DRILL

Standing on one leg with your weight forward (as in a running motion), keep the non-weight-bearing leg in the air parallel to the ground and in line with your back (see figure 7.5). The key is that you can draw a straight line from your back through your ankle. Activate your gluteals to keep your free leg up. The benefits of this drill are multifaceted: First, it trains the gluteus to fire in order to support the landing leg. Most runners underutilize their gluteus muscles, which means they are unable to properly push off and are likely placing stress on their back (putting them at greater risk for injury). This drill also trains your planted foot to handle body weight. Over the course of a marathon, your feet are required to support your entire body weight for thousands of foot strikes! This exercise trains all the small muscles, tendons, and ligaments to effectively handle the foot strike phase.

Figure 7.5   747 drill.

PULLEY DRILL

The pulley drill involves attaching a pulley system to your ankle and simulating the running motion. Standing on one foot, drive the foot attached to the pulley up and down (similar to a running motion), and also move your arms as if you were running, as shown in figure 7.6. Finish with the leg extended behind your body without arching your back. Your body weight should be toward the forefoot of the planted foot in order to simulate the weight bearing of running. Focus on using your gluteus muscles to drive the engaged foot and keep your abs tight with a slight pelvic tilt.

Figure 7.6   Pulley drill.

More Power Exercises

The functional training that my physiotherapist, Steve Hill, designed for me involves exercises that target cycling and running and that train me to generate power in the range of motion specific to those sports. We integrate exercises such as squats, jump squats, one-legged lunges, side lunges, and broad jumps. These exercises must be done quickly, yet precisely, because high turnover is important in both cycling and running. In between these leg-dominant exercises, I incorporate abdominal work as recovery. These recovery exercises include using the Swiss ball and the medicine ball. I usually do three to six rounds of my circuit with 20 to 30 seconds of each exercise. A typical circuit includes the following:

- 20 seconds of quick squats.
- 20 seconds of hands-on physio ball planking.
- 20 seconds of jump squats—the key is to activate the glutes as I leave the ground and jump from the squat position.

- 20 seconds of medicine ball exercises.
- 20 seconds of lunges.
- 20 seconds of hands-on physio ball planking tracing the alphabet.
- 20 seconds of broad jump—focus is on exploding from the set position to the jump position.
- 20 seconds of medicine ball exercises.
- Repeat this sequence four to six times.

ALTERNATIVE STRENGTHENING

Yoga and Pilates are other great tools for gaining flexibility, increasing range of motion, and strengthening your core muscles. Because the movements are very precise and the focus is on breathing, both of these tools also incorporate a "calming effect" that can be beneficial in helping you "slow down" and absorb your training. Keep in mind that it is very easy to do yoga and Pilates incorrectly. Be sure to join a class with a certified instructor. I have excellent core strength and stability, and yet there are very few yoga and Pilates movements that I can do perfectly. Allow yourself to be a beginner if you don't have experience in these exercise methods. Do a modified version (prescribed by the instructor) if you cannot do the demonstrated activity correctly. By doing exercises imperfectly, you risk creating muscle imbalances that can negatively affect how you swim, bike, and run. Conversely, when performed correctly, both yoga and Pilates can correct muscle imbalances caused by swimming, biking, and running; increase overall core strength; and add power to your performance.

TESTING PERFORMANCE

Performance feedback is another critical link in the triathlon training chain. For a long time, I measured my training based on perceived effort. Now, however, I use a heart rate monitor to gauge my effort and determine exactly how hard I am pushing. I also use a PowerTap on my bike to determine my power output so that I can work on increasing my wattage on key bike rides. When riding indoors, my Computrainer measures wattage, and I can set the wattage to a certain level and force myself to ride for an extended period at that effort. On the run, I use a speed and distance system to tell me my pace, average pace, and distance covered. Often, I do my runs off the bike on a mile loop around my home, and I push the "lap" button on my heart rate monitor to compare laps. Friends tell me this sounds terribly boring, but I just love to see how fast I can go on each lap. Feedback like this can be a great motivator to get you out the door, to push the pace when necessary, and to gauge changes in fitness. Once you try it, you'll live for it.

Using Heart Rate and Lactate Threshold Training

A heart rate monitor is one of the most effective tools for monitoring training intensities, recovery, and general health. The first step in maximizing the use of a heart rate monitor is to determine an athlete's individual heart rate training zones. There are a variety of ways to obtain this information, including using generalized formulas, but the most effective method is to have a coach or exercise scientist test you either on a treadmill or stationary bike.

The most accurate of these tests is a lactate threshold test. This involves pushing an athlete to her aerobic limit, or the point at which the body is unable to take up enough oxygen for energy and produces more lactic acid in the bloodstream than the body can clear. By measuring the content of lactate in an athlete's blood, the tester can determine the heart rate at which the athlete produces lactic acid. The buildup of lactic acid is the great limiter of athletic performance. When you produce more lactic acid than your system can clear at any one time, your body slows down to compensate. The key to enhancing athletic performance is to raise your aerobic threshold—that is, the heart rate at which you produce lactic acid—and to increase your body's efficiency at ridding itself of the metabolic waste. Using myself as an example, my max heart rate is approximately 184 beats per minute (bpm), and my lactate threshold is about 175 bpm. Notice how close my lactate threshold is to my maximum heart rate. This means I can exercise at a very high heart rate, almost my max, before I will produce lactate. That is especially beneficial to me as an Ironman athlete because it means I can race at my anaerobic threshold (lactate threshold) for the entire race, which is almost the same pace that I would hold during an Olympic-distance event.

Your lactate threshold is completely individual and is something that must be tested to ensure accuracy. It is best tested by a coach or exercise professional; however, triathlon and cycling coach Bettina Younge has provided some self-tests in the sidebar on page 90 to give you an idea of your LT.

Once you determine your lactate threshold, you can tailor your workouts according to this magic number (see table 7.1). To increase your lactate threshold, you will need to train very close to that number for an extended period. For example, tempo runs and bikes are usually done just below threshold. This is where your heart rate monitor comes into play. When your schedule calls for you to do a tempo session, you use your monitor to gauge your effort and stay in a zone that is neither too hard nor too easy.

Keep in mind, however, that training by heart rate alone can be misleading. Your heart rate is subject to other conditions such as air temperature, humidity, nerves, diet, and general health. Some days, no matter how hard I work, I can't get my heart rate to rise high enough. Those are usually days when I am fatigued from training hard. Training in a fatigued state is sometimes necessary when training for an Ironman because it is an extreme endurance

Measuring Lactate Threshold

There are several different ways to estimate or measure heart rate at lactate threshold:

Blood Test

Usually done in a laboratory

Required equipment: watch, trainer, heart rate monitor, power measurement, lactate analyzer

This is the most accurate test for determining heart rate at lactate threshold. Protocols may vary depending on the testing institution. Often, wattage is increased by 20 to 30 watts every three minutes once the test has begun.

Conconi Test

Usually done with a coach

Required equipment: watch, trainer, heart rate monitor, odometer

It is sometimes difficult to find the deflection point on the graph of speed versus heart rate. The observation of a ventilatory threshold may help in estimating lactate threshold.

Other Estimations

Estimate lactate threshold on your own

Required equipment: watch, heart rate monitor

Possible procedures:

- On a bike, find a steady climb or 10K time trial and, after a 10- to 15-minute warm-up, ride it at the highest sustainable pace you can. The average heart rate in this time trial should be close to the heart rate at your lactate threshold.

- On a bike, find a steady climb or 10K time trial and, after a warm-up, pick an effort level and continue increasing your effort every few minutes (look at your heart rate monitor and bump it up about five beats every few minutes). When you need to back off from a pace because you feel like you can't sustain it for 20 minutes, try to continue riding at just a few beats per minute below the effort level that you were not able to hold. You should find a level that is quite uncomfortable but that you are able to maintain (just barely). The heart rate at this effort level should be close to your lactate threshold.

Heart rate zones will vary for each athlete and need to be refined through testing and observation. Heart rate zones need to be adjusted slightly on a daily basis because the lactate threshold depends on factors such as fatigue, dehydration, or altitude changes. It will also vary with fitness, so you should redo the test at regular intervals. Also remember that lactate threshold and heart rate zones vary significantly among different sports.

Bettina Younge, PhD

TABLE 7.1 **Lactate Threshold and Rating of Perceived Exertion (RPE) Training Zones**

Zone	Swim pace	Percent of lactate threshold heart rate (bike)	Percent of lactate threshold heart rate (run)	Rating of perceived exertion or RPE (Borg scale)	Breathing and perception using running as the example	Purpose and cross-reference of terms commonly used to describe each zone
1	Work on form; no clock watching	80 and less	84 and less	6-9	Gentle rhythmic breathing. Pace is easy and relaxed. For running, intensity is a jog or trot.	Easy, aerobic, recovery
2	T-pace (race pace) + 10 sec. per 100 meters	81-88	85-91	10-12	Breathing rate and pace increase slightly. Many notice a change with slightly deeper breathing, although still comfortable. Running pace remains comfortable, and conversations are possible.	Aerobic, extensive endurance, aerobic threshold endurance Ironman-distance race pace for beginners is typically within zones 1 and 2.
3	T-pace + 5 sec. per 100	89-93	92-95	13-14	Aware of breathing a little harder; pace is moderate. It is more difficult to hold a conversation.	Tempo, intensive endurance Ironman-distance race pace for experienced athletes is typically within zones 1 to 3.
4	T-pace	94-99	96-99	15-16	Starting to breathe hard; pace is fast and beginning to get uncomfortable, approaching all-out 1 hr. run pace.	Subthreshold, muscular endurance, threshold endurance, anaerobic threshold endurance
5a	T-pace	100-102	100-102	17	Breathing deep and forceful; many notice a second significant change in breathing pattern. Pace is all-out, sustainable for 1 to 1 1/2 hr. Mental focus required, moderately uncomfortable, and conversation undesirable.	Lactate threshold endurance, anaerobic threshold endurance, superthreshold, muscular endurance Olympic-distance race pace is typically zones 4 to 5a for experienced athletes and zones 1 to 3 for inexperienced athletes.
5b	T-pace - 5 sec. per 100	103-105	103-106	18-19	Heavy, labored breathing. Pace is noticeably challenging but sustainable for 15 to 30 min. Discomfort is high but manageable.	Aerobic capacity, speed endurance, anaerobic endurance Sprint-distance race pace is typically zones 4 to 5b, with limited 5c for experienced athletes.
5c	As fast as possible	106+	107+	20	Maximal exertion in breathing; pace is sprinting effort, with high discomfort that is unsustainable for over 1 min.	Anaerobic capacity, power

Note that the training zones used by some coaches vary from these definitions. The "newer" zones are as as follows: zone 1—recovery and endurance; zone 2—tempo; zone 3—lactate threshold; zone 4—long and short intensive repetitions; zone 5—sprinting. By simply referring to the definitions of these two training zone guidelines, it's easy to make conversions when needed.

event that requires your body to continue moving even when it is tired. On these days, I rely on feelings of perceived exertion to keep me in the right training zone (see figure 7.7). Then, when I begin to hit my peak training phase where I am trying to maintain speed, I will be more rested for these workouts, and my heart rate should respond accordingly.

6	No exertion at all
7	Extremely light
8	
9	Very light
10	
11	Light
12	
13	Somewhat hard
14	
15	Hard (heavy)
16	
17	Very hard
18	
19	Extremely hard
20	Maximal exertion

Borg RPE scale
© Gunnar Borg, 1970, 1985, 1994, 1998

Figure 7.7   Borg's rating of perceived exertion scale.

A heart rate monitor is also very beneficial on easier training days. As everyone knows, you can't complete threshold workouts every day or you'd become overtrained and your performance would decline. So, a heart rate monitor can keep you working at easier efforts that will most likely fall between 65 and 70 percent of your threshold heart rate. These workouts might be designed for recovery, or they might be long base workouts that lay the foundation for your in-season training.

Lastly, your heart rate monitor can help you gauge how quickly you can recover from your intervals. The more fit you become, the quicker your heart rate will drop from your interval effort heart rate to about 60 percent of your threshold heart rate. When your heart rate falls into this "recovered" zone, it is time to do another interval.

Using Wattage Training

Power measured in watts, which can be utilized in bike training, is probably the best gauge of training intensity. It is a direct measure of the rate of work produced by an athlete. It is not influenced by the heat or by your mood or your environment. For example, on a particular ride, your average speed can vary dramatically depending on the wind, heat, and so on. You may finish a ride feeling deflated when you see that your average speed is lower than anticipated. On the other hand, if you had used a power meter, you likely would have found that your average wattage was significantly higher than normal. This means that your training intensity was higher and that the training effect was more beneficial than the ride you did the week before in perfect conditions at a higher average speed. The more power you can generate, the greater your potential for improved performance.

I use a Computrainer to gauge my fitness level from week to week. I set my wattage on my Computrainer and then "force" myself to maintain that level. Each week, I try to increase my wattage for a particular workout set, such as 2 × 20K time trials with 20 minutes of recovery. I set my watts at 200 and then hammer for as long as I can. If I notice that my heart rate is significantly lower than my threshold, I increase the watts and see if I can boost the cadence to support the increase. I keep going until either my cadence falls below 90 revolutions per minute or my heart rate gets close to my threshold.

If I am riding outside, I use a PowerTap to gauge my power. After first using my PowerTap, I noticed that my power really drops on the descents. So, besides trying to push the highest possible watts on the flats and on the hills, I also try to keep my wattage high on the downhills. These little techniques and subsequent improvements can lead to a substantial difference in race performance.

Using Racing to Determine Performance Levels

Despite all the technology used to measure heart rate, lactate threshold, wattage, speed, and distance, nothing can take the place of getting out there and actually racing. When you race, you gain experience and push your body harder than you would ever push it in a workout. Racing allows you to practice your mental preparation and determine which mental state creates the best race performance zone for you. It allows you to troubleshoot your nutrition, test your sight and draft on the swim, and gain confidence dealing with a mass start. Racing puts you in a competitive arena that training cannot—neck and neck with another athlete on the bike or the run; in a possible illegal drafting position on the bike; and in cornering situations with other athletes. Best of all, racing allows you to break the finish line tape and truly assess your performance—physically, mentally, and emotionally.

Getting Set for Sprint Racing

Gale Bernhardt

A sprint-distance triathlon is an excellent way to achieve fitness and experiment with the sport of triathlon. Most often, it takes just one experiment before the addiction sets in. One triathlon never seems to be enough—it's simply too much fun to stop there! Once you become hooked on the sport, sprint triathlon can be a great way to test and improve your speed, and it can also serve as a powerful stepping stone toward longer distances if you so desire.

Sprint-distance triathlons usually involve swimming 400 to 500 meters, biking 11 to 15 miles, and running 3.1 miles (5K). While the longer events tend to get all the glory, training to maximize your genetic potential at this short distance is no easy feat. Those who specialize in sprint racing—and who in fact race it "all out"—will attest that it can be very uncomfortable.

Before training to go all-out fast and maximize your ability to sprint, a foundation of fitness is essential. In this chapter, two training plans are provided, one plan for beginner triathletes who are reasonably fit and one plan for intermediate-level triathletes. The plans can be used as stand-alone programs or can be used consecutively.

PLAN GOALS AND ATHLETE PROFILES

The training plan you select depends on your fitness level prior to beginning training and on your goals for the event. This section provides an athlete profile (description of fitness level and current activity) and goal statement for each plan.

Fit Beginner Plan

The goal when using the beginner plan is to comfortably complete a sprint-distance triathlon consisting of approximately 500 meters of swimming, 15 miles of cycling, and 3.1 miles of running.

Before beginning this plan, you are in reasonably good shape. Although you are fit, it has been a while since you have been in the pool, but you can comfortably swim 25 meters without stopping. For swimming as well as the other sports, you lack endurance. You are looking to the plan to help you build swimming and triathlon-specific endurance.

You are currently riding your bike (indoor or outdoor bike) three times per week. On two of the days, your ride length is about 45 minutes, and you do a longer ride of about an hour on the third day. You are capable of running three times per week for 15 to 20 minutes per session. (If you are

© Human Kinetics

Once you get your feet wet in triathlon, you can use sprint racing to improve your speed.

not capable of this level of training, work up to it and return to the plan when you are ready.) Your available weekly training hours range from 3.5 to about 5 hours.

Intermediate Athlete Plan

The goal when using the intermediate plan is to comfortably complete a sprint-distance triathlon—consisting of approximately 500 meters of swimming, 15 miles of cycling, and 3.1 miles of running—at a faster pace than your last race or faster than your current fitness allows.

This plan is designed as the next step after the beginner plan. Many new triathletes like to use a beginner's plan to start their season, and after a taste of competition, they want to do a second, faster race at the end of the season. This plan will help you do just that.

Although the intermediate plan was designed with the beginner plan in mind, it can be used as a stand-alone plan for anyone who is fit enough to complete it.

Before beginning the plan, you can comfortably swim 500 meters. You are riding a bike three times per week. Two of the rides are about 45 minutes long, and the third ride is an hour to an hour and 15 minutes. You are running two or three days per week for about 30 minutes per session. Your available weekly training hours range from about 3.5 to 6.5 hours.

INTENSITY FOR BOTH PLANS

For all workouts, you must determine your intensity. Doing all workouts at an all-out intensity will lead to injury or burnout and will do little to build true fitness. For the plans in this chapter, use a rating of perceived exertion (RPE) scale or a heart rate monitor to judge intensity and speed. Heart rates and RPE values are referred to by "zone." A reference scale for heart rate, RPE, and the related zone can be found in table 7.1 on page 91. This chapter does not detail how to determine lactate threshold heart rate, but more information can be found in chapter 7.

GENERAL INSTRUCTIONS FOR BOTH PLANS

Every workout should include a period of warm-up and cool-down. At minimum, 10 minutes of warm-up should be performed at intensity zone 1 and some zone 2. For cool-down, 5 to 10 minutes works well. Warm-up and cool-down time is included in the total workout time shown on the charts.

When a range of intensities is specified for a workout—for example, "ride at intensity zones 1 to 2"—the goal is not to maximize time in the higher zone (in this case, zone 2). If you are feeling good, it is fine to include more time in zone 2; however, if you are feeling tired, more zone 1 is appropriate.

The training plans utilize abbreviations and special terms to optimize space on the chart. Those abbreviations and terms are as follows:

5 × 3 min. (1 min. RI) into zone 3 intensity: This is a shorthand example for three-minute intervals performed five times with a one-minute rest interval. After the warm-up, begin timing the interval as soon as you begin the effort. Heart rate as displayed on your monitor takes some time to catch up to the perceived effort. Once you achieve zone 3 on your heart rate monitor or perceived effort, hold that intensity until the end of the interval time assigned. Take a one-minute recovery in zone 1 between each work bout.

Accels: Accelerations. A gentle buildup of speed. Not an all-out sprint.

Brick: A bike ride immediately followed by a run.

Cadence: On the run, count left (or right) foot strikes for 15 seconds. The value should be 22 or more. On the bike, if you do not have a cadence meter, count the number of times your left or right foot reaches the bottom of the pedal stroke. On the bike, this is also known as revolutions per minute (rpm), and you are aiming for 90 or more rpm in the form workouts.

ILT: Isolated leg training. On the bike, rest one leg in or out of the pedal while the other leg does 90 to 100 percent of the work. Begin by working one leg only 20 or 30 seconds and accumulating about 3 minutes of total ILT work per leg. As you gain fitness, increase the total amount of work per leg to about 10 minutes.

Min.: Minute

Negative split: A workout in which the second half of the assigned distance or time is faster than the first half.

RI: Rest interval

Rpm: Revolutions per minute

Sec.: Second

For all workouts more than an hour long, carry fluids and fuel. See chapter 13 for more details on this subject.

The plans in this chapter do not include specific recommendations for strength training. If your main goal is triathlon success, your strength training program should not make your arms and legs fatigued for the endurance workouts.

BEGINNER PLAN DETAILS

The fit beginner plan for sprint-distance racing is presented in table 8.1 on pages 100-101. Notice that the swim days are Monday and Wednesday, while brick days are Tuesday and Thursday in nonrest weeks and Saturday in rest weeks. Long runs are scheduled on Saturday, and long bike rides are on Sunday. If it works better for you to rearrange the workout days, that's no problem. Just try to keep 48 hours between similar workouts. For example, swim on Tuesday and Thursday as opposed to Tuesday and Wednesday.

To save space on the chart, the swim workouts are noted by workout number. The swim workouts for the beginner plan are listed here:

Swim Workout Number and Main Set Description for the Beginner Plan

1. 20 × 25 meters (10-second rest interval [RI])
2. 10 × 25 meters (5-second RI), 10 × 25 (10-second RI)
3. 5 × 50 meters (20-second RI), 10 × 25 (10-second RI)
4. 5 × 50 meters (15-second RI), 10 × 25 (5-second RI)
5. 10 × 50 meters (20-second RI)
6. 8 × 75 meters (20-second RI)
7. 4 × 75 meters (20-second RI), 6 × 50 (20-second RI); swim 50s faster than 75s
8. 4 × 100 meters (20-second RI), 4 × 50 (20-second RI); swim 50s faster than 100s
9. 5 × 100 meters (20-second RI)
10. 4 × 150 meters (20-second RI)
11. 3 × 200 meters (20-second RI)
12. 500-meter steady swim
13. 1 × 200 meters (20-second RI), 2 × 100 (20-second RI), 4 × 50 (20-second RI). Each swim set faster than the previous one.
14. 6 × 50 meters (20-second RI); each 50 faster than the previous one.

Notice that only the main set is assigned, and this is the minimum recommended swimming distance for each numbered workout. If you have more swimming skill or more time, include a warm-up set of 100 to 300 meters and a similar cool-down.

If you are looking to minimize pool time, make the first few meters a gentle warm-up and the last few meters a gentle cool-down. Keep most of the swimming intensity in zone 1 or zone 2. Some of the workouts include faster swimming. "Fast" in this case means your goal race pace or slightly faster.

Week 1 begins with a swim on Monday, followed by a brick on Tuesday. The brick workouts can be done on your own at home or at the gym. Either way, each brick workout has a recommended intensity and a focus prescription. The prescription for each workout has an intended benefit for your fitness. General workout purposes include building endurance, improving economy (the oxygen cost of a particular pace), improving the ability to work at faster speeds, recovery, neuromuscular form work, and learning to appropriately pace yourself, to name a few.

TABLE 8.1 *Getting Set for Sprint Racing–Beginner Plan*

	Monday	Tuesday	Wednesday	Thursday	Friday	Saturday	Sunday
Week 1	**Swim:** Workout #1	**Brick:** 1:00 **Bike:** 45 min. Ride a flat course (in zones 1 to 2). **Run:** 15 min. Run a flat course (zone 1).	**Swim:** Workout #2	**Brick:** 1:00 **Bike:** 45 min. Ride a mostly flat course (in zones 1 to 2 at 90+ rpm). **Run:** 15 min. Run a mostly flat course (zones 1 to 2); count cadence and aim for 22+.	Day off	**Run:** 20 min. Run a mostly flat course in zones 1 to 2.A soft surface such as a treadmill, dirt, or grass is good.	**Bike:** 1:00. Ride a mostly flat course at zone 1 to 2 intensity.
Week 2	**Swim:** Workout #3	**Brick:** 1:00 **Bike:** 45 min. **Run:** 15 min. For both sports, negative split an out-and-back course. Go out zone 1 and back in 2.	**Swim:** Workout #4	**Brick:** 1:00 **Bike:** 45 min. Mostly zones 1 and 2. Include 6 × 30 sec. accels (1:30 RI). **Run:** 15 min. Mostly zones 1 and 2. Include 3 × 30 sec. accels (1:30 RI).	Day off	**Run:** 30 min. Run on a mostly flat course in zones 1 and 2.	**Bike:** 1:15. Ride a mostly flat course in zones 1 to 2.
Week 3	Day off	**Bike:** 1:00 Mostly zone 1 to 2 intensity; include ILT work.	**Swim:** Workout #5	**Run:** 30 min. Run mostly in zones 1 and 2. Count cadence and aim for 22+.	Day off	**Brick:** 1:15 **Bike:** 45 min. **Run:** 30 min. For both sports, negative split an out-and-back course. Go out zone 1 and back in 2. Count cadence on both sports going out; aim for 90 rpm on the bike, 22+ for the run.	Day off
Week 4	**Swim:** Workout #6	**Brick:** 1:00 **Bike:** 45 min. Ride 20 min. zone 1, 15 min. zone 2, and 10 min. zone 3. **Run:** 15 min.All zone 1 to 2.	**Swim:** Workout #7	**Brick:** 1:00 **Bike:** 30 min. **Run:** 30 min. Both sports in zone 1 to 2. Count cadence on both sports going out; aim for 90 rpm on the bike, 22+ for the run.	Day off	**Run:** 30 min. Run a rolling course at intensity zones 1 to 3. Accumulate 10 min. in zone 3.	**Bike:** 1:30. Ride mostly in zones 1 to 2. Accumulate about 30 min. in zone 2.

	Monday	Tuesday	Wednesday	Thursday	Friday	Saturday	Sunday
Week 5	Swim: Workout #8	Brick: 1:00. Bike: 45 min. Run: 15 min. Both sports at zone 1 to 2 intensity, based on how you feel.	Swim: Workout #9	Brick: 1:00. Bike: 30 min. Zones 1 to 2. Run: 30 min. Begin in zones 1 to 2, then 5 × 3 min. (1 min. RI) into zone 3 intensity.	Day off	Run: 45 min. Run a rolling course in zones 1 to 2.	Bike: 1:30. Ride a rolling course in zones 1 to 3. Accumulate about 30 min. in zone 3.
Week 6	Day off	Bike: 1:00. Mostly zone 1 to 2 intensity; include ILT work.	Day off	Run: 45 min. Run a mostly flat course (zones 1 to 2); count cadence and aim for 22+.	Day off	Race simulation day: Swim: 500 yards Bike: 45 min. Run: 15 min. All three sports in a negative split manner. First half in zones 1 to 2, second half in zones 2 to 3.	Day off
Week 7	Swim: Workout #10	Brick: 1:00. Bike: 45 min. Begin in zones 1 to 2, then 4 × 4 min. (1 min. RI) into zone 3 intensity. Run: 15 min. Zones 1 to 2, based on how you feel.	Swim: Workout #11	Brick: 1:00. Bike: 30 min. Run: 30 min. Both sports in zones 1 to 2. Count cadence on both sports going out; aim for 90 rpm on the bike, 22+ for the run.	Day off	Run: 30 min. Run at zone 1 to 3 intensity; no more than 15 min. in zone 3.	Bike: 1:30. Ride a rolling course at zone 1 to 2 intensity.
Week 8	Swim: Workout #12	Brick: 1:00. Bike: 45 min. Begin at zone 1, move to zone 2, with the last 15 min. steady in zone 3. Run: 15 min. Begin at zone 1, move to zone 2, with the last 7 min. steady in zone 3.	Swim: Workout #13	Brick: 1:00. Bike: 20 min. Run: 25 min. Both sports in zones 1 to 2. Count cadence on both sports going out; aim for 90 rpm on the bike, 22+ for the run.	Day off	Run: 30 min. Run in zones 1 to 2 on a rolling course.	Bike: 1:00. Ride mostly in zones 1 to 2. Within the ride, include 4 × 90 sec. working up to zone 3 intensity and hold it steady. Take 3 min. RIs between each 90 sec.
Week 9	Day off	Swim: Workout #14	Day off	Run: 20 min. Run mostly at zone 1 to 2 intensity. Include 3 × 30 sec. accels (1:30 RI).	Day off	Bike: 30 min. Ride mostly in zones 1 to 2. Check all gears and do a couple of accels.	Race day!

Notice that each brick workout has the total time listed, such as 1:00 on Tuesday. In addition to the total time, the time for each sport within the brick is listed as well. For the Tuesday workout previously mentioned, the bike ride is 45 minutes of the total time, and the run is 15 minutes. The total workout time may go slightly over 1:00, because it takes some time to transition from one sport to the next. Transitions count toward your overall race time, so minimizing transition time is good practice.

The long Saturday run begins at 20 minutes, and the long ride at 1:00. The time of these long workouts builds over the course of the plan. Note that the longest ride builds to 1:30 and the longest run to 45 minutes.

This particular plan uses three-week cycles. There are two weeks of higher volume followed by a reduced-volume rest week. Rest weeks are where fitness gains are made; do not cheat on rest!

In the week prior to race week, check all of your equipment to make sure it's working properly, and try to drive the course if possible. Plan to use the same gear you have tested in workouts on race day.

On race day, plan to arrive with plenty of time to spare to reduce stress. Because you have practiced setting up your swim-to-bike and bike-to-run transitions, the routine should feel comfortable. When the gun goes off, try to keep your speed (intensity) equal to what you practiced in training. During the event, be sure to look around and enjoy the moment. You have built great fitness; enjoy it!

INTERMEDIATE PLAN DETAILS

The intermediate plan for sprint-distance racing is outlined in table 8.2 on pages 104-105. This plan includes more volume and intensity than the beginner plan. It requires a higher level of base fitness prior to beginning the plan. Because there are many similarities between the two plans, if you have not done so already, read the previous description for the beginner plan. The text that follows assumes you have read the beginner plan information.

Like the beginner plan, swim days are scheduled for Monday and Wednesday. The swim workouts follow a repeating pattern and are listed here:

Swim Workout Number and Main Set Description for the Intermediate Plan

1. 5 to 8 × 100 meters (20-second rest interval [RI])

2. T-pace test: After a good warm-up, swim 3 × 100 meters with 20 seconds rest between each swim. Determine your average pace per 100 based on the three swims. This average pace is called your T-pace. As you improve your speed, this average pace should decrease (get faster).

3. Warm-up: 100 to 300 swimming, 100 to 300 kicking, 100 to 300 swimming

Main set: 5 to 8 × 100 at T-pace plus 1 to 3 seconds, zone 1 to 2 intensity (10- to 15-second RI)

Cool-down: 100 to 300 swimming

4. Warm-up: 100 to 300 swimming, 100 to 300 form drills, 100 to 300 swimming

Main set: 6 to 10 × 50 at T-pace minus 1 to 5 seconds (1-minute RI)

Cool-down: 100 to 300 swimming

5. Warm-up: 300, your choice

Main set: 500 swim, negative split where the second 250 is faster than the first

Cool-down: 100 to 300 swimming

6. Warm-up: 300, your choice

Main set: 4 × 50 at race pace (10-second RI)

Cool-down: 100 easy swimming

Notice that the swimming in the intermediate plan utilizes your personal speed. Learning to watch the pace clock to monitor your pace becomes more important with this plan and as you continue to try to improve performance.

Many of the swim workouts include a range of intervals. At the start of the plan, begin with the lower number of intervals. As the plan and your fitness progress, you can increase the distance you swim within a single workout. Although the workouts assigned here can do the job, some people prefer more variety. More workouts are available at local Masters swimming sessions and in my book *Workouts in a Binder™ for Triathletes*.

On Monday and Wednesday, in addition to a swim, a run workout is planned. On Monday, the run is optional and is intended for those with more running experience and training time. In this particular plan, the weekday runs and bike rides are longer than in the beginner plan. For this reason, and other plan design reasons, the rides and runs are scheduled on different days.

There are several similarities between the two plans, but the intermediate plan contains more volume and more intensity. If you find that the intensity is making you too tired, modify the plan by decreasing the number of intervals within a workout.

As with the beginner schedule, plan to race at the intensities you practiced in training. By pacing yourself, you can enjoy a strong kick at the end of the event.

Both the beginner and intermediate plans will go a long way toward increasing your level of fitness and your skills as a triathlete. If fun is your main objective, sprint racing is a great, nonintimidating way to enjoy triathlon racing. If speed is your strength, consider specializing in sprint-distance racing and seeing how competitive you can become. And, if you're looking to use sprint racing as a springboard to longer distances, turn to chapter 9 to learn about entering the exciting world of Olympic-distance triathlon.

TABLE 8.2 Getting Set for Sprint Racing—Intermediate Plan

	Monday	Tuesday	Wednesday	Thursday	Friday	Saturday	Sunday
Week 1	**Swim:** Workout #1 **Run:** (optional) 20 to 30 min. (zone 1)	**Bike:** 45 min. Ride a mostly flat course in zones 1 to 2. Keep cadence at 90+ rpm.	**Swim:** Workout #2 **Run:** 30 min. Run an out-and-back course, negative split mode. Go out in zones 1 to 2; come back in zones 2 to 3. Leave enough time for cool-down.	**Bike:** 45 min. Ride a rolling course at zones 1 to 2 intensity.	Day off	**Run:** 30 min. Run mostly in zones 1 and 2. Count cadence and aim for 22+.	**Bike:** 1:15. Ride a rolling to hilly course at intensity zones 1 to 5a. Accumulate about 20 min. in zones 4 to 5a.
Week 2	**Swim:** Workout #3 **Run:** (optional) 20 to 30 min. (zone 1)	**Bike:** 45 to 60 min. Ride a mostly flat course in zones 1 to 2. Keep cadence at 90+ rpm.	**Swim:** Workout #4 **Run:** 45 min. After a good warm-up, do 4 to 6 × 3 min. to intensity zone 4 to 5a (1 min. RD). Cool down after.	**Bike:** 45 to 60 min. Ride a rolling course at zones 1 to 2 intensity.	Day off	**Run:** 45 min. Run mostly in zones 1 and 2. Count cadence and aim for 22+.	**Bike:** 1:30. Ride a rolling to hilly course at intensity zones 1 to 5a. Accumulate 20 to 30 min. in zones 4 to 5a.
Week 3	Day off	**Bike:** 1:00. Within a ride that is mostly at zone 1 to 2 intensity, include 4 × 90 sec. at intensity zone 4 to 5a (1 min. RD).	**Swim:** Workout #5	**Run:** 30 min. Run mostly at zone 1 to 2 intensity. Include 3 or 4 × 30 sec. accels (1:30 RD).	Day off	**Brick:** 1:30 **Bike:** 1:00 **Run:** 30 min. For both sports, keep intensity mostly in zone 1 to 2. Include a few 30 sec. accels as you please. Long rest intervals.	Day off
Week 4	**Swim:** Workout #3 **Run:** (optional) 20 to 30 min. (zone 1)	**Bike:** 1:00. Ride a mostly flat course in zones 1 to 2. Keep cadence at 90+ rpm.	**Swim:** Workout #4 **Run:** 45 min. After a good warm-up, do 4 or 5 × 4 min. to intensity zone 4 to 5a (1 min. RD). Cool down after.	**Bike:** 45 to 60 min. Ride a rolling course at zones 1 to 2 intensity.	Day off	**Run:** 45 min. Run mostly in zones 1 and 2. Count cadence and aim for 22+.	**Bike:** 1:30. Warm up 20 min. in zones 1 to 2. Then do 3 × (10 min. building to zones 4 and 5a and holding steady, then 10 min. at zones 1 to 2).

	Monday	Tuesday	Wednesday	Thursday	Friday	Saturday	Sunday
Week 5	Swim: Workout #3 Run: (optional) 20 to 30 min. (zone 1)	Bike: 1:00. Ride a mostly flat course in zones 1 to 2. Keep cadence at 90+ rpm.	Swim: Workout #4 Run: 45 min. After a good warm-up, do 5 × 3 min. into zone 5b (3 min. RI). Can be on the track. Be sure to leave enough time for a cool-down.	Bike: 45 to 60 min. Ride a rolling course at zones 1 to 2 intensity.	Day off	Run: 45 min. Run mostly in zones 1 and 2. Count cadence and aim for 22+.	Bike: 1:30. Warm up 45 min. in zones 1 to 2. Then do 4 or 5 × 6 min. building to zones 4 and 5a and holding steady (2 min. RI).
Week 6	Day off	Bike: 1:00. Within a ride that is mostly at zone 1 to 2 intensity, include 4 × 90 sec. at intensity zone 4 to 5a (1 min. RI).	Swim: Workout #2	Run: 30 min. Run mostly at zone 1 to 2 intensity. Include 3 or 4 × 30 sec. accels (1:30 RI).	Day off	Brick: 1:30 Bike: 1:00 Run: 30 min. For both sports, keep intensity mostly at zone 1 to 2. Include a few 30 sec. accels as you please. Long rest intervals.	Day off
Week 7	Swim: Workout #3 Run: (optional) 20 to 30 min. (zone 1)	Bike: 1:00. After a good warm-up, do 5 × 3 min. into zone 5b (3 min. RI). Can be on an uphill course. Be sure to leave enough time for a cool-down.	Swim: Workout #4 Run: 45 min. Run on a flat to gently rolling course in zones 1 and 2.	Bike: 30 to 45 min. Ride a mostly flat course at intensity zones 1 to 2 at 90+ rpm.	Day off	Brick: 1:30 Bike: 1:00. After a warm-up, do 4 or 5 × 5 min. into intensity zones 4 to 5a (2 min. RI). Run: 30 min. Run on an out-and-back course in a negative split manner; out in zones 1 to 2, back at zones 4 to 5a.	Bike: 1:30. Ride a flat course at zone 1 intensity. Easy and fun ride.
Week 8	Swim: Workout #3 Run: (optional) 20 to 30 min. (zone 1)	Bike: 1:00. After a good warm-up, do 5 × 1 min. building speed to nearly all-out (4 min. RI). Be sure to leave enough time for a cool-down.	Swim: Workout #4 Run: 45 min. Run on a flat to gently rolling course in zones 1 and 2.	Bike: 30 to 45 min. Ride a mostly flat course at intensity zones 1 to 2 at 90+ rpm.	Day off	Brick: 1:30 Bike: 1:00. Ride an out-and-back course in a negative split manner. Go out at zone 1 to 2 intensity, and back at zones 4 to 5a. Run: 30 min. Run an out-and-back course in a negative split manner. Go out at mostly zone 2 intensity, and back at zones 4 to 5b.	Bike: 1:30. Ride a flat course at zone 1 intensity. Easy and fun ride.
Week 9	Day off	Bike: 1:00. Within a ride that is mostly at zone 1 to 2 intensity, include 4 × 90 sec. at intensity zone 4 to 5a (1 min. RI).	Swim: Workout #6	Run: 30 min. Run mostly at zone 1 to 2 intensity. Include 3 or 4 × 30 sec. accels (1:30 RI).	Day off	Bike: 30 min. Ride mostly in zones 1 to 2. Check all gears and do a couple of accels.	Race day!

Succeeding at the Olympic Distance

Siri Lindley

I'll always remember my first Olympic-distance race, which took place in Ashland, Massachusetts. I loved the fact that I had to first focus on completing the distance (I had only done sprint triathlons until then) but could also throw in a big effort to keep things fast. The race wasn't long enough to scare me away and not short enough to have me going too hard and blowing up.

It's this "best of both worlds" aspect of Olympic-distance racing that makes it a perfect test for competitors who want to go the distance while also having the option of mixing in some speed. It's also a perfect challenge for anyone who has been competing in sprint racing and wants to increase her endurance.

The Olympic distance is sometimes classified as a middle distance. In reality, there is a range of middle-distance triathlons held throughout the world, most of which are a variation of the traditional 1.5K swim, 40K bike, and 10K run that make up the Olympic distance. For the purposes of this chapter, I will focus on Olympic-distance racing since it is the most popular of the middle distances.

STRATEGIZING FOR OLYMPIC-DISTANCE RACING

How you approach triathlon training and the way you execute your training on race day are just as critical to your overall success as the many swim, bike, and run workouts you'll be doing to increase your strength and endurance. Think of the following techniques as the building blocks of your Olympic-distance racing plan and your training and fitness will fall into place.

Know Your Weakness

One of the biggest mistakes you can make in triathlon training is focusing on what you love. If you're an experienced runner who uses the run leg to move yourself up in the results, you are most likely limiting your potential in the other two disciplines, and ultimately, in the sport. As discussed in chapter 1, triathlon is about becoming as efficient as possible in *three* sports and putting the disciplines together as powerfully as possible. To do this, you must concentrate on your weaknesses.

I entered this sport as a nonswimmer—I could splash around, but swim training was totally foreign to me. Therefore, if I was going to do a triathlon, my first goal was to learn how to swim.

During my eight years in competitive triathlon, I made the swim my main focus. This was particularly important because my professional career involved competing in draft-legal racing, which meant that if I didn't exit the water in time to join a lead pack on the bike, I would be fighting a losing battle on the run. I knew that if I wanted to win races and be the best, I had to advance my swim far enough to compete with the Barb Lindquists, Loretta Harrops, and Sheila Taorminas of the world. So, even as my swim improved, I treated it as my weakness and did everything in my power to make it my strength. In the end, I earned a world championship title and walked away knowing I had become the best possible triathlete I could be.

Although you won't likely be competing in draft-legal racing, you should consider how working on your own weaknesses can be used to your best advantage. This doesn't mean you won't work hard in the other disciplines; it simply means you should not ignore any aspect of triathlon training, and that turning your weakness into a strength can lead to performance breakthroughs.

Know the Key Components

I believe there are four key components involved in training well for an Olympic-distance triathlon: fitness, strength, form, and the ability to stretch your thresholds for training.

Using swimming as an example, I spent many years working on my technique and strength in the water. It wasn't until I began working with coach Brett Sutton in Australia that I realized I wasn't pushing myself hard enough to reach the next level. I used to say, "I'm giving all I have" and "I can't push any harder." Coach Sutton recognized that I *could* push harder, that there was more there, and that I should not be afraid to push that little bit extra. In doing so, I reached a whole new level of training and realized that in addition to increased fitness and strength, as well as proper form, this would lead me to faster swims and faster finishing times.

Of course, this does not mean that you should always push yourself to your limits. Triathlon training, as covered in chapter 2, involves stressing the body, giving it time to adapt, and then stressing it some more to increase fitness. Therefore, the time to really push yourself beyond what you think is possible is on the day when your schedule calls for you to go hard—and never on your easy days or rest days.

Focus on Quality

The smartest way to train as a triathlete is to focus on *quality* of work as opposed to quantity. Working hard is important, but training efficiently is critical for long-term success. To do this, athletes must set realistic goals. These goals depend on the potential and qualities of the athlete. To reach peak form, a certain number of stages must be achieved. Set small goals every day; work to become fitter, faster, and stronger through your training; and don't focus too closely on an end result—the results will come as your short-term goals are met.

© John Segesta

Olympic-distance racing will do wonders to improve strength, endurance, and even speed.

TRAINING PLANS

Since this book is for triathletes with varying abilities and fitness levels, keep in mind that you may need to make adjustments to the training programs to suit your level. To help you do this, ranges are provided in both the level I and level II plans. Use your judgment based on individual fitness as well as how you feel on a given day to determine where your workouts should fall within the ranges.

For the first four to eight weeks of the plans, you will gradually build training time. During this phase, the focus is on aerobic endurance, and intensity is not a consideration. You should organize your sessions so that they are spread throughout the week and so that you're not doing workouts in the same discipline back-to-back. Here is an example:

Monday: Swim

Tuesday: Run

Wednesday: Bike

Thursday: Swim

Friday: Rest

Saturday: Run

Sunday: Swim and bike

Assuming you have an adequate aerobic base to begin a structured program, you will need eight weeks of structured training to adequately prepare for the Olympic distance. During this time, intensity will be added along with strength work. A lot of hill work is included in the programs because, in my opinion, it is the best way to develop strength, which leads to speed (as well as mental toughness!). It's also important to schedule an easy day or full recovery day each week to refresh the body and mind, and to give them time to adapt to the training you're introducing.

Based on my experience, two sessions per discipline each week is the minimum work required to successfully complete an Olympic-distance triathlon, and three per discipline is ideal.

We will begin with an eight-week program for the level I athlete.

LEVEL I OLYMPIC-DISTANCE TRAINING

For the purposes of this chapter, a level I athlete is defined as someone who has successfully completed one or more sprint-distance triathlons and who has an adequate aerobic base that includes 8 to 12 weeks of performing low-intensity workouts in each of the three disciplines. The level I athlete may also have completed an Olympic- or middle-distance triathlon and is looking to improve via a structured program. Details of the program are given below, and a summary is presented in table 9.1 on page 117.

Weeks 1 to 3

Day 1

Swim 45 minutes

Warm-up:

200-meter swim freestyle

8 × 50 meters:

2 × swim on 10 seconds rest

2 × kick on 10 seconds rest

2 × swim on 10 seconds rest

2 × kick on 10 seconds rest

12 × 25 drill and freestyle swim on 10 seconds rest

On odd-numbered lengths, do drills: catch-up drill, fingertip drag drill, kick drill (descriptions of these drills are provided on page 128); on even lengths, do freestyle swim, incorporating what you worked on in the drill.

10 minutes of continuous freestyle swimming; focus on your technique and changing pace throughout the swim.

Cool-down: easy 200 meters of your choice

Day 2

Bike and run session

Ride 1 hour to 1 hour and 30 minutes.

Run 20 to 30 minutes off the bike.

Day 3

Swim 45 minutes

Warm-up:

200 meters easy:

50 swim, 25 kick, 50 swim, 25 kick, 50 swim

8 × 25: Fast start for a half length; do the rest easy. 20 seconds rest.

6 × 50 swim freestyle:

Descend 1 to 3, meaning first one easy, second one moderate, third one strong (twice through).

100-meter easy swim

Test set:

4 × 100 meters—best effort with 5-second rest between each. Take note of your time for each 100. At the end, find your average time. Add 5 seconds to this average time and use that as your hard effort intervals for the future. Add 10 seconds to the average and you can get your hardest aerobic threshold (AT) effort interval for the future.

Here's an example:
#1 100 time: 1:50
#2 100 time: 1:52
#3 100 time: 1:54
#4 100 time: 1:49
Average time = 1:51

In the near future, if you're doing a hard set of 8 × 100, do them on an interval of 2:00 and try to make all the 100s within that interval.

If you are doing a shorter set in which you are giving your best effort the whole way (for instance, 4 × 100), do them on 1:55. The goal here is to make the interval.

Cool-down: easy 200-meter swim

Day 4

Run session

45 minutes easy. The goal is to keep the pace conversational, meaning you can comfortably talk to a friend while running.

Day 5

Recovery day

This can be a complete recovery (rest) or it can incorporate active recovery: go for a walk, attend a yoga class—anything active but nothing hard!

Day 6

Long bike

1 hour and 30 minutes to 2 hours and 30 minutes, easy to moderate pace

If you live near hills, try doing this ride on a hilly course to help develop strength and mental toughness.

Day 7

Long run

If you have already built a proper running base, your aim should be to run 1.5 times the 10K race distance, which is 15K or 9.3 miles. This run should be done at an easy, conversational pace.

Weeks 4 and 5

At this point, incorporate strength work in the pool. Find a pair of paddles and a pull buoy, and be sure to get some instruction on how to use them properly. These will be very useful in developing swim-specific strength, which in turn will lead to stronger and faster swimming.

Day 1

Swim 1 hour

Warm up:

> 200 meters easy freestyle
>
> 4 × 25 kick with 15 seconds rest
>
> 4 × 25 swim with half a length fast and half a length easy
>
> 100-meter easy swim

3 × 200 meters with paddles and pull buoy. 1 easy, 1 moderate, 1 strong effort (15 seconds rest after each).

4 × 100 meters freestyle, no equipment. 1 easy, 1 moderate, 1 strong, 1 easy (15 seconds rest after each).

5 × 50 freestyle; 1 easy, 1 moderate, 1 strong, 1 moderate, 1 easy (15 seconds rest after each).

200-meter easy swim:

> 25 kick and 75 swim × 2

Day 2

Bike and run session

Ride 1 hour to 1 hour and 30 minutes, with 3 or 4 × 10 minutes of tempo work (just under your goal race pace) and 5 minutes easy between each effort. Run 15 minutes at a moderate pace off the bike, and then 15 minutes easy.

Day 3

Swim 1 hour: speed session

Warm-up:

> 400-meter swim: 175 freestyle, 25 kick × 2
>
> 8 × 25: half a length FAST, half a length easy (with 15 seconds rest after each)
>
> 4 × 100 with paddles for strength. Moderate effort with 20 seconds rest after each.

25 FAST as you can go, 20 seconds rest

50 FAST as you can go, 30 seconds rest

25 FAST as you can go, 20 seconds rest

100 FAST as you can go, 1 minute rest

Swim 100 very easy.

(Do this two or three times through.)

300-meter swim with paddles and pull buoy, easy effort

100-meter easy swim

Day 4

Run session

45 minutes to 1 hour

Warm-up: 10 to 15 minutes with 4 × 15-second strides

Find a hill about 200 to 400 meters long. Do 6 to 8 × 1-minute efforts uphill; recover with an easy jog or by walking back down to the bottom.

Cool-down: easy run of 5 to 10 minutes

Day 5

Recovery

Complete rest or active recovery

Day 6

Long bike

35 to 50 miles, easy to moderate pace

Day 7

Long run

Easy 9 to 12 miles

Weeks 6 and 7

Day 1

Swim 1 hour with some aerobic threshold work

This type of work will develop your ability to increase your threshold and will allow you to hold faster speeds for longer periods. They are mainly short rest sets.

Warm-up:

200-meter swim, easy freestyle

10 × 50 meters:

2 × kick with 15 seconds rest

2 × with 25 drill, 25 free (15 seconds rest)

2 × kick with 15 seconds rest

4 × with 25 STRONG, 25 easy (20 seconds rest)

4 × 100 with paddles; hard effort on an interval with 5 seconds rest only

50-meter easy swim

4 × 100 swim freestyle, no equipment; again, hard effort on an interval with 5 seconds rest

100-meter easy swim

8 × 50 hard effort; short rest of 5 seconds

300-meter easy swim:

    25 kick, 75 swim easy × 3 to cool down

Day 2

Bike and run session

Bike 1 hour to 1 hour and 30 minutes, with a 30- to 45-minute time trial effort. Run immediately off the bike, 4 × 3 minutes hard, 2 minutes easy; cool down by running easy 10 to 15 minutes.

Day 3

Swim 1 hour all aerobic

This means that you stay within your aerobic heart rate zone throughout the entire session. Focus on good technique and strength work.

Warm-up:

    400-meter easy swim

300 meters: kick 25, swim 75 × 3 easy

200 meters: drill 25, swim 25 × 4

100-meter easy swim

Paddles:

    10-minute swim. Focus on good technique and using the paddles to give you better strength and efficiency.

100 meters: kick

200 meters: drill 25, swim 25 × 4

300 meters: the first 10 meters of every 100 meters quick, the rest easy

400 meters: easy

Day 4

Long run

Easy 9 to 12 miles

Day 5

Recovery

Day 6

Track workout

Warm up easy with some 100-meter pick-ups.

Speed set should include fast 200-meter to 800-meter efforts with equal rest. Focus on speed and good form. Here's one example:

    4 × 200 meters FAST, easy 200 recovery jog or walk

    2 × 400 meters FAST, easy 400 recovery jog or walk

1 × 800 meters FAST, easy 400 recovery jog or walk

2 × 400 meters FAST, easy 400 jog or walk

4 × 200 meters FAST, easy 200 jog or walk

Cool-down: easy run 5 to 10 minutes

Day 7

Long ride

35 to 50 miles easy, including hills if possible

Race Week (Week 8)

Day 1

Swim 45 minutes with some short, fast efforts

Warm-up:

200-meter easy swim

4 × 75 meters: drill 25, swim 50 (15 seconds rest between each)

8 × 25 with paddles: 1 FAST, 15 seconds rest, 1 easy, 10 seconds rest (4 times through)

100-meter easy swim

4 × 50: 25 FAST as you can go, 25 easy (20 seconds rest)

6 × 100 meters:

Descend 1 to 3: first 100 easy, second 100 moderate, third 100 FAST; twice through. Take 30 seconds rest after each.

Cool-down: 400-meter easy swim

Day 2

Bike and run session

Ride 1 hour. Do 2 × 5-minute race pace efforts (5 minutes easy between each). Run off the bike 6 × 30 seconds FAST, 1 minute easy; then jog 15 minutes easy.

Day 3

Swim 45 minutes

Warm-up:

200-meter easy swim

4 × 50: kick (15 seconds rest)

4 × 50: drill down, swim back (15 seconds rest)

2 × 100: build speed each length to last length FAST (20 seconds rest)

12 × 25:

1 FAST, 30 seconds rest, 2 easy (repeat 4 times)

400-meter easy swim and done

TABLE 9.1   Level I Olympic-Distance Training Plan

	Monday	Tuesday	Wednesday	Thursday	Friday	Saturday	Sunday
Week 1	Swim 45 min.	Brick: Bike 1:00-1:30 Run 20-30 min. off the bike	Swim 45 min.	Run 45 min. easy	Rest or active recovery	Long bike: 1:30-2:30, easy to moderate pace	Long run: 9 miles
Week 2	Swim 45 min.	Brick: Bike 1:00-1:30 Run 20-30 min. off the bike	Swim 45 min.	Run 45 min. easy	Rest or active recovery	Long bike: 1:30-2:30, easy to moderate pace	Long run: 9 miles
Week 3	Swim 45 min.	Brick: Bike 1:00-1:30 Run 20-30 min. off the bike	Swim 45 min.	Run 45 min. easy	Rest or active recovery	Long bike: 1:30-2:30, easy to moderate pace	Long run: 9 miles
Week 4	Swim 1:00	Brick: Bike 1:00-1:30 (with tempo work) Run 30 min.	Swim 1:00 speed session	Run 45 min. to 1 hr.	Rest or active recovery	Long bike: 35-50 miles	Long run: 9-12 miles easy
Week 5	Swim 1:00	Brick: Bike 1:00-1:30 (with tempo work) Run 30 min.	Swim 1:00 speed session	Run 45 min. to 1 hr.	Rest or active recovery	Long bike: 35-50 miles	Long run: 9-12 miles easy
Week 6	Swim 1:00 with AT work	Brick: Bike 1:30 (with 30-45 min. TT effort) Run 25 min.	Swim 1:00 easy	Long run: 9-12 miles easy	Rest day	Run: Track workout	Long bike: 35-50 miles easy with hills
Week 7	Swim 1:00 with AT work	Brick: Bike 1:30 (with 30-40 min. TT effort) Run 25 min.	Swim 1:00 easy	Long run: 9-12 miles easy	Rest day	Run: Track workout	Long bike: 35-50 miles easy with hills
Week 8	Swim 45 min.	Bike 1:00 Run 20 min.	Swim 45 min.	Bike 1:30 easy	Rest day	Swim 10 min. easy Bike 20 min. easy Run 15-20 min. easy (with 3 × 15 sec. strides)	Race day!

Note: The above training plan indicates the general workout and duration for each day. For specific details on the workouts, refer to the descriptions on pages 111 to 118.

117

Day 4

Ride 1 hour and 30 minutes easy

Day 5

Recovery

Day 6

Day before the race—swim 10 minutes easy; bike 20 minutes to check bike and just spin the legs; jog 15 to 20 minutes with 3 × 15-second strides.

Day 7

RACE! Have fun and do your best—you are ready!

LEVEL II OLYMPIC-DISTANCE TRAINING

For the purposes of this chapter, a level II triathlete is defined as someone who has experienced success racing at the sprint distance, or someone who is looking to take her performance in the Olympic distance to the next level. Details of the program are given below, and a summary is presented in table 9.2 on page 127.

Weeks 1 to 3

Day 1

Morning: Swim 1 hour

Warm-up:

400-meter swim with 100 kick, 100 free, 100 doing drill work on the first 25 and swimming on the return 25, 100 freestyle

Strength work:

3 × 400 meters:

1 with paddles and pull buoy: focus on technique and getting the most power per stroke you can get. Rest 30 seconds.

1 with paddles only, same thing. Rest 30 seconds.

1 with paddles and pull buoy doing 25 meters strong, 75 easy × 4. Rest 30 seconds.

800-meter swim, continuous

Each week, you can increase the distance of this session by about 800 meters (you can add another 400 to the warm-up and a 400 on the cool-down). By week 3, this session should be 3,200 meters.

Afternoon: Run at an easy pace

Week 1: 30 minutes

Week 2: 35 to 40 minutes

Week 3: 45 minutes

Focus on technique.

Day 2

Brick workout

Week 1: 1 hour to 1 hour and 30 minutes on the bike, easy pace; run 20 minutes off the bike, easy.

Week 2: 1 hour and 30 minutes on the bike, easy; run 30 minutes off the bike, easy.

Week 3: Bike 2 hours at easy to moderate pace. Immediately off the bike, run 20 minutes, moderate pace.

Day 3

Swim 1 hour to 1 hour and 15 minutes

Warm-up:

400-meter easy swim

4 × 100 with 25 kick, 75 free, 15 seconds rest

400 meters with paddles and pull buoy

4 × 100 with 25 up-tempo, 75 easy

12 × 50 meters:

4 easy on interval with 15 seconds rest

4 moderate on interval with 10 seconds rest

4 very solid on interval with 5 seconds rest

400-meter swim: build intensity on each 100 from easy to moderate to strong to hard.

200 meters easy and done

Week 1: 600-meter swim, build in effort and pace each 200

Week 2: 400 meters easy to cool down

Week 3: 800-meter swim, build by 200; 500 to 600 meters easy to cool down

Day 4

Morning: Run session

Tempo run:

Warm up by running 10 to 15 minutes easy.

Do 3 × 15-second pick-ups with 45 seconds easy between each.

Try to find a road with rolling hills; run the flats easy, and pick up the intensity to a solid effort uphill. Perform a total of 20 to 40 minutes of this tempo work. Efforts should be anywhere from 20 seconds to 2 minutes long.

Cool down by running 5 to 15 minutes easy, for a session total of 1 hour to 1 hour and 15 minutes.

On alternate weeks, substitute the following:

Warm up with 10 to 15 minutes easy jogging and 3 × 15-second pick-ups.

10 minutes up-tempo

5 minutes easy

5 minutes up-tempo

5 minutes easy

10 minutes up-tempo

5 minutes easy

Cool down easy

This workout can be done on flat or rolling terrain. Intensity should be at the high end of your aerobic zone at a pace that would make it uncomfortable to talk while running.

- In the first three weeks, this tempo is still at an aerobic heart rate (you are not yet going HARD). Week 1 tempo is an aerobic pace, just faster than your warm-up pace. 30 to 35 beats below your maximum.
- Week 2: Tempo is within your mid-aerobic heart rate zone, 25 to 30 bpm below your maximum heart rate.
- Week 3: Tempo is within your higher end aerobic zone, 20 bpm below your maximum.

Afternoon: Swim session

Warm-up:

   4 × 50 kick with a board to loosen up legs (week 2: 6 × 50; week 3: 8 × 50)
   400-meter swim

12 × 50 with 15 seconds rest, building the intensity through the 50. For instance, 12.5 meters easy, 12.5 meters moderate, 12.5 meters strong, last 12.5 meters FAST.

8 × 100 meters:

   2 on interval with 20 seconds rest
   2 on interval with 15 seconds rest
   2 on interval with 10 seconds rest
   2 on interval with 5 seconds rest

1000-meter swim, continuous

100 easy; 100 with 25 fast, 75 easy; 100 with 50 fast, 50 easy; 100 with 75 fast, 25 easy; 100 all fast (Do this twice through.)

100-meter swim, easy

100 meters with paddles and pull buoy; focus on technique

100 meters, paddles only

100 meters free (easy cool-down)

(Add 50 meters each week to these intervals so that in week 2 you do 150s, week 3 you do 200s.)

Day 5

Recovery

Complete rest or active recovery (including a walk, a light jog, or light swim)

Day 6

Long bike

Week 1: 2 hours

Week 2: 2 hours and 30 minutes

Week 3: 3 hours

Easy effort—just get the miles into your legs and have fun.

Day 7

Run 9 to 12 miles easy. If you have already built up a good pace before starting this eight-week plan, you can start with your longest base work run and add 10 percent onto that each week.

Weeks 4 and 5

Day 1

Swim 1 hour to 1 hour and 30 minutes

Warm-up:

4 × 200 (20 seconds rest after each):

1 freestyle easy

1 kick 50, swim 150

1 with paddles and pull buoy, moderate

1 with paddles and pull buoy—25 FAST, 175 easy swim

10 × 100 hard effort on interval with 5 seconds rest

200-meter easy swim

10 × 50 with 15 sprint, 35 easy

400-meter easy swim and done

Day 2

Bike and run session

Bike 1 hour and 30 minutes.

Warm-up: 30 minutes easy, then do the following:

4 to 6 × 5 minutes hard effort, 3 minutes easy spin recovery; after the last one, run 1 minute hard, 1 easy; 2 minutes hard, 2 easy; 3 minutes hard, 3 easy; 3 minutes hard, 3 easy; 2 minutes hard, 2 easy; 1 minute hard, 1 easy. Jog easy for an additional 12 to 15 minutes.

Day 3

Swim 1 hour to 1 hour and 30 minutes

Warm-up:

400-meter swim, easy

300 meters with 100 easy, 100 moderate, 100 stronger

200 meters: kick 50, swim 50

100-meter swim with 25 FAST, 75 easy

6 × 200 with paddles:

1 on interval with 20 seconds rest (moderate to easy effort)

1 on interval with 15 seconds rest (solid effort)

1 on interval with 10 seconds rest (hard effort)

Twice through that sequence

400-meter easy swim

6 × 100 freestyle (same as above):

1 with 20 seconds rest

1 with 15 seconds rest

1 hard with 10 seconds rest

Twice through

400 meters easy

Day 4

Run session

Run 45 to 60 minutes; use rolling hills if possible.

15-minute warm-up

30 minutes of tempo work; for example,

10 minutes at heart rate 25 below max

10 minutes at heart rate 20 below max

10 minutes at heart rate 15 below max

15-minute cool-down, easy

Swim off run if possible:

Kick 8 × 50

Swim 1 × 200

6 × 50: drill 25, swim 25

8 × 25: 1 FAST freestyle, 1 easy (15 seconds rest)

400-meter easy swim to cool down

Day 5

Recovery

Day 6

Long bike

Ride 2 hours and 30 minutes to 3 hours and 30 minutes, preferably on hills for strength.

Day 7

Long run

Easy 9 to 12 miles. Incorporate hills for strength.

Weeks 6 and 7

Day 1

Morning: Swim session

Warm-up:

10-minute swim

10 × 50:

2 × kick with 15 seconds rest

2 × drill down, swim back (15 seconds rest)

2 × kick with 15 seconds rest

4 × 25 fast, 25 easy (20 seconds rest)

12 × 100 with paddles on interval that gives you 10 seconds rest going at moderate intensity

200-meter easy swim and done

Afternoon: Bike session

Ride 2 to 3 hours on rolling hills for strength and endurance.

Day 2

Brick workout

2-hour bike including a time trial of 20 to 40 minutes, race pace, with hard effort. Run immediately off the bike half the distance of your key race. So, for an Olympic-distance race, run 5K hard off the bike.

Cool-down easy running for 15 to 20 minutes

Day 3

Swim 1 hour to 1 hour and 30 minutes

Swim 400 meters freestyle, easy.

4 × 100: kick 25, swim 75 (15 seconds rest)

8 × 50 (descend every 4):

> 1 easy effort
>
> 1 moderate effort
>
> 1 strong effort
>
> 1 fast
>
> all with 15 seconds rest

3 × 500:

> 1 easy freestyle
>
> 1 with paddles and pull buoy, strong effort
>
> 1 best effort

200-meter easy swim and done

Run: 45 minutes to 1 hour easy. Give yourself plenty of rest (3 to 4 hours if possible) before this session.

Day 4

Track session

Here are three workouts to consider:

Session #1:

> 5- to 10-minute warm-up
>
> 4 × 400 FAST with 200 easy recovery between each
>
> 1 mile STRONG: 10 seconds per 400 slower than 400-meter repeats
>
> 1 lap easy recovery
>
> 1 mile strong (same as above)
>
> 4 × 400 with 200 easy recovery between each
>
> Cool down easy

Session #2:

> 5- to 10-minute warm-up
>
> 1 × 400 with 200 recovery very easy (walking is okay)
>
> 1 × 800 with 200 recovery
>
> 1 × 1K with 400 recovery
>
> 1 × 1 mile with 400 recovery (advanced athletes: do another 1 × 1 mile after this one before coming back down the ladder)
>
> 1 × 1K with 400 recovery
>
> 1 × 800 with 200 recovery
>
> 1 × 400 with 200 recovery
>
> Cool down easy

Session #3:

> 5- to 10-minute warm-up
>
> 4 × 200 FAST, equal rest
>
> 2 × 400 FAST, equal rest
>
> 4 × 200 FAST, equal rest
>
> 2 × 400 FAST, equal rest (Intermediate athletes: you are done here. Advanced athletes: do the last 4 × 200 as well.)
>
> 4 × 200 FAST, equal rest
>
> Cool down

Afternoon: Easy 1- to 2-hour recovery ride. Try to give yourself a few hours rest before this.

Day 5
Recovery day

Day 6
Long bike

> Ride 35 to 50 miles easy.

Day 7
Long run

> Easy 9 to 12 miles

Race Week (Week 8)

Day 1
Swim 1 hour with some fast speed work

> Warm-up:
>
> > 8 × 100 with 15 seconds rest:
> >
> > 1 × easy freestyle
> >
> > 1 × drill 25, swim 25
> >
> > 1 × kick 25, swim 75
> >
> > 1 × freestyle moderate intensity
> >
> > Do this sequence twice through.
>
> 8 × 25: 1 FAST, 1 easy (15 seconds rest after each)
>
> Speed set:
>
> > 2 × through this set:
> >
> > 25 FAST, 25 very easy, 30 seconds rest
> >
> > 50 FAST, 50 easy, 30 seconds rest
> >
> > 100 FAST, 100 easy, 30 seconds rest

Day 2

Brick workout

Bike 30 minutes.

Warm up with 3 × 20-second pick-ups.

3 × 5 minutes hard at race pace; 5 minutes easy between each one

Run off the bike: 5 minutes at race pace, 20 minutes easy

Day 3

Swim 45 minutes to 1 hour aerobic easy to moderate effort

3 × 400-meter swim freestyle:

1 very easy with 50 drill, 150 swim × 2

1 with paddles and pull buoy

1 building intensity every 100 to strong, not FAST

3 × 200 same as above

3 × 100 same as above

100 meters easy and done

Bike 1 hour to 1 hour and 30 minutes easy if time permits.

Day 4

Run session

Run 35 minutes with 4 × 20-second race pace pick-ups.

Day 5

Recovery day

Day 6

Transition workouts

Swim 15 to 20 minutes with 4 × 15-second sprints.

Bike 30 minutes easy on course (to check out bike).

Run 20 minutes with 3 × 15-second pick-ups.

Day 7

RACE! Have fun and do your best—you are ready!

As you can see in the training schedule, Olympic-distance training will get your body into excellent shape and will do wonders to increase your strength, endurance, and even your speed. Unlike the longer races (half Ironman and Ironman), Olympic-distance triathlon doesn't require huge amounts of training time, but it offers a challenge that is long enough and great enough to earn you some pretty big bragging rights! If you do have aspirations to go long, there's no better way to motivate yourself toward the long-distance challenge than by putting a few stellar Olympic-distance performances under your belt.

TABLE 9.2 Level II Olympic-Distance Training Plan

	Monday	Tuesday	Wednesday	Thursday	Friday	Saturday	Sunday
Week 1	Swim 1:00 Run 30 min.	Brick: Bike 1:00-1:30 Run 20 min.	Swim 1:00-1:15	Tempo run + swim (see plan for details)	Rest or active recovery	Long bike: 2:00	Long run: 9-12 miles easy
Week 2	Swim 1:00 Run 35-40 min.	Brick: Bike 1:30 Run 30 min.	Swim 1:00-1:15	Tempo run + swim (see plan for details)	Rest or active recovery	Long bike: 2:30	Long run: 9-12 miles easy
Week 3	Swim 1:00 Run 45 min.	Brick: Bike 2:00 Run 20 min.	Swim 1:00-1:15	Tempo run + swim (see plan for details)	Rest or active recovery	Long bike: 3:00	Long run: 9-12 miles easy
Week 4	Swim 1:00-1:30	Bike/run session: Bike 1:30 with run intervals (see plan for details)	Swim 1:00-1:30	Run 45 min.-1 hr. with hills	Rest day	Long bike: 2:30-3:30 with hills	Long run: 9-12 miles with hills
Week 5	Swim 1:00-1:30	Bike/run session: Bike 1:30 with run intervals (see plan for details)	Swim 1:00-1:30	Run 45 min.-1 hr. with hills	Rest day	Long bike: 2:30-3:30 with hills	Long run: 9-12 miles with hills
Week 6	Swim Bike 2:00-3:00 on rolling hills	Brick: Bike 2:00 Run 15-20 min.	Swim 1:00-1:30 Run 45 min.-1 hr. easy	Run: Track workout (see plan for details) Bike 1:00-2:00 easy	Rest day	Long bike: 35-50 miles easy	Long run: 9-12 miles easy
Week 7	Swim Bike 2:00-3:00 on rolling hills	Brick: Bike 2:00 Run 15-20 min.	Swim 1:00-1:30 Run 45 min.-1 hr. easy	Run: Track workout (see plan for details) Bike 1:00-2:00 easy	Rest day	Long bike: 35-50 miles easy	Long run: 9-12 miles easy
Week 8	Swim 1:00 with speed work	Brick: Bike 30 min. Run 25 min.	Swim 45 min.-1 hr. easy Bike 1:00-1:30 easy	Run 35 min. with strides	Rest day	Swim 15-20 min. with sprints Bike 30 min. easy Run 20 min. with strides	Race day!

Note: The above training plan indicates the general workout and duration for each day. For specific details on the workouts, refer to the descriptions on pages 118 to 126.

127

Swimming Drills

CATCH-UP FREESTYLE

Start in a streamlined position (while lying flat in the water, both your arms are in front of your head at the surface of the water). Begin the drill by taking one entire freestyle stroke with your right arm only. When your right hand returns to the start position, take one full stroke with your left arm and then return it to the starting position. This completes one full cycle of catch-up freestyle.

FINGERTIP DRAG DRILL

This drill helps promote correct recovery for the freestyle stroke. It's performed by swimming regular freestyle and exaggerating the elbow position during recovery. As your hand exits the water at your hips, bend your elbow and pull it up to the sky. Then drag your fingertips along the surface of the water underneath your elbow. Enter your hand in the water in front of your shoulder.

KICK DRILL

Start with your arms in front of your face in a streamlined position. While kicking strongly, take a pull with your right arm but stop the hand at your hip. Your other arm will remain in front of your face. Rotate onto that side and kick while in this position. Stay in this position for a four count. Then recover your right arm to the front while pulling your left arm to your hip. You will now be on your right side and remain there kicking for a count of six. Repeat the motion.

Taking the Long-Distance Challenge

Lori Bowden

There's something special about the challenge of a long-distance triathlon. Short triathlons are a great challenge, too, but the long ones, especially the Ironman-distance events, have a unique appeal. It's sort of like the allure of Mount Everest for climbers: If you're going to climb mountains, you might as well climb the biggest! I know some people who wanted to do an Ironman triathlon before they had even done a sprint triathlon. They saw the Hawaii Ironman on TV and were so inspired they decided they had to do it themselves (after they learned how to swim, of course). More often, people start thinking about long-distance triathlons after getting hooked on the sport through shorter races. But sooner or later, one way or another, most dedicated triathletes do set their sights on the ultimate challenge.

What's so special about going long? For me there are two major attractions. The first is the lifestyle of training for long-distance races. You'd better enjoy training if you're going to put in the time to prepare properly for an Ironman, and I really do enjoy it. A lot of triathletes start off enjoying training but allow themselves to get too serious and too focused on the race itself, and training winds up becoming a burden. I'm constantly being asked what advice I would give to triathletes preparing for their first Ironman, and it's always this: Enjoy the process! Keep it fun. And if it starts becoming a chore, take a mental time-out and remind yourself why you're doing it.

The other factor that keeps me coming back is the amazing personal journey that I experience in each Ironman race. It seems like I'm tested in a new way and learn something new about myself each time. There's no such thing as an easy long-distance triathlon; they're always challenging, and the biggest challenge is mental. First-timers need to be prepared for this reality. No matter how well trained you are, 4 to 17 hours of swimming, bicycling, and running will be a mental struggle. You need to keep a positive attitude, stay focused, and make smart decisions. I truly believe that preparing mentally for a long-distance triathlon is as important as preparing physically. How do you do that? Mainly by working on keeping a positive attitude, staying focused, and making smart decisions in your workouts and through the training process as a whole. (For specific tips on mental training, refer to chapter 11.)

WHEN TO GO LONG

Triathletes who are thinking about doing their first long-distance triathlon often ask me if I think they're ready, or when I think they'll be ready, based on their training and racing experience and sometimes on other factors such as their age. A typical question of this variety goes something like this:

"Lori, I'm 38 years old, and I've been doing triathlons for two years. So far I've done three sprints and two Olympic-distance races, and I'm getting a little faster each time. I want to do an Ironman, and there's one in my area in six months. Do you think I can do it, or is it too soon? Should I do a half Ironman instead and save the Ironman for next year?"

I never know quite how to answer these questions because, truly, there are no absolute rules for when a person is ready to do her first long-distance race. I know some people who have successfully completed an Ironman with less experience and training than I might have thought they should have. But it's still best to be cautious. Due to the exploding popularity of long-distance racing, more and more new triathletes are doing their first Ironman too soon and are having a less than ideal experience because of it.

Let me offer some general guidelines, with the understanding that each case is unique and you have to take responsibility for making your own objective judgment about when the time is right to take the long-distance plunge. I think the average triathlete should have two years of consistent, year-round training under her belt before doing an Ironman. You should have done at least four shorter triathlons, including a half Ironman-distance event, ideally.

Training experience and race experience are important for different reasons. Racing experience is critical because there are many ways to make mistakes in a triathlon, and beginners tend to make a lot of mistakes in their first few races. Some examples are starting too fast in the swim, getting psyched out by the physical contact that is inevitable during a mass swim start, eating too many packets of energy gel on the bike, and forgetting to put on sun block. Even apart from mistakes, those first few triathlons teach you important lessons that you can use to have a better race next time. You learn things such as how to draft in the swim, how to set up your gear for a more efficient transition, and what sort of nutrition strategy works best for you. You also become less nervous before races and better able to handle the discomfort of racing and setbacks that occur during races (e.g., cramps and flat tires). The cost of making mistakes and doing things inefficiently is so much greater in a long-distance triathlon than in a shorter one. You invest too much time, energy, and even money in preparing for a long-distance race to spoil it with "rookie" mistakes.

The function of accumulating training experience before signing up for that first long-distance triathlon is to develop a base fitness level that will allow you to handle a heavy training load without getting injured or overtrained. Two-time Hawaii Ironman champion Tim DeBoom said, "You have to train to train for Ironman." His specific point was that an elite triathlete must slowly and patiently build her training load for years in order to eventually be able to handle the kind of training it takes to win an Ironman, but the same general rule applies to first-timers on a smaller scale. You can't go straight from the couch to long-distance triathlon training. Patiently training at a moderate and gradually increasing level for a couple of years will put you in a much better position to effectively absorb and benefit from heavier training.

TRAINING REQUIREMENTS FOR A FIRST LONG-DISTANCE TRIATHLON

Trying to establish minimum training requirements for a first long-distance triathlon is fraught with the same difficulties as trying to establish minimum experience requirements. Genetic fitness levels are widely varying, and responses to training are highly individual, too. Someone who is genetically designed for endurance might be as fit on the first day of training as a less gifted athlete is after nine weeks or even nine months of training. Aside from genetic fitness, some athletes are "fast responders," while others are "slow responders." The fast responders, it seems, only have to look at a bicycle or a pair of running shoes or swim goggles and their heart gets bigger and they lose three pounds of body fat. Others have to train consistently for a long time to achieve the same results.

So, once again, I'm putting a caveat ahead of my training recommendations for first-time long-distance triathletes. In a phrase, the caveat is this: There are no one-size-fits-all guidelines. But, as a general rule, I think it's best for all first-timers to be conservative in two directions in establishing training parameters. On the one hand, you want to pad the numbers a bit (and by numbers I mean the length of the ramp-up and the average and maximum weekly training hours) just to be sure you're ready. You want to do a little more than the absolute minimum you think you could get away with. Even if your goal is to "just finish," this doesn't mean you'd be content to suffer miserably all day, walk most of the marathon, and then be hauled away in an ambulance as soon as you've crossed the finish line. You want to finish upright and smiling.

On the other hand, you want to be conservative in the other direction as well—that is, you want your training numbers to be close to the minimum you need so that you don't overtrain, so you don't get sick of training and stop having fun, and so you still have time for work and family! If you've been training consistently for at least a year and therefore have a solid base level of fitness, then 16 weeks of dedicated long-distance training should be enough to prepare you for an Ironman-distance triathlon. Eighteen weeks would be even better, and 20 weeks would probably be ideal (see Ironman program in table 10.1 and half Ironman program in table 10.2, pages 134-137). You should swim, cycle, and run each at least three times a week. Assuming you are at least a serviceable swimmer, three swims are plenty, but if you can build up to four rides or runs a week, at least some weeks, there will be additional benefit. In the early weeks of training, you should do about 10 total hours of training. In your heaviest week of training, which will be the third or fourth week before the race, you should do about 14 to 16 hours of training.

It's okay if most of your training hours are grouped together on the weekends. Too many triathletes overwhelm themselves by trying to squeeze in multiple workouts and training hours during the workweek. It's just not necessary to train hard or do multiple workouts every day. One long workout per week in each of the three disciplines is enough, and it's fine to do all three on the weekend if necessary. After all, the objective of training for a long-distance triathlon is to prepare your body to exercise all day on one specific day—always a Saturday or a Sunday. So bunching together half of your weekly training hours on Saturday and Sunday makes more sense than trying to spread out your weekly training hours across six or seven days. Of course, if you have the luxury of using those extra days, there's no harm in that either.

TRAINING TIPS

There's a big difference between training to win an Ironman and training to finish an Ironman. But that big difference can be captured in one small word: *volume.* The professional triathletes who train to win an Ironman, and the age-groupers who train to win their age group, simply have to do a lot more training than first-timers who aren't going to be caught up in who's ahead of them and who's behind them. But the other aspects are the same. Both types of triathlete should follow the same basic training format. Following are some specific things I do in my training that you should also do in yours.

Train Progressively

There's one simple thing you don't have enough of at the beginning of training and you want to have a lot more of by race day: endurance. There isn't a human on earth who has enough natural endurance to complete an Ironman without training specifically for it. So the most important objective of training for a long-distance triathlon is to gradually build your endurance to a high enough level to get you to the finish line smiling.

Each week you should do one long, steady swim; one long, steady bike ride; and one long, steady run. These are your most important workouts (along with your brick workouts, discussed below). In the first week of training, these workouts should be just slightly longer than the longest workouts of each type that you've done recently. The following week, make them a little longer, and so on. Never increase the duration of these workouts by more than 10 percent at a time, and don't make them longer every single week. If you rush it, you'll get injured or develop overtraining fatigue. Also, you don't need to do these long workouts every single week. Three out of every four weeks is enough (build for three weeks and then back off for one).

If you're training for an Ironman, your longest swim should be at least 2.4 miles (the distance of the race swim itself). It can be slightly longer, if you wish. Your longest bike ride should be about 100 miles. And your longest run should be 20 to 22 miles. These peak workouts should be done three to four weeks before race day. When you're planning your training, mark these workouts on your training calendar as well as your very first (and much shorter) long workouts, and then "connect the dots" between them. This is a good way to ensure that your training is progressing gradually and steadily.

Monitor Your Intensity

Many of the training programs you get from magazines, books, and some coaches include lots of high-intensity interval workouts in all three disciplines. I have found that very little of this sort of training is needed for

Building endurance gradually and training mental strength are keys to the long-distance triathlon.

TABLE 10.1 Ironman Training Program

Before beginning this program, gradually build your fitness to the point where you are able to cycle for 2 hours comfortably, run for 1 hour, and swim for 45 minutes without a break.

Note: Workout key is at the end of the training plans on page 137.

	Monday	Tuesday	Wednesday	Thursday	Friday	Saturday	Sunday
Week 1	Rest	Swim short intervals Easy bike	Steady run	Short, easy brick	Swim long intervals	Long bike: 2:00	Long swim: 40 min. Long run: 50 min.
Week 2	Rest	Swim short intervals Easy bike	Steady run	Short, easy brick	Swim long intervals	Long bike: 2:15	Long swim: 40 min. Long run: 55 min.
Week 3	Rest	Swim short intervals Easy bike	Steady run	Short, hard brick	Swim long intervals	Long bike: 2:30	Long swim: 40 min. Long run: 1:00
Week 4	Rest	Swim short intervals Easy bike	Steady run	Hilly bike	Swim long intervals	Brick: Long bike: 2:30+ Run: 20 min.	Long run: 1:15
Week 5	Rest	Swim short intervals Easy bike	Steady run	Short, hard brick	Swim long intervals	Long bike: 3:00	Long swim: 50 min. Long run: 1:20
Week 6 (Recovery)	Rest	Swim short intervals Easy bike	Steady run	Short, easy brick	Swim long intervals	Long bike: 2:00	Long swim: 45 min. Long run: 55 min.
Week 7	Rest	Swim short intervals Easy bike	Steady run	Short, hard brick	Swim long intervals	Long bike: 3:30	Long swim: 50 min. Long run: 1:30
Week 8	Rest	Swim short intervals Easy bike	Steady run	Hilly bike	Swim long intervals	Brick: Long bike: 2:30 Run: 30 min.	Long run: 1:40
Week 9	Rest	Swim short intervals Easy bike	Steady run	Short, hard brick	Swim long intervals	Long bike: 4:00	Long run: 1:50 Optional swim: 50 min.

	Monday	Tuesday	Wednesday	Thursday	Friday	Saturday	Sunday
Week 10 (Recovery)	Rest	Swim short intervals Easy bike	Steady run	Short, hard brick	Swim long intervals	Long bike: 2:30	Long run: 1:00 Optional swim: 45-50 min.
Week 11	Rest	Swim short intervals Easy bike	Steady run	Short, hard brick	Swim long intervals	Long bike: 4:30	Long run: 2:00 Optional swim: 30 min.
Week 12	Rest	Swim short intervals Easy bike	Steady run	Hilly bike	Swim long intervals	Brick: Bike: 3:00 Run: 40 min.	Long run: 2:00 Optional swim: 45-50 min.
Week 13	Rest	Swim short intervals Easy bike	Steady run	Short, hard brick	Swim long intervals	Long bike: 5:00	Long swim: 1:10 Long run: 2:20
Week 14 (Recovery)	Rest	Swim short intervals Easy bike	Steady run	Short, easy brick	Swim long intervals	Long bike: 3:00	Long swim: 1:10 Long run: 1:10
Week 15	Rest	Swim short intervals Easy bike	Steady run	Hilly bike	Swim long intervals	Brick: Long bike: 5:30 Run: 30 min.	Long swim: 1:20 Long run: 2:00
Week 16	Rest	Swim short intervals Easy bike	Steady run	Hilly bike	Swim long intervals	Brick: Long bike: 6:00 Run: 50 min.	Swim 45-50 min. easy Long run: 2:15
Week 17	Rest	Swim short intervals Easy bike	Steady run	Short, hard brick	Swim long intervals	Brick: Long bike: 6:00 Run: 30 min.	Long run: 2:40 Optional swim: 30-40 min.
Week 18	Rest	Swim short intervals Easy bike	Steady run	Hilly bike	Swim long intervals	Brick: Bike: 3:00 Run: 45 min.	Swim: 1:00 Long run: 2:50
Week 19 (Recovery)	Rest	Swim short intervals	Easy run	Easy bike	Swim long intervals	Brick: Bike: 2:30 Run: 20 min.	Swim 45 min. easy Run: 1:00
Week 20 (Recovery)	Rest	Swim short intervals	Easy run	Easy bike	Easy swim	Rest	Ironman triathlon

TABLE 10.2 Half Ironman Training Program

Before beginning this program, gradually build your fitness to the point where you are able to cycle for 90 minutes comfortably, run for 45 minutes, and swim for 40 minutes without a break.

	Monday	Tuesday	Wednesday	Thursday	Friday	Saturday	Sunday
Week 1	Rest	Swim short intervals Easy bike	Steady run	Short, easy brick	Swim long intervals	Long bike: 1:30	Long swim: 40 min. Long run: 45 min.
Week 2	Rest	Swim short intervals Easy bike	Steady run	Short, easy brick	Swim long intervals	Long bike: 1:45	Long swim: 40 min. Long run: 50 min.
Week 3	Rest	Swim short intervals Easy bike	Steady run	Short, hard brick	Swim long intervals	Long bike: 2:00	Long swim: 40 min. Long run: 55 min.
Week 4 (Recovery)	Rest	Swim short intervals Easy bike	Steady run	Short, easy brick	Swim long intervals	Long bike: 1:30	Long swim: 45 min. Long run: 45 min.
Week 5	Rest	Swim short intervals Easy bike	Steady run	Short, hard brick	Swim long intervals	Long bike: 2:15	Long swim: 50 min. Long run: 1:00
Week 6	Rest	Swim short intervals Easy bike	Steady run	Short, hard brick	Swim long intervals	Long bike: 2:30	Long swim: 55 min. Long run: 1:10
Week 7	Rest	Swim short intervals Easy bike	Steady run	Short, hard brick	Swim long intervals	Long bike: 2:45	Long swim: 50 min. Long run: 1:20
Week 8 (Recovery)	Rest	Swim short intervals Easy bike	Steady run	Easy bike	Swim long intervals	Long swim: 50 min. Long run: 1:00	Brick: Bike: 1:30 Run: 20 min.
Week 9	Rest	Swim short intervals Easy bike	Steady run	Short, hard brick	Swim long intervals	Long bike: 3:00	Long swim: 55 min. Long run: 1:30
Week 10	Rest	Swim short intervals Easy bike	Steady run	Short, hard brick	Swim long intervals	Long bike: 3:15	Long swim: 1:00 Long run: 1:40

	Monday	Tuesday	Wednesday	Thursday	Friday	Saturday	Sunday
Week 11	Rest	Swim short intervals Easy bike	Steady run	Short, hard brick	Swim long intervals	Long bike: 3:30	Long swim: 1:00 Long run: 1:50
Week 12 (Recovery)	Rest	Swim short intervals Easy bike	Steady run	Easy bike	Swim long intervals	Long swim: 50 min. Long run: 1:20	Brick: Bike: 2:00 Run: 20 min.
Week 13	Rest	Swim short intervals Easy bike	Steady run	Short, hard brick	Swim long intervals	Long bike: 3:45	Long swim: 1:10 Long run: 2:00
Week 14	Rest	Swim short intervals Easy bike	Steady run	Short, hard brick	Swim long intervals	Long bike: 4:00	Long swim: 1:00 Long run: 2:00
Week 15 (Recovery)	Rest	Swim short intervals	Easy run	Easy bike	Swim long intervals	Bike: 2:00	Swim: 45 min. Run: 1:00
Week 16 (Recovery)	Rest	Swim short intervals	Easy run	Easy bike	Easy swim	Rest	Half Ironman triathlon

Workout key (for both Ironman and half Ironman plans):

Short swim intervals: A pool workout with a main set consisting of 25- to 100-meter intervals. The total duration of this workout should be about 40 minutes at the beginning of the program and about 1 hour at the end.

Easy bike: Ride at an easy pace for whatever duration feels right (up to 90 minutes).

Steady run: Run at a moderate pace for 40 minutes to 1 hour and 10 minutes. The pace and duration of the workout should increase gradually throughout the program (except in recovery weeks, when it should be slower and shorter).

Short, easy brick: Ride easy for 30 minutes to 1 hour, and then run easy for 15 to 30 minutes.

Long swim intervals: A pool workout with a main set consisting of 100- to 400-meter intervals. The total duration of this workout should be about 40 minutes at the beginning of the program and about 1 hour at the end.

All weekend workouts: Maintain a steady, comfortable pace for the specified duration.

Short, hard brick: Ride at a challenging intensity level for 30 minutes to 1 hour, and then run moderately hard for 15 to 30 minutes.

Hilly bike: Ride on a hilly route for 1 to 2 hours. The intensity and duration of the workout should increase gradually throughout the program (except in recovery weeks, when it should be slower and shorter). If there are few hills in your area, simulate hills by riding in a high gear.

Easy run: Run at an easy pace for 20 to 40 minutes.

long-distance racing. It's fine to do lots of intervals in swimming, because they don't wear you out as much as high-intensity cycling and running do. As mentioned in chapter 3, probably the best way to swim train for triathlons of any distance is to work out with a Masters swim club, and these workouts are always interval based. You can prepare perfectly well for an Ironman swim by simply swimming laps at a steady, moderate pace, but this is very boring. Doing intervals will not only make you faster, but will also keep you from getting "black line fever!"

As for cycling and running, there's really no need to do killer intervals, especially if you're training for your first long-distance race. I don't do any formal high-intensity running workouts, yet running is usually my strongest leg in races. I do run hard sometimes, but not on the track, and only when I feel like it. One form of high-intensity training that I do recommend is hill climbing. You should work some good, hard hill climbs into your cycling and running each week, especially if there will be hills in your chosen race (for more specific bike and run training tips, refer to chapters 4 and 5).

Stay Healthy

An injury or a bout of the flu could ruin your big race before it even begins—forcing you to drop from the event and wait a long time for another opportunity. So your highest priority (alongside having fun) in your training should be to stay healthy.

Minimizing your risk of getting sick or injured requires that you take a number of small preventive measures. Here are the little things you can do to keep from getting a viral or bacterial infection:

- Rest when you need rest (it's easy—if you feel overly fatigued or if your plan calls for a rest day, don't train!).
- Get eight hours of sleep every night.
- Maintain a healthy diet.
- Drink a sports drink before and after workouts (hard workouts suppress the immune system; the carbohydrates in sports drinks reduce this effect).
- Eliminate all unnecessary stressors from your life.

Here are the little things you can do to prevent injuries:

- Rest when you need rest.
- Stretch and strength train regularly. Many overuse injuries are caused by muscle imbalances—that is, when muscles on one side of a joint are too tight and muscles on the opposite side are too weak. Muscles that tend to become too tight in triathletes are those of the calf, the hamstrings, the hip flexors, the piriformis (the muscle under your gluteus maximus),

the internal shoulder rotators, the neck extensors, and the chest muscles. Two major tendons, the iliotibial band and the Achilles tendon, also tend to become tight. The muscles that are typically underdeveloped in triathletes are the medial and frontal shin muscles, the hip abductors, the gluteal muscles, the abdominals, the scapular stabilizers, and the rotator cuff muscles, all of which you should proactively strengthen with resistance exercises.

- Consume carbohydrates and protein immediately after workouts. Your muscles will repair themselves much faster if you do this than if you wait until your next meal.

- Buy your running shoes from experts who know how to set you up with the right shoe. Get orthotics if you need them. And replace your running shoes frequently (every 300 to 500 miles depending on the shoe).

- Be sure to train on a bike that fits you, and that your bike is set up properly. Many knee and lower back injuries are caused by ill-fitting bikes and improper bike setup.

- Don't run too much. The vast majority of overuse injuries that triathletes suffer are caused by running, due to its high-impact nature. Try to do just enough running to develop the running fitness you'll need for your long-distance race, and no more.

For more information on avoiding injury, refer to chapter 14.

Do Frequent Brick Workouts

Bike/run "brick" workouts are probably your most important workouts because they involve the same challenge of running immediately after getting off the bike that you will face in the race itself. You should do at least one brick workout every other week, and preferably one each week. Like your long rides and long runs, your brick workouts should get progressively longer as the race draws nearer.

Feel free to mix up the formats. A lot of triathletes like to do "transition workouts," which involve a long ride followed by a short run (20 minutes). Since the hardest part of running and cycling is *starting* to run after cycling, these workouts are helpful, but I wouldn't rely on them exclusively. A standard brick workout should involve approximately the same ratio of bike time to run time as a long-distance race (which is about 5:3 for the typical triathlete). But you can also do some brick workouts that emphasize the run more. You can even throw in some swim/bike/run bricks. This is an especially good idea if you aren't planning to do many shorter races before your long race. You can mix up the intensity of your bricks, too, but most of them should be done at or near Ironman race pace (in other words, steady, not all out).

As with your long rides and long runs, your longest brick workout should be done three to four weeks before your big race.

Take Advantage of Recovery Weeks

Every three or four weeks, you should cut back on your training volume by about 20 percent in order to absorb the training of the past two or three weeks and to prepare your body for the higher training volumes to come. Intuitively, many triathletes feel that each week they should do more training than the previous week, but this is not the best way to maximize your fitness. Ultimately, you will be able to handle more training in your heavy training weeks if you take regular recovery weeks than you would without them.

The most important recovery weeks are, of course, the last two or three weeks before your race. In the final week before the race, you should do only about 20 percent as much training as you did in your peak week of training. You'll be bouncing off the walls with pent-up energy, but that's a good thing, because you're going to need that energy on race day!

Practice Nutrition

Individual athletes vary a lot in terms of how much fluid consumption they can tolerate and how much carbohydrate they can absorb during exercise. Too often, triathletes try to follow one-size-fits-all recommendations that could fall way below or drastically exceed their personal limitations. You can only determine your nutritional needs, limitations, and preferences by testing them in training.

On the bike, train yourself to drink a sports drink frequently throughout rides. You should be able to drink 1.0 to 1.2 liters (equal to a little more than a quart) per hour during harder, warmer rides. Try different brands and flavors of sports drink until you find a favorite. On your longer rides, experiment with carbohydrate gels and solid foods such as energy bars during the later stages. Some long-distance triathletes get by on fluids alone, but most feel the need to consume something a little more substantive after three or four hours of pedaling.

On your longer runs, carry a squeeze bottle of sports drink in a fluid belt and drink from it every 10 minutes or so. It's not possible to drink as much while running as you can while cycling, yet you sweat more and burn more energy while running, so it's important that you train yourself to drink as much as you can tolerate. Gels work well for supplemental carbohydrate during running, but be wary of combining too much gel with sports drink, because it could easily lead to gastrointestinal discomfort. It's better to wash down gels with water.

Once you've determined the nutrition schedule that works best for you while cycling and running, turn this schedule into a precise plan for the race. You should have a good idea of exactly what, how much, and how often you will drink and eat on the bike and during the run. For more recommendations on nutrition, see chapter 13.

RACE DAY

A long-distance triathlon is sort of like parenthood: No matter how much you prepare for it, you're never totally prepared for it. You just have to prepare as best you can, then take the plunge and give it your best shot. No long-distance triathlon is ever flawless, and you can spoil the fun of it by expecting it to go perfectly and by driving yourself crazy beforehand trying to prepare for everything that could possibly happen. But there are certain things you absolutely should do in order to avoid unnecessary setbacks during your race. Here are a few.

Know the Course

In short races, you can get by without studying the course beforehand. Just follow the people in front of you, right? But in preparing for a long-distance race, it's much more important to get to know the course and conditions well beforehand. This can help in a variety of ways. The first thing you should do (many weeks before the race) is study online or printed course maps—and especially elevation charts for the bike and run courses. This will enable you to train on similar topography. Also find out about the water temperature and climatic conditions you can expect, so that you can prepare for these, too.

If it's feasible, visit the race location well in advance of the event for a training weekend on the course. Some triathlon training outfits such as Multisports.com sponsor special on-site training camps at various Ironman venues. If this isn't feasible, don't sweat it; just be sure to arrive at the race location several days before the race so you can take the time to familiarize yourself with the lay of the land. Do the swim course at least once (easy!), ride portions of the bike course, run portions of the run course, and drive the full bike course (and perhaps bike the full run course). This will not only prevent you from making terrible mistakes such as taking a wrong turn or thinking the run is two laps when it's really three, but it will also prepare you for what certain parts of the race are going to feel like—what that windy stretch on the bike course will feel like, what that killer hill at the beginning of the run will feel like, and so forth.

Pay special attention to the transitions. You should be able to visualize every move you're going to make from the time you step out of the water until the time you mount your bike, and from the time you dismount your bike until the time you exit the transition on foot. This means you must do a complete walk-through the day before. Other important things to know about the course are where aid stations will be and where special needs bags will be (if there are any).

One last benefit of getting familiar with the course is that it allows you to create a good spectating plan for your supporters.

Practice Simple Bike Repairs

As covered in chapter 4, I strongly recommend that you get comfortable changing tires, replacing dropped chains, and making small derailleur adjustments before you do your first long-distance race. Easily fixed mechanical problems could ruin your race if you don't have the basic know-how you need to deal with them. So don't let your friend the gearhead change all your flats for you on training rides. Change them yourself, and it's not a bad idea to time yourself while you're at it. See how fast you can get.

Know the Rules

Disqualification is probably the most discouraging way not to finish (or not to officially finish) a long-distance triathlon. So be sure to study the race rules, not just before the race itself, but before you even travel to it. By far the most common infraction in triathlon is drafting on the bike. That's pretty easy to avoid doing. But there are many other infractions that could surprise you. For example, in some Ironman events, competitors are not allowed to leave the second transition without reflective tape on their shoes and jersey. Other no-nos are riding your bike in the transition area and receiving outside assistance from supporters (nutrition, pacing, technical help, and so forth).

Check and Double-Check Your Equipment

Another terrific way to spoil your first long-distance triathlon is to forget an important piece of gear or to experience some kind of avoidable equipment failure. Even if everything seems fine with your bike, have a mechanic give it a once-over before you check it in. On the morning of the race, give it one last inspection yourself. Top off the air pressure in the tires, and make sure your bike is set in an appropriate gear.

Before you travel to the race, make an exhaustive packing list, and don't leave home without every item checked off. Make a separate list of items you'll need in your transition bag, and make sure you have all of them in the bag before you leave the hotel on race morning. And always—always!—pack a backup pair of swim goggles.

11

Winning the Mind Game and Staying Motivated

Joanna Zeiger, PhD

As a competitive athlete for 26 years—16 as a swimmer and 10 as a triathlete—I have experienced a full spectrum of emotions, from the highs of achieving or exceeding expectations to the anguish of coming up painfully short in difficult races and of being sidelined from major competitions due to injury. During the low periods, I often questioned whether the struggle was worth it. But after many hours of hand-wringing consideration, it became clear that giving up without exhausting all options was out of the question. The pain of not going on would simply outweigh the emotional pain of not having given my all. This approach has seen me through races that seemed futile and patches of training that seemed like I'd hit rock bottom. It also brought me to one of the biggest lessons I've learned in sport: No matter how well you train, you will never reach your ultimate potential if your mind isn't as strong as your body.

Although building mental muscle is no easy task, once certain skills are mastered, they will greatly enhance your sports performance and overall enjoyment of triathlon. This chapter focuses on the following mental strategies: goal setting, visualization, overcoming prerace anxiety, "getting in the zone," and coming back stronger after disappointment.

GOAL SETTING

In my own training and racing, I complete my list of goals long before the season begins. Setting goals helps give me focus and direction. Additionally, it allows me to plan my training regimen, increases my motivation and confidence, and keeps me excited about the sport during the long winter months. I set my goals early in the year to provide myself ample time for both physical and mental preparation. First, I select my key races for the year, and then I fill in the season with races that are preparatory, fun, or located in desirable locations.

Before you set your own goals, you must decide on your level of commitment to the sport. Ask yourself how much time you have to train each week (factoring in what your objectives are) and how many races you can attend. Family and work will certainly dictate the amount of time spent training and racing. And from one season to the next, your desire to train and race may wax and wane. If you have a coach, she should have an active role in helping you formulate appropriate goals.

When setting goals for the season, make them realistic, specific, and measurable. You want to challenge yourself, but keep in mind that setting goals that are too lofty will not only end in disappointment but also lead to decreased self-confidence, which will likely hinder future performance. For instance, if you've completed a handful of Olympic-distance races, and you are considering moving up to the Ironman distance, don't set out to win your age group or achieve a 10-hour performance your first time out. Your goal for your first Ironman should be to finish on two feet, injury free. More challenging goals can be set once you've learned from your experience and identified your strengths and weaknesses. The key is to set challenges that force you to rise to the occasion, and avoid aiming for long shots that set you up for failure.

It's also important to make your goals as specific as possible and to set both short- and long-term goals. Short-term goals will help keep you motivated during the season and will let you know whether you are on track to reach your ultimate goal.

Sport psychologist Tom Holland explains that goals can be divided into three types: outcome, performance, and process.

An *outcome goal* is oriented toward a long-term result such as, "To qualify for age-group nationals next year." An athlete sometimes has little control over outcome goals (e.g., a flat tire or extreme weather conditions can impede the chance of achieving this type of goal). A *performance goal* is generally independent of other competitors and the specific outcome of the race. An example is improving your time in a specific distance or coming out of the water with the lead group. Finally, a *process goal* includes such things as perfecting swim strokes or honing run form.

The most accomplished athletes employ a combination of all three of these on their road to success. Creating your own combination of these three types of goals will increase your motivation by allowing you to reach goals at all stages of training and racing.

Pump Yourself Up

Employ these five strategies to stay motivated during training and racing:

- *Post your goals.* Write them down and post them where you can see them daily (on your refrigerator, on your bathroom mirror, or at your desk). This will keep you on task, and once you begin achieving them, they'll motivate you to aim higher.

- *Surround yourself with other athletes.* Finding training partners or joining a triathlon club will keep you from missing workouts and make training a lot more fun.

- *Check your attitude.* During tough moments, see challenges, not problems, and look for the silver lining. Remind yourself how far you've come, how much your fitness has increased, how blessed you are to be healthy, or how beautiful the day is. These mental tricks will propel you forward and keep your head positive.

- *Praise yourself.* Positive self-talk ("I'm a machine!" "I'm fast!") during training and racing will help you avoid the rough patches.

- *Mix up your training.* Take recovery days when they are planned, and use cross-training to avoid injury and burnout. There's nothing like time off from a sport you love to get you pumped for your next workout!

VISUALIZATION

When I was competing as a collegiate swimmer, part of our practice routine involved participating in group visualization sessions before or after practice. We would lie on our backs while the coach talked us through various racing scenarios. This never quite worked for me; I could only visualize diving off the blocks and landing a belly flop. Today, I've learned to incorporate visualization successfully into my training, but it is less conventional than in my swimming days. Race images pop into my head when I am on the bike, running, or lying in bed. I do not usually picture myself racing against my competitors in these situations (although that might work for you). Instead, I visualize the perfect race where I am swimming, biking, and running flawlessly and fast.

Former pro triathlete Jennifer Gutierrez, a member of the 2000 American Olympic triathlon team, utilized a step-by-step visualization process in her quest for Olympic glory. She explains, "I went through the race in my mind from start to finish. I would do this several times during the day before the race as well as race morning. I went through the tough race spots over and over again." This is much easier to do when you are familiar with the course, so if you have not raced at a venue, drive it or ride it prior to race day to give you a mental picture of how the race will unfold. This will boost your race day confidence because you'll know where to push yourself, where to conserve your energy, and where you'll need to rely on your mental muscle most.

If you have never engaged in visualization, initially try following a more formal program and then tailor it to your specific needs. Just like any form of training, using trial and error will help you pinpoint the intricacies that work best for you. Holland suggests several steps to take you through a successful visualization session:

Step-by-Step Visualization

1. Find a quiet place, get in a comfortable position, and allow your body and mind to relax. Progressive muscle relaxation (consciously relaxing one muscle group at a time) and deep breathing exercises will help achieve this relaxed state.

2. Close your eyes and begin to practice imagery by visualizing a large circle. Make the circle smaller and smaller until it disappears. Visualize another large circle but this time filled with a color, and shrink that one down until it disappears as well. Do this with several different colored circles.

3. Visualize a sports setting. Begin to fill in the setting—the weather, the people, and so on; use rich detail.

4. Picture yourself in a triathlon alongside other competitors. Visualize yourself performing successfully in each discipline. Hear the sounds, smell the smells, taste the sweat that drips down your face as you experience a great performance.

5. End by taking a few slow, deep breaths and opening your eyes.

In the beginning, Holland suggests practicing visualization for three to four minutes; when you lose your attention and focus, then it is time to stop. Ultimately, the optimal time will be individual, and trying to force visualization may result in diminishing returns. Consistency and quality are more important than quantity. Mental practice can and should be performed prior to training, on rest days, or during periods of injury. Begin with visualization on rest days, and then add in sessions prior to training and competition.

OVERCOMING PRERACE ANXIETY

Everyone deals with prerace jitters differently. To stay calm and focused before a race, I follow the same routine each time. This involves getting my bike ready and packing my bag the night before, and I always eat the same breakfast on the morning of a race. I also like to chat with other competitors to ease the tension at the start line. Instead of viewing competitors as adversaries, which can cause intense anxiety, pro triathlete and Ironman champion Michael Lovato uses the following tactic: "Rather than ignore other competitors and/or spectators, I attempt to draw energy from them, in one way or another," he says. "I am generally stronger when others are around to push me."

If you suffer from prerace anxiety, you're not alone. Jennifer Gutierrez finds it to be the worst part of competing. She says, "You can race over 100 times and still be just as nervous as your first. My anxiety usually started the day before the race and lasted until the start of the race. If I had to, I would cry to ease the pain."

While this may sound extreme, a certain amount of stress prior to a race is actually beneficial. Low levels of stress (some call it "nervous energy") increase adrenaline and alertness and ready the body for physical demands. When stress levels increase too much, however, impaired judgment, negative emotions, muscle tightness, and decreased self-confidence can result.

Anxiety occurs when an athlete loses the ability to deal with the factors that cause stress or when an athlete feels she has no control over her situation. Performance invariably suffers when this occurs.

You can combat prerace anxiety with the following tips:

- *Relaxation techniques.* Deep breathing, progressive muscle relaxation, or listening to music can reduce anxiety. Visualization, as discussed earlier, can help alleviate negative thoughts.

- *Positive self-talk.* Many athletes don't realize how many negative thoughts they have during training and racing. It's important to recognize these and replace them with a key phrase that gives you

© Nigel Farrow

Relaxation techniques and positive self-talk can reduce stress to a level that's actually beneficial.

self-confidence ("You are strong!" "You can do this!" "You're a machine!"). These phrases can be repeated to yourself in any combination, at any time, especially when you feel your confidence waning. Self-talk can begin several days before an event and continue right up to or during competition.

• ***Take control of the things you can.*** Train hard and smart; make sure your equipment works properly; have a nutritional plan. All of these things will increase your confidence and give you a sense of power.

• ***Don't let past negative experiences influence the future.*** In other words, if you've had a bad experience racing in the heat in the past and have addressed the issue in your training, feel confident that this time out you will succeed!

• ***Implement realistic expectations.*** For instance, if you are competing in a race to test your fitness (your peak race is six weeks away), don't make the mistake of setting the same goals for this race as you would for your peak event. In this instance, your expectation should be to complete the event successfully and to find out where your fitness lies in relation to your goals.

© John Segesta

Recalling visual images practiced prerace can help you push past mental barriers.

GETTING IN THE ZONE

In more than 10 years as a triathlete, I've had only a handful of races I consider to have been "perfect" (the 2000 Sydney Olympic triathlon being one such race), where everything felt effortless, my focus was complete, and I was able to enjoy the moment. These feelings are examples of being "in the zone" or "flow."

The zone is a perceived experience in which the mind and body work synchronously. The zone can occur during training or racing. Characteristics include "Zen-like" feelings of relaxation, confidence, focus, effortlessness, and lack of conscious thought. Although this state often emerges unpredictably, certain conditions increase its likelihood. These include low levels of stress, feeling prepared for an event, allowing yourself enough time and space to focus, being relaxed, and keeping your thoughts positive. On the other hand, high stress, illness or injury, trying too hard, and inability to deal with distraction will decrease your chances of achieving flow and getting in the zone.

Apply these ideas to help achieve flow:

- Improve your focus through meditation or visualization.

- Practice mood control—use positive self-talk prior to and during training and competition. Do not allow mistakes or feeling fatigued to consume you.

- Learn to cope with distractions; they are inevitable. Do not dwell on events that are out of your control. Develop a plan to refocus when distractions arise. Turn your thoughts positive ("It's a beautiful day! Look how far I've come!").

- Channel your stress into energy that propels you, and avoid letting it draw energy from you.

COMING BACK STRONGER AFTER DISAPPOINTMENT

A swim coach once told my team that it wasn't the good workouts or races that made us better, stronger, and mentally tougher—it was the bad ones. Slogging through endless yards in the pool and many less-than-perfect swim meets, I thought he was crazy. In the interim years, after grueling workouts, disappointing races, and injuries that have tested me physically and mentally, I now appreciate the meaning of these words. It is easy to maintain motivation when everything feels good, but when injury, commitments outside the sport, or a stretch of poor performances occur, your resilience is tested. Can you battle back after extreme disappointment?

If an athlete believes her happiness and well-being are contingent on a good race performance, an unachieved goal will result in depression. This is especially true for a race that requires considerable amounts of time and effort for preparation, such as an Ironman. Amanda Gillam, a long-time age-grouper turned pro triathlete, says, "After a bad race, I am sometimes discouraged and withdrawn. To offset these feelings, I surround myself with friends who are positive. I also find it comforting to talk to my coach about a bad race. He helps me keep my confidence high for the next race."

Whether or not you achieve the results you are aiming for, the end of the season can be a difficult time. You may find that your motivation suddenly disappears, illness occurs, negative thoughts overtake the positive ones, and a sense of purpose has disappeared. Combat these feelings by taking some time off to rejuvenate and gain perspective. This can involve a few weeks of complete rest (spending time with friends and family, catching up on chores at home, or reading some good novels) or spending time cross-training (learning a new sport or participating in some great off-season conditioning such as cross-country skiing or snowshoeing). When you feel ready, ease back into training. Take this opportunity to evaluate your performances; recognize your successes with pride and determine where improvements can be made for the future. Start formulating your goals for next season, and sign up early for a race you look forward to. Most important, take some time off so that you will be mentally (and physically) fresh when it's time to start training again. And, remember the best motivator of all: Keep it fun!

Gearing Up
for Triathlon

Liz Dobbins

It's no secret—triathlon is an extremely equipment-intensive endeavor. With different gear requirements for three separate sports, it's possible to devote whole books to the equipment used in triathlon. For the purposes of this book, I'll keep things easy, covering what a well-educated triathlete should know about gear and pointing you in the right direction for more information when needed.

Throughout this chapter, keep in mind that the most important requisite for your gear—whether you intend to merely complete a triathlon, be competitive in your age group, or go for an overall placing—is a comfortable fit. A good fit translates to greater efficiency, more mental energy, and better enjoyment of the sport.

Let's start by listing essential equipment for each discipline before moving into specifics.

- Swimming: Swimsuit, wet suit, goggles, swim cap, sunscreen, fins and paddles, fist gloves, pull buoys, kickboards
- Biking: Bike, wheels, tires, helmet, bike shoes, pedals, sunscreen, bike jersey, bike saddle, cycling shorts, gloves, tool bag and tools, sunglasses
- Running: Running shoes, running apparel (shorts, top, hat or visor, socks), glasses, sunscreen

SWIM GEAR

To finish a triathlon swim, all you really need is a swimsuit, cap, and goggles. However, there are some things to consider when choosing each of these, and there's a lot more swim equipment that can make both your swim training and your race much more comfortable and a lot more fun. Consider the following when selecting swim gear.

Swimsuit

A comfortable, reasonably snug fit is essential for a swimsuit, whether you'll use it for training or racing. Many manufacturers (such as Orca, Louis Garneau, Arena, Speedo, Iron Girl, and others) offer triathlon-specific women's suits in both one- and two-piece styles.

Ideally, the suit you compete in should be comfortable for biking and running as well as swimming. Although it's not a requirement that you continue your race in your swimsuit, many people enjoy the ease of not having to change during transitions. Likewise, many race suits feature a small padded chamois, allowing for extra saddle comfort and freedom of run stride. Test different race suits in training until you find a comfortable style and cut. Once you do, consider buying a few at a time, because styles may change with the seasons.

For swim training only, some manufacturers make thicker, ultra-chlorine-resistant suits that can last up to a year (five swims a week). If you need more specific information, specialty swim shops or triathlon stores will have a large variety of suits in stock and can usually order what you need.

Wet Suit

Wet suits are typically allowed in triathlon swims that are held in waters cooler than 76 degrees Fahrenheit. They aid in insulation and buoyancy, making swimming easier for weaker swimmers. When selecting a wet suit, a proper fit is critical. Trying the suit on is a must to ensure that you are buying the right size (size varies greatly among manufacturers). Likewise, many triathlon retail stores offer demo models that can be tested in the water. If you have an opportunity to test your suit, do not pass it up. An uncomfortable fit—whether too snug or too loose—will limit your swim potential and get your race off to a disappointing start. When testing a suit, make sure to practice getting out of it to ensure that the zipper is easily accessible and that you can slip out of it with relative ease.

Your wet suit should feel very snug on land. In the water, it will feel considerably less restrictive due to water pressure. An important feature is the shoulder area (gusset). A good suit will feature supple, easy-to-stretch shoulder gussets that allow nonbinding, low-resistance range of motion at the shoulder joint. This allows for a natural stroke with no restrictions in your range of motion.

Wet suits range in price from about $175 to $450. The more expensive suits are made of (you guessed it) a higher quality rubber. This can make a difference in performance, but if a lower-end suit fits you well, a more expensive suit will not make a huge performance difference. Consider what your needs are (how competitive you plan to be), and if you find a comfortable suit that works, go with it.

An important note: Although you'll see many triathletes in the transition area applying nonstick cooking spray to ease the process of putting on their wet suit, resist this temptation. Sprays such as this can damage the rubber of your wet suit and decrease its wear life. Instead, look to your wet suit manufacturer for nonstick products that are specially made for wet suits. Before you do this, however, try getting in and out of your suit without the aid of extra products. If your suit is a good fit, it shouldn't feel impossible to put on.

If possible, test a wetsuit before buying it, and always practice getting in and out of it before racing.

Goggles

Goggles are one of the most affordable pieces of triathlon gear you'll purchase, but they are no less important in terms of fit, function, and comfort. There are different models for racing, training, low-light conditions, and sunny days. And remember that not all goggles fit the same. Different brands and models offer different shapes and contours. Athletes with smaller faces may find better luck with a "junior" model featuring contours that fit a smaller face better. The test? At the store, hold a pair of goggles to your eyes (without putting the strap over your head) and gently press them into your sockets, testing suction hold. Look for a snug fit with a reasonable degree of suction created when you press on them. If they fall away immediately, look for another model until you get one that holds to your face for a few seconds. As with swimsuits, when you find a pair that works well for you, consider buying several pairs at once. You should have at least one backup pair of goggles at all times and have pairs for cloudy conditions (featuring a clear or light-colored tint) as well as for sunny conditions (darker, reflective lenses). You may also want to try a "mask" style goggle, which offers increased peripheral vision and, for some, more comfort.

For people who wear prescription glasses, some manufacturers offer prescription goggles at a reasonable cost. Consult your local swim store or triathlon shop for suggestions.

Swim Cap

Swim caps generally come in one size, although smaller youth sizes can be found. Caps are usually made of latex or silicone. Your local swim shop will carry a wide variety of different caps. Most of them will fit just fine. A quick note: Silicone caps tend to last the longest of the general-use caps, are more supple, and may cause less skin irritation.

For cold open-water swims, a neoprene "squid lid" can mean the difference between a good swim and one that smarts of "ice-cream headache" and a cold body core. Brands such as Quintana Roo offer a neoprene cap that aids in retaining body heat in the area where you're most likely to lose it. Wearing a standard latex or silicone cap under *and* over a neoprene cap will further aid in critical heat retention.

Sunscreen

Triathlon exposes you to harmful rays anywhere from over an hour to 12 hours. To protect your skin and allow for a more comfortable race, a quality, water-resistant sunscreen is a must. Look for a broad-based sunscreen or sunblock that protects against both types of ultraviolet rays—UVA and UVB. For maximum protection, look for one with the ingredients *micronized titanium dioxide* and *zinc oxide* (which help prevent melanoma), and an SPF of 30 or higher to provide the longest protection possible.

Test different types (lotions, gels, spray-on) until you find an effective one that does not clog your pores (which raises your core body temperature). Keep in mind that sunscreens must be applied 30 minutes prior to sun exposure, while sunblocks provide immediate protection. Your skin may react differently to each, so test different varieties in training before committing to one or the other. Also remember to reapply sunscreen in both T1 and T2. Taking an extra second to do this can make your race (not to mention the day after your race) a lot more comfortable.

Training Aids

Pool training devices are a great way to improve both technique and strength, and also to add variety to your swim workouts. Prior to using any aid, consult a Masters coach or experienced swimmer to learn how to use it correctly, as misuse can lead to injury and wasted hours in the pool. Following are some of the most effective training devices.

Pull buoys and paddles   There are a few simple, inexpensive "pool toys" that will aid in lowering your times and moving you up lanes during Masters workouts. Two essentials come in the form of pull buoys and paddles. A pull buoy, which is an hourglass-shaped closed-cell foam "floatie" that is braced between the thighs, levels the body with the water surface while swimming and eliminates the need for kicking. This isolates the upper body and aids in strengthening.

Paddles also aid in upper-body strengthening. Strapped over the wrist and fingers, the paddles increase surface area propulsion, building muscles integral to the pull phase of the swim stroke. Being too aggressive with paddles can stress and potentially injure the shoulders, however. Learning to use any training aids should be done under the instruction of a coach.

Fist gloves   As discussed briefly in chapter 3, fist gloves—rubber gloves that fit a balled fist—prevent the swimmer from extending her fingers, forcing her to "feel" the water and incorporate the use of the forearm as a source of propulsion. Swimming after doing drill work with fist gloves will give you a heightened sense of feel for the water, aiding in the catch and pull phase of your stroke.

Kickboards   The fluttering leg kick, originated from the lower body, is important too. The use of a simple kickboard helps build lower-body and leg power and speed, as well as a continuous kicking motion.

Fins   Fins are used to build leg strength and provide extra propulsion while working on other areas of your stroke. Use shorter fins to work on lower-body strength, but make sure not to overuse fins. Practicing swimming without them is critical since they are not allowed during racing.

BIKE GEAR

If there's any area of triathlon where it's easy to rack up charges on your credit card, it's the bike. Not only will your bike be the most expensive piece of equipment you'll buy, but there are countless accessories you can outfit yourself with in pursuit of a faster split—everything from cycling socks and tires to carbon forks and ultralight componentry. Following is a look at the many gear considerations for triathlon's second leg.

Bike

The bike is one piece of equipment where comfort is certainly paramount. Considering that the largest percentage of your training and racing hours will be spent on this particular piece of equipment, you will be well served choosing the most comfortable bike possible. This will also be the most expensive piece of equipment you will purchase, which is all the more reason to make an informed decision.

Fit

Women have, on average, longer legs and shorter torsos than men. By manipulating seat height and stem length, a very comfortable fit can be achieved for many women. However, a significant number of women, especially smaller riders, have difficulty attaining a comfortable position on bikes that are by and large built for male riders. Luckily for these women, some bike manufacturers (such as Trek, Cannondale, Softride, Specialized, and Terry) have addressed this problem by producing bikes specifically to fit a woman's body structure—many of these bikes include lower stand-over height, a shorter top tube for easier reach to the handlebars, short-reach brakes, narrower handlebars, and smaller 650c wheels. These bikes have made it possible for even the smallest, most-difficult-to-fit women riders to achieve a comfortable, efficient fit.

If you plan on using a single bike for both triathlon and social road riding with friends on the weekends, you might consider buying a road bike and purchasing add-on aerobars separately (if you find a model that's comfortable). After the triathlon season, you can easily unbolt the aerobars and join your buddies for casual off-season bike rides. You might also want to consider an entry-level tri bike that features road-style drop handlebars, a relatively relaxed seat angle, and a set of clip-on aerobars.

But if you plan to become a competitive triathlete who rides a triathlon-specific bike, you'll have a few more options to consider, such as bar-end shifting and cowhorn-style aerobars. These types of bikes usually have a steeper seat angle than the typical road bike, allowing the rider to settle into a more aerodynamic riding position and stay there for the duration of the bike ride.

Choosing the right frame size is critical. Frame sizing for road and triathlon bikes is based on a measurement in centimeters from the center of the bottom bracket (where the crank arm bolt fixes to the frame) to either the center of the top tube/seat tube axis or the top of the top tube (referred to as "center to center" or "center to top").

I suggest finding a few bike shops within your area—preferably at least one triathlon-specific shop—where you can test ride bikes from different manufacturers. Doing so will give you an idea of which frame materials feel best, and which manufacturer provides the best fit for you. Then, it's up to your personal preference and budget. When possible, call in advance to make sure a shop has bikes in your size to test ride. (The shop will be able to determine your approximate size over the phone, from your height and inseam.)

Upon purchase of any bike, you should have the bike shop personnel fit the bike exactly to your body's specifications. Your position on the bike has the greatest effect on your energy expenditure, and an improper fit can translate to reduced power output. If you sit upright when you ride (instead of in a tucked, aerodynamic position), you will create significantly more air resistance, requiring more energy to overcome it. After you become comfortable on your new bike, return to the shop to achieve a more aerodynamic position while still maintaining comfort. This will, of course, reduce the amount of energy you expend to maintain a given speed.

If you are looking to be competitive in triathlon, consider getting professionally fit by a bike fit expert outside your local shop. Look to your local triathlon club for suggestions, and use the Internet to research the subject further. There are an increasing number of businesses that perform bike fit services, measuring your power output while analyzing everything from stem length and handlebar width to seat position and aerobar position. If you are serious about the sport, investing in a professional bike fit is well worth the cost (anywhere from $50 for a basic fit to $1,000 and up for wind tunnel analysis). You will not only end up with the most efficient riding position possible, but the fit could also save you from injury and will most certainly leave you with increased comfort and performance.

Frame Material

Frame material should be considered after determining how much money you plan to spend on a bike. Bikes are made from many different materials: steel, aluminum, titanium, and carbon fiber being among the most popular. Frame material has a significant impact on how a bike "feels" or rides—be it soft, stiff, or supple. While some people want nothing more than all-day comfort out of a bike, others value complete stiffness for total power transfer while pedaling. The following assessment of each material and its ride characteristics will help you decide what best suits your needs.

Steel   Steel is by far the least expensive frame material, and it has the favorable ride characteristic of liveliness—it's stiff out of the saddle but is capable of inherently absorbing high-frequency vibration. Rust is the greatest concern with steel bikes, making good maintenance critical.

Aluminum   Aluminum is a popular choice because it is one of the lightest and stiffest materials, as well as affordable and able to accommodate a high polish finish. The drawback is that ride quality can be rougher than with other materials. As with any material, make sure to test it before committing to purchase, and buy from manufacturers that have long-standing experience building aluminum frames.

Titanium   This increasingly popular frame material has the unique capability of being light and stiff while also being very compliant and comfortable on bumpy roads, particularly for lighter riders. Ti bikes are also corrosion resistant, and with low-fatigue characteristics, they have a very high life expectancy. The drawback is cost. A ti frame will cost as much as $500 more than the equivalent steel frame.

Carbon fiber   Carbon fiber is light and stiff where you want it to be, and also compliant and forgiving where you want it to be. How? Good carbon frame builders (such as Kestrel) have become adept at orienting carbon fiber layers to create a desired ride characteristic—adding more layers of composite material at high-stress areas (such as the bottom bracket) and using less material at low-stress areas (such as the down tube and top tube). It all adds up to a light ride with nearly custom ride characteristics. Once considered less durable than other frame materials, carbon frames are enjoying greater life expectancy as more manufacturers become adept at working with the material. If you choose this option, make sure to buy from a manufacturer that has a long history of producing carbon bikes.

A 15-minute test ride on roads similar to what you train on can make a huge difference when selecting frame material. Seek out both rough and smooth sections of road, and see how the frame feels beneath you.

Componentry

Allow your bike shop personnel to explain the different componentry on the bikes they offer. Of the two offerings in the components realm—Shimano and Campagnolo—most bikes will be outfitted with Shimano. The company offers a hierarchy of components (which consist of integrated shift/brake levers, a rear and front derailleur, cassette, and brake calipers) ranging from their new top-end 10-speed Dura-Ace to more moderately priced Ultegra, to an entry-level 105, Sora or Tiagra group set. Regardless of your choice, they'll all be reliable and functional; the difference generally comes down to weight, with higher end groups such as Dura-Ace and Ultegra being the lightest and having a discernible performance edge.

Budget Considerations

If you plan to use the bike for at least five years, I suggest investing more up front and buying a better bike in the beginning. Just think of the bike you could buy for the price of both an introductory bike and the new bike you will likely upgrade to after a season or two of racing. If you take this approach, however, make sure to do your homework. Road bikes are priced anywhere between $500 and $5,000 (and beyond!). In my opinion, the best equipment for the money is between $1,000 and $2,500. In this range, you will find virtually every frame material and very good, durable componentry. Bikes in this range will give you many years of trouble-free performance. That being said, if you have the resources, and you are a competitive age-grouper, it might be worth your time to research high-performance bikes priced beyond $2,500. These bikes provide very lightweight frames, top-end componentry, and an extremely comfortable fit (again, if you are in this category, invest in a professional fit).

Similar to cars, the time to get the best deal on a bike is in the fall. In late summer, bike shops start dropping prices and liquidating their stocks to make room for next year's bikes—not unlike automobile manufacturers. If you are lucky enough to find your size, you could save hundreds of dollars, and you can spend the off-season getting acquainted with your new bike.

Wheels

Depending on your height, you could be considering two different wheel sizes. The most widely used wheel diameter—ridden by Lance and the rest of the Tour competitors—is 700c. But if you're under five-foot-six, smaller 650c wheels are a good alternative. The benefit? For shorter women, 650c wheels allow for better bike handling. When you put 700c wheels on a small frame (which features a shorter wheel base), there's a risk of foot/wheel overlap during turns, causing instability and greater risk for crashing. To avoid this, a smaller diameter wheel (650c) is used to bring the wheel out to a more manageable distance with increased clearance. Many of the best women triathletes, from Gina Kehr to Natascha Badmann to Paula Newby-Fraser, ride 650c wheels, while others, such as Swiss Ironman competitor and time trial specialist Karin Thuerig, are tall enough to require a 700c wheel set.

Some triathletes will use the same set of wheels for racing as they do for training—and that's just fine. Most bikes on the market come with reasonably light and very durable OE (original equipment) wheels that are great for all-around use. Some triathletes will go the extra step and buy a very lightweight, aerodynamic wheel set (see figure 12.1a). Often comprised of lightweight carbon fiber, these race wheels are significantly lighter and more aerodynamic (configured specifically to slice through the wind with less resistance) than most all-around wheels—and, as a result of the high-tech materials and labor, they are also more expensive. However, if used properly, they can provide substantial time savings over the length of the bike leg, especially in the longer events. The lighter weight makes the bike more nimble since the wheels accelerate and climb better with less energy. The aerodynamic advantage starts to come into play when the flow of air past the wheels exceeds 20 miles per hour (mph). The faster you go, the greater the benefit, since wind resistance (drag) increases exponentially.

If you're thinking about getting a set of race wheels, consider the type of courses you plan to race on. If you race under hilly or windy conditions, a shallower dish (or aero cross-section to the rim) might be a better choice since they handle better in crosswinds and are lighter for climbs (see figure 12.1b). If flat courses, such as Ironman Florida, are on the docket, a deeper dish aero section will provide more aerodynamic advantage (see figure 12.1c). Even greater aerodynamic advantage can be gained by using a solid carbon fiber disc wheel in the rear, provided you don't expect to be in windy conditions.

Aerodynamic wheels are configured to offer as little resistance to the flow of air as possible, thereby requiring less energy on your part to maintain a given speed. At low speeds (15 to 20 mph), there is very little air resistance. At higher speeds (20 to 25 mph), there is a very distinct increase in drag. At very high biking speeds (25 to 35 mph), the drag produced is extreme and so is the amount of energy required to overcome it.

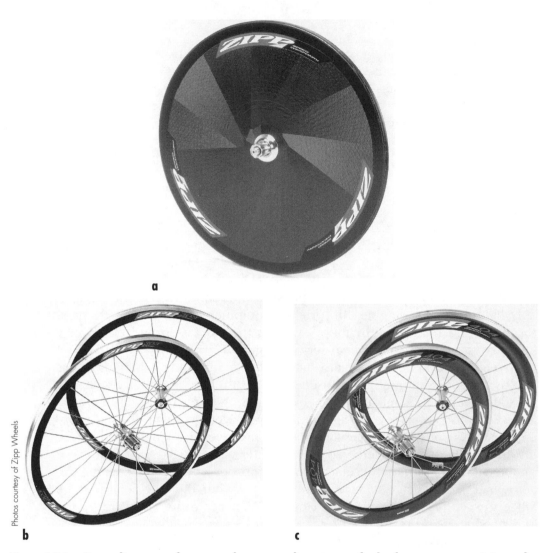

a

b   c

Figure 12.1 Depending on preference and purpose, three types of wheels are common: *(a)* aerodynamic carbon-fiber wheels, *(b)* shallow-dish wheels, and *(c)* deeper-dish aero wheels.

To be clear, you do not need to ride at 25 mph to gain a benefit from aerodynamic wheels. If you are riding at 17 mph into a 5 mph head wind, the airflow past the wheel is 22 mph—plenty fast enough to gain an advantage. Also, when you ride downhill at speeds of 25 to 35 mph, the advantage of aerodynamic wheels is keenly felt.

Tires

There are two main types of tires—clincher and tubular. A clincher tire is placed on the wheel rim, and the tube is placed inside the tire. The tire is designed to "clinch" to a lip on the rim. In the case of tubular tires, the tube is sewn into the tire, and the tire is actually glued to the wheel rim. Virtually every bike comes with wheels requiring clincher tires. That is good. For an overwhelming majority of people, clincher tires are far easier to use. They are very simple and quick to mount, and they allow for very swift flat tire repair during rides. When a tubular tire punctures (unless you have a sealant in the tire), there is no way to fix it, and your ride is over. However, some racers prefer tubular tires because they offer a slight weight savings paired with the lighter tubular rim (it requires no extra lip) and have a better road "feel."

Helmet

The helmet is one of the most critical but least-heralded pieces of equipment in your arsenal. You don't have to go for the high-end $150 model; the lower-end $50 model will protect you just as well. The benefits that come with the higher end models include better ventilation with increased and deeper vent channels, and adjustable retention devices that help keep the helmet snug to your head. As with wet suits, if you find a lower-end model that works for you, go with it.

Again, fit is critical. Too many cyclists negate the benefits of a helmet by using one that fits improperly on the head. The goal is to find a helmet that fits snugly—not so tight that it's uncomfortable (allow for just enough room to slip a finger between your forehead and the helmet) and certainly not so loose that it rattles around on your head or moves forward or backward. Your local shop can help you determine the right size and show you how to adjust the straps correctly. A few manufacturers (including Bell Helmets and Giro) make a women-specific model with a smaller shell, also taking into account the ever important "ponytail factor."

Shoes

The advantage of a cycling shoe is its stiffness, which leads to better power transfer. Cycling shoes are vastly stiffer than running shoes, and combined with a clipless pedal system, greatly improve your cycling efficiency. Go to any bike shop or triathlon store and try on several brands. Different brands use different lasts so some will simply fit your foot better than others. Unlike running shoes, you don't need a lot of space between your big toe and the end of the shoe, since you won't be running down any hills in them. A comfortable, nonrestrictive fit with no binding or pressure on your toes in the toe box (front of the shoe) will serve you well, especially on longer rides. There are numerous cycling shoes on the market. There are even a fair number of triathlon-specific models (e.g., Pearl Izumi, Carnac, Sidi). In addition, if you wear orthotics in your shoes or have orthopedic issues that require special consideration, there are a few companies (such as Rocket7) that will make custom cycling shoes for you with an orthotic built into the sole—at a price that's competitive with higher end, off-the-rack, cycling shoes.

Pedals

From both a safety and energy savings standpoint (not to mention comfort), clipless pedals are without question the way to go. They are easy to get in and out of (although some practice will be required) and much more efficient at transferring energy than a pedal and strap system. By completely engaging the cleat on the cycling shoes, the clipless pedal enables constant, even contact during the entire pedal stroke, creating better efficiency and conserving energy.

Again, a huge number of clipless pedals are on the market, each offering different features. Several companies (such as LOOK, Time, Crank Brothers, and Shimano) offer centering that allows for a biomechanically centered pedal stroke, eliminating the possibility of a splayed, inefficient stroke that can lead to injury. Others (including Speedplay) allow free "float," a blessing for cyclists with knee problems and biomechanic issues. Those who walk with "duck feet" (pointed outward) or those who are "pigeon-toed" can greatly benefit from these types of pedals because they allow the foot and knee to fall where they naturally want to throughout the pedal stroke. If you can, test your pedals before buying. Some bike shops will allow you to test different systems, particularly if you're buying shoes from them.

Bike Saddle

Being one of three contact points on the bike, the saddle is critical to riding comfort. Fortunately, there are now many manufacturers of women-specific saddles (including top models made by Fizik, Terry, and Specialized). They have gel padding, foam padding, cutouts to relieve nerve pressure, and carbon or titanium rails to shave saddle weight. For some women, a firmer saddle is more comfortable; others require more cushion. I suggest hopping on your friends' bikes to get an idea of how their saddles feel. Bike shops will, of course, allow you to test ride any bikes they have—which will, additionally, give you an opportunity to test several different saddles. Most bike shops will even let you test-drive some saddles if you are buying a bike from them. If you're buying a bike and you aren't keen on the stock saddle, request that the shop substitute another of the store's aftermarket choices and offer to pay any cost difference. A new bike should start with a comfortable ride!

Bike Clothing

Choosing the right clothing for cycling can make a huge difference in terms of comfort and performance. Following are the top considerations when selecting high-performance cycling clothing.

Bike jersey. I see many women wearing nothing but a jog bra or racing singlet when biking in warm weather. Instead, I encourage wearing a comfortable and colorful bike jersey when training. First, a bike jersey offers substantially more protection from the sun, and in the case of a fall, it offers a buffer between the asphalt and your skin. Second, and perhaps even more important, a colorful jersey is more likely to capture the eyes of a road-weary or distracted motorist. When I know I'm going to be cycling on busy roads, I wear a neon yellow jersey. Leave the earth tones for hiking!

Bike shorts. Bike shorts are an essential you don't want to skimp on. Virtually every major manufacturer has taken into consideration the anatomical differences between men and women and has created gender-specific pads (or chamois) sewn into their shorts to cushion and alleviate chafing while cycling. A comfortable pair of shorts can make the difference between having an enjoyable experience riding or a miserable one. Before buying a pair, try them on at your local bike shop. Make sure there is no bunching of material between the legs and look for a snug, even fit. You shouldn't feel any rough seams along the pad sewn into the shorts. Bike shorts range in price from $25 to $200. You can always be lucky and have the inexpensive ones fit you well, but more realistically, you'll probably have to go to the better-constructed shorts (they use more panels of fabric for a more contoured fit) to find a comfortable pair (expect to pay $75 to $125).

Gloves. Gloves are important for two reasons: First, they protect your hands and palms from chafing due to the pressure from holding and leaning on the handlebars. Second, they provide excellent protection for your palms in the event of a fall. Again, gloves that fit well work well. Try them on and make sure they don't bind between the fingers. Many people prefer a glove with gel pads to alleviate some of the pressure at the base of the palms, especially on longer rides.

General bike clothing. For most people, the climate where they live isn't warm year-round, and even warm climates have temperature variations. With just a few articles of cycling apparel, you can greatly extend your comfortable cycling temperature range. A long-sleeve jersey, a windbreaking vest, some leg warmers, a pair of shoe covers, and some long-fingered gloves can keep you comfortable in brisk temperatures. Depending on whether or not you opt for indoor training, you can layer up to withstand some significantly cold weather. However, when it is very cold outside, your reflexes become slower, and your bike-handling skills suffer. If you are uncomfortable even with added clothing, it's a sign you need to hop on an indoor wind trainer.

Bike Tools

Any good bike shop can handle virtually any repair job. However, as covered in chapter 4, it is extremely beneficial for triathletes to be reasonably self-sufficient when it comes to simple repairs and adjustments (your trusty shop mechanic won't be out there when you experience a flat tire 25 miles out of town). A small saddle bag (secured under the saddle) containing a

Tri Gear Essentials

Following is a list of essential items you'll need to participate in triathlon on a regular basis, along with a range of costs geared toward a beginner to semicompetitive athlete. Keep in mind that you may find better deals than indicated here, and you can certainly spend beyond the higher range, depending on the quality of product you desire.

Equipment	Approximate cost
Swimsuit	$50-$75
Wet suit	$150-$400
Goggles and swim cap	$20-$30
Bike	$1,000-$2,500
Bike shorts	$50-$100
Helmet	$50-$150
Running shoes	$85-$120
Miscellaneous apparel	$150-$250
Total	**$1,555-$3,625**

spare tube, two tire levers, an Allen wrench set, a minipump or CO_2 cartridges plus inflator, and a few dollars will help you deal with any minor mishap. Replacing a punctured tube and adjusting or tightening the brakes, handlebars, or cycling shoe cleats can be dealt with hassle free if you carry the aforementioned items.

See if your local shop offers a workshop in basic bike repair. If not, you might find a mechanic who is willing to show you how to make basic repairs to your bike if you frequent his shop. This way you will be able to complete just about every bike ride you begin.

A couple of quick notes: Make sure the stem (air valve) on your spare tube is long enough to go all the way through the rim of your wheel. Today's rims are increasingly deep, and many require tubes with a longer stem length. Ask your bike shop employee to tell you which stem length your wheels require. Also, in rare instances due to a tire puncture, the tire tread and casing can suffer enough damage that the replacement tube will push through the tire wall and result in another, almost immediate flat tube. To avoid this, simply fold a piece of an energy bar wrapper (or a dollar bill, cardboard, newspaper—almost anything will suffice) and place it on the inside of the tire (over the puncture hole or tear) when you put in your replacement tube. The pressure of the air in the tube will push the "patch" against the tire and keep it in place, and you'll be able to make it home.

Eyewear

Eye protection is vital. When you train for triathlon, you will undoubtedly spend many hours outdoors in the wind, and on rare occasions, in inclement weather. Good glasses will be distortion free and will fit to your face well, shielding you from wind, dust, bugs, hail, tossed gravel, and whatever else may be flying through the air. Also, the tint or coating of the lens should protect your eyes from the glare and potential damage of UV rays.

I suggest going to a local optometrist to find out which brands have safe lenses that will truly protect your eyes from UV rays. Some brands, including Oakley, even offer prescription lenses with their sport-specific frames. An important note: Cheaply constructed sunglasses, while shielding you from debris, can actually allow your eyes to become damaged by the sun. A dark lens will cause your pupil to dilate, and if the lens isn't a quality protective lens, it will allow far more of the sun's damaging rays to pass through and penetrate deep into your eyes than if you wore no glasses at all.

RUN GEAR

Running is the simplest of disciplines when it comes to tri gear. For the most part, running equipment comes down to shoes and apparel, and both have special considerations if you're looking for top performance.

Running Shoes

Selecting the right running shoes for your specific biomechanics goes without saying, given that running poses the greatest risk for triathlon injury. As such, it's critical to buy from a specialty running or triathlon store where expert staff can either watch you run on a treadmill or examine the wear patterns on an old pair of shoes. Most people will be given several different brand choices. Try them all on until you find a pair that feels right (never purchase a brand just because a fellow triathlete has had success with it!). A few running stores will allow you to test shoes before making a final decision. If you have access to such a store, take advantage of this policy. As with other critical gear items, if you find shoes that you love, consider buying two pair at once since models are regularly modified or even discontinued. If necessary, pay a little extra and get the best shoes possible. Many manufacturers make great shoes in the $85 to $110 range.

If you wear orthotics, bring them with you when buying shoes to ensure that your new shoes will accommodate them comfortably.

Running Apparel

An increasing number of manufacturers are making stylish, high-tech women's running apparel, making it one of the most fun aspects of tri gear shopping. Make sure you purchase fabrics that both breathe and wick sweat away from the body, regardless of whether they are for hot or cold weather.

To protect yourself from the harmful rays of the sun, run in both a hat and sunglasses, and look for apparel that includes a sun protection factor. Hats should be ventilated and light in color to reflect the sun.

Another critical item that all women rely on is the sports bra. As with running shoes, invest some time and money in finding what works best for you, and then stock up!

From shorts to singlets, socks to lace locks, tights to jackets, you can meet most any training and racing need at a specialty running or triathlon store.

ACCESSORIES

The list goes on. In addition to the previously mentioned gear items, triathletes can consider purchasing a heart rate monitor to aid in training. These cost anywhere from about $60 for the basic models to $200 for advanced models, and they can greatly assist in keeping your workouts in the proper range. Another accessory to consider is a stationary trainer, which allows you to perform bike training in the comfort (and safety) of your home when riding outside is undesirable. Various models are available (fluid, fan units, rollers) and range in cost from about $150 to $350.

Considering all the gear possibilities in triathlon can be overwhelming. To keep things under control, take it one discipline and one item at a time. Obtaining triathlon equipment is a cumulative process. Start with the basics and keep your friends and family updated on your needs—it will make birthday and holiday shopping a snap!

Fueling for Optimal Performance

Kimberly Brown, MS, RD

Nutrition has long been the unsung hero of endurance training. Many athletes put all their energy into the physical side of training, ignoring the nutrition component altogether, and hence cheating themselves of their true performance potential. Proper nutrition not only helps to optimize energy production and utilization (giving you greater power!), but it also helps prevent injuries that lead to diminished performance. This chapter will provide you with the nutritional strategies you need to get the most out of your triathlon training program.

ESSENTIAL NUTRIENTS FOR TRIATHLON SUCCESS

There are six nutrients that are essential for peak triathlon performance: carbohydrate, protein, fat, vitamins, minerals, and water. Carbohydrate, protein, and fat—otherwise known as macronutrients—are the only nutrients capable of providing a person with direct energy, and they are measured in calories. Vitamins and minerals—otherwise known as micronutrients—are found in all types of foods, which makes restriction of certain foods problematic, especially since many of these nutrients play an essential role in the breakdown and conversion of macronutrients into energy. And finally, water is essential in regulating core body temperature, lubricating muscles and joints, and maintaining proper metabolic function.

Carbohydrates

Put simply, carbohydrates are sugars and starches that fuel the body much like gas fuels a car. Each gram of carbohydrate yields approximately 4 calories of fuel. Just like a car storing its fuel in a tank, the human body stores carbohydrates as glycogen in both the muscles and liver. These glycogen reserves are relied on to stabilize blood sugars and aid in optimal muscle function. Women athletes who balance their meals with 45 to 65 percent carbohydrate while meeting daily energy demands can expect to store about 2 grams (8 calories) of glycogen per pound of muscle tissue and an additional 0.55 gram (2 calories) of glycogen per pound of body weight within the liver. This amount of glycogen will supply the energy needed to train for approximately two hours at a moderate intensity.

Unfortunately, with weight loss being a common goal among many female triathletes, particularly beginners, both calories and carbohydrate are often restricted. This can lower the amount of glycogen stored within the muscles and liver by as much as 75 percent, leading to premature depletion of glycogen, reduced power output, and decreased endurance capacity. Two terms are often used to describe how it feels when glycogen stores are depleted. *Bonking* refers to depletion of liver glycogen stores, causing a shortage of glucose being sent to the brain and ultimately leading to profound dizziness, lethargy, and possibly staggering on the course. The minimum amount of carbohydrate needed to supply adequate glucose for proper brain function is 130 grams, meaning athletes who follow extremely low-carbohydrate diet plans, such as the Atkins diet, are at heightened risk for bonking not only during exercise, but also at rest.

In addition to mentally bonking, a low carbohydrate intake can also lead to "hitting the wall," which occurs as a result of depleting muscle glycogen during the early stages of training. In this state, athletes experience muscle cramping and extreme fatigue, and they are at heightened risk for muscular injury due to catabolism of lean body mass. In response to low muscle glycogen levels, the liver starts making glucose from amino acids (building blocks of protein) and sending it back to depleted muscles as well as to the "bonking" brain. In the end, not only are glycogen reserves depleted, but protein levels are compromised, making recovery a long, slow process. Therefore, severe restriction of calories and carbohydrate is not advised for triathletes and will lead to diminished performance.

Determining Daily Carbohydrate Needs

Daily carbohydrate needs will vary greatly among athletes depending on the amount of training completed each day. Those training for half Ironman and Ironman-distance triathlons (training two to four or more hours a day) should expect to consume four to six grams of dietary carbohydrate per pound of lean body weight each day, whereas those training for sprint- and Olympic-distance triathlons require a daily carbohydrate intake of approximately three to four grams per pound of lean body weight (see table 13.1 for instructions on determining lean body weight). Note that a high volume of training is not an invitation to splurge on cookies, cake, chips, or chocolate. Your health and performance will thrive only when you fuel your body with the right types of carbohydrates at rest and during training.

TABLE 13.1 Daily Carbohydrate Needs Based on Lean Body Weight

Carbs per pound LBW*	LEAN BODY WEIGHT (POUNDS)*							
	90	95	100	110	120	130	140	150
3 grams	270	285	300	330	360	390	420	450
4 grams	360	380	400	440	480	520	560	600
5 grams	450	475	500	550	600	650	700	750
6 grams	540	570	600	660	720	780	840	900

*Lean body weight (LBW) can be determined with body fat analysis. Body fat testing is generally available at most gyms and universities. The Tanita Body Fat Scale will also give you an estimate of body fat percentage. Note that most women triathletes will have approximately 15 to 25 percent body fat. To determine lean body weight, subtract your percentage of body fat from 100 to achieve your percent of lean mass and then multiply by your total body weight. For example, a triathlete whose weight is 140 pounds and body fat 20 percent carries a lean body weight of 112 pounds (100 − 20 = 80 percent lean mass; .80 × 140 = 112 pounds of lean body weight).

Choosing the Right Types of Carbohydrate

The general consensus among health professionals used to be that a diet rich in complex carbohydrates (including potatoes, rice, and wheat) with inclusion of a smaller amount of simple sugars (such as sucrose or table sugar) was the ideal diet for optimal health and peak fitness performance. This changed when scientists found that frequent and excessive consumption of certain forms of carbohydrates, including complex carbohydrates, actually increased fat storage and increased the risk for the number one killer among women—cardiovascular disease. It is now understood that not all carbohydrates are created equal. Over the past 10 to 15 years, the term *glycemic index* has essentially replaced the terms *simple sugar* and *complex carbohydrate* when discussing the effect of different carbohydrate sources on overall health and performance.

Glycemic index simply refers to a carbohydrate-rich food's ability to cause a rise in blood glucose. Foods with a high glycemic index—such as refined flours (white bread), corn and rice cereals, potatoes, and baked goods (cookies, doughnuts, cake)—solicit a rapid rise in blood glucose that causes the body to respond by secreting insulin, which helps to shuttle those sugars into working cells. Consider this analogy: Hundreds of triathletes (representing carbohydrates/glucose) sprinting down the road (bloodstream) toward a tiny finish chute (entrance into your muscle cells) and all competing for a top 10 finish. The race director (your pancreas) is nervous about how to control the chaos so she recruits some volunteers (insulin) to assert control. Some of the volunteers (insulin) shuttle the top 10 triathletes (carbohydrates) into the "winner's" chute (muscles); the other volunteers (insulin) create another chute (entrance to fat cells) for the other 90 triathletes to filter through. To avoid this overflow, it's important to balance glycemic levels by eating no more than 10 percent of high-glycemic foods in your diet.

Low- to moderate-glycemic carbohydrates (100 percent whole grains, fruit, legumes, dairy) have a much more positive effect on energy levels and performance. Instead of a mass rush of triathletes sprinting toward that finish chute, picture a more filtered stream of competitors all being able to enjoy the same finish without anyone being pushed to the side. By maintaining glycemic levels, you help stabilize your energy levels, increase muscle glycogen, and prevent unwanted fat storage. Note that a person can only utilize and store so much carbohydrate, so overconsumption of any type of carbohydrate, as well as fat or protein, can lead to fat gain.

You should also note that the healthfulness of any carbohydrate can't be based solely on glycemic index. For example, many of the fruits and vegetables on the high glycemic list contain a multitude of health-enhancing benefits (see table 13.2). Furthermore, the portions of these foods typically consumed actually do not solicit a high-glycemic response. For example, one cup of raw carrots, which is a typical portion of carrots, does not stimulate insulin in the same manner as a typical portion of soda (one can). And unlike soda, which is nutritionally void, carrots are rich in beta-carotene, a potent antioxidant that may protect healthy cells from damage that occurs from ingested pollutants, lactic acid buildup, and exposure to chemicals, making it an excellent addition to any diet. Healthful carbohydrate choices that carry a high glycemic index, such as basmati rice, raisins, and potatoes, can be balanced out with an equal portion of lean protein (e.g., cottage cheese, chicken breast, or nuts) to promote a more desirable insulin response.

TABLE 13.2 Glycemic Index of Common Food Sources of Carbohydrates

High glycemic (60 and above)	Moderate glycemic (between 50-60)	Low glycemic (under 50)
Glucose (most sports drinks)	Cheese pizza	Old-fashioned oatmeal
Tofu frozen desserts	Bran muffin	Green peas
Dried dates, raisins	Blueberry muffin	Grapefruit juice
French bread	Shredded Wheat, Bran Chex cereal	Canned baked beans
Soft drinks		Bulgur
Instant rice, rice pasta, rice cakes	Canned fruit, heavy syrup	Parboiled rice
	Pita bread	Long-grain rice
Most cereals (corn and rice cereals being highest)	Orange juice	Pineapple juice
	White rice	Canned beans
Potatoes	Sweet corn	Orange, grapes
Pretzels	Popcorn	All-Bran, Kashi Go Lean cereal
Jelly beans	Oatmeal cookies	Hummus
Grape Nut Flakes, Total cereal	Pasta (<10 g. protein)	Apple juice
Vanilla Wafers, graham crackers	Brown rice	Tomato soup
Waffles, plain pancakes	Sweet potato	Whole wheat pasta (or pasta with >10 g. protein)
French fries	Balance Bar, Harvest Bar, PowerBar	Apple, pear
Doughnuts, pastries	Special K cereal	Fat-free milk
Saltines, Wheat Thins, corn chips	Pound cake	Baby lima beans
Cream of Wheat, instant	Potato chips	Soy milk, unsweetened
Bread stuffing	Pumpernickel, 100% whole wheat bread	Dried apricots, cherries
Bran flakes		Peach; canned peaches in juice
Honey	Banana (unripe), kiwifruit, mango	Pearled barley
Watermelon, pineapple		Plum, grapefruit
Carrots	Low-fat ice cream	Fructose (fruit sugar)
Bagel, plain; bread, white and wheat	Cheese tortellini	Peanuts, other nuts
Couscous		Low-fat yogurt (without sugar)
Beets		
Table sugar (sucrose); baked goods		

Protein

In Greek, *protein* means "to take first place," a feat many triathletes would like to accomplish. Scientifically speaking, proteins are large, complex molecules that make up 20 percent of a person's body weight in the form of muscle, bone, cartilage, and skin, as well as other tissues and body fluids. During digestion, protein breaks down into at least 100 individual chemical building blocks known as amino acids that form a little pool within the liver and are used to build muscle; grow skin, hair, and nails; and maintain healthy eyes, hormones, enzymes, antibodies, and nerve chemicals. Inadequate protein intake leads to a dehydrated amino acid pool and a consequent breakdown of healthy cells without repair, ultimately leading to elevated injury risk, slowed recovery time, and increased feelings of lethargy. Furthermore, recent research indicates that a low protein intake is also associated with increased risk for stress fractures and osteoporosis, a disease that is becoming increasingly prevalent among female athletes. On the flip side, excessive protein intake can cause the amino acid pool to overflow, ultimately leading to health problems such as diminished kidney function, calcium excretion, and dehydration. Therefore, finding an appropriate protein intake for your athletic needs is not only essential to performance, but will also play a big role in your overall health and well-being.

Determining Protein Needs

Just like carbohydrate, protein needs will vary among athletes depending on lean body weight and activity level. Likewise, women athletes who are pregnant or lactating require additional protein. Most women triathletes require approximately 0.50 to 0.80 grams of daily protein per pound of lean body weight to support growth, repair, and development of cells during training (see table 13.3 for instructions on determining your protein needs). For most, this equates to two to three servings of dairy and 5 to 6 ounces of meat/meat alternative per day and approximately 10 to 20 percent of total calorie intake.

TABLE 13.3 Daily Protein Needs

Protein per pound LBW	LEAN BODY WEIGHT (POUNDS)							
	90	95	100	110	120	130	140	150
0.50 grams[1]	45	48	50	55	60	65	70	75
0.60 grams[2]	54	57	60	66	72	78	84	90
0.70 grams[3]	63	67	70	77	84	91	98	105
0.80 grams[4]	72	76	80	88	96	104	112	120

[1]Appropriate daily protein consumption for women training up to 1 hour.
[2]Appropriate daily protein consumption for women training 1 to 2 hours.
[3]Appropriate daily protein consumption for women training 2 to 3 hours.
[4]Appropriate daily protein consumption for women training 3+ hours.

Finding Protein in Food

Just like carbohydrate, not all protein sources are created equal. Powerhouse protein sources, also known as "complete" proteins, are those that provide all 20 amino acids necessary to rebuild and repair damaged tissue. Complete protein sources are found in animal foods such as chicken, turkey, fish, eggs, and milk, as well as soy foods. In contrast, many vegetarian protein sources, including legumes and nuts, are missing several of the amino acids needed to rebuild tissue. Fortunately, research has shown that by including a variety of plant-based foods, such as beans and grains, throughout the day, these missing amino acids will be accounted for. As a general rule, aim for meals in which 25 percent is made up of quality proteins (see table 13.4 for suggested sources).

TABLE 13.4 Good Sources of Protein

Source	Amount	Grams of protein
Soy milk	1 cup	7
Nonfat milk	1 cup	8
Miso soup	1 cup	6
Pinto beans, cooked	1 cup	15
Cottage cheese, nonfat	1 cup	28
Lean beef	3 oz.	24
Soybeans, boiled	1 cup	28
Chicken breast	Half (3 oz.)	26
White tuna, canned	4 oz.	27

Protein During Pregnancy and Lactation

Because protein is required for all growth processes, women athletes require additional protein when pregnant and lactating. In fact, there is profound evidence that women who eat too little protein during pregnancy run a higher risk of having a low-birth-weight baby who will be more susceptible to heart disease and diabetes later in life. Women who maintain a low level of activity during pregnancy or lactation are recommended to add 6 to 10 extra grams of protein per day, equivalent to about two tablespoons of peanut butter, one cup of nonfat milk, one serving of string cheese, or a half cup of beans.

Protein for the Vegetarian Athlete

Protein is perhaps the most recognized nutrient of concern in vegetarian athletes due to the incomplete nature and reduced digestibility of most plant sources of protein. With the exception of soybeans, milk, and egg whites, other vegetarian-based foods don't have all the essential amino acids necessary for maximal tissue growth and repair. Most vegetarian-based foods need to be combined to attain all the essential amino acids; for example, tortillas and beans, rice and lentils, peanuts and wheat bread. The World Health Organization suggests that vegetarian endurance athletes consume 110 percent of their normal protein requirement because of the reduced protein digestibility of plant foods, which is attributable to their high fiber content. Vegetarian diets providing adequate energy and a variety of protein-containing plant foods will supply all the essential amino acids needed for efficient protein metabolism, thereby enhancing recovery from exercise and helping to prevent muscular injury.

Fat

Within the triathlon world, many women athletes have become overly obsessed with fat intake, virtually eliminating all high-fat foods from their diet as a means of controlling body weight. What many women athletes fail to realize is that fats are just as essential to good health and optimal performance as protein or carbohydrate. As the most energy-dense nutrient, providing more than twice as much energy per gram than either carbohydrates or protein, fat supplies the female athlete with much needed energy for performance. It also provides essential fatty acids necessary for transportation of fat-soluble vitamins and synthesis of hormonelike substances that are ultimately important for overall growth and healthy skin.

Determining Fat Needs

Endurance athletes appear to perform best when they consume a diet made up of approximately 30 percent fat. Most health professionals agree that the *minimal* amount of fat needed for bodily functions in a woman athlete is approximately 30 grams, which is equivalent to approximately two tablespoons of olive oil. Lower fat intakes have been associated with hormonal imbalances, loss of bone mass, and compromised athletic performance. On the flip side, an excessive intake of fat, which is a problem among the nonathletic American population, has been associated with obesity and increased risk for chronic disease, including heart disease and cancer. As a general rule, aim at consuming a balance of 20 to 30 percent of your total calories as fat, which equates to approximately a half gram of fat per pound of body weight.

Choosing the Right Fats

There are four types of fats: saturated, transfats, monounsaturated, and polyunsaturated. Saturated fats, which are solid at room temperature, are mostly found in foods of animal origin, including egg yolk, whole milk, cheese, beef, and chicken skin. Transfats, byproducts of partial hydrogenation, can be found in margarine, fried foods, packaged foods such as chips, cookies, and crackers, frozen foods, and sweet treats. There is profound evidence that a high intake of saturated fats and transfats increases cardiovascular risk and therefore should not make up more than 10 percent of an athlete's total calorie intake.

In contrast, monounsaturated and polyunsaturated fats, which are liquid at room temperature, are found mostly in foods of plant origin, including avocado, nuts, seeds, and olives, as well as some seafood such as salmon and albacore tuna. Some scientific evidence suggests that inclusion of mono- and polyunsaturated fats in an athlete's diet may fight inflammation and muscle soreness and may even boost immunity. As a general rule, women athletes should focus primarily on plant fats and seafood, limiting the intake of saturated fats to no more than 10 percent of total calories.

Vitamins and Minerals

Vitamins and minerals can be compared to the oil that makes an engine run efficiently. Without an adequate amount, the engine does not run smoothly, and excessive amounts can actually cause harm (although the body does a fairly good job of ridding itself of excess nutrients through urine). The best source of vitamins and minerals is from whole foods. Neglecting certain foods—which is common among some women athletes looking to achieve an ideal body shape—can increase the risk of vitamin and mineral deficiencies.

The most prevalent nutritional deficiencies among women endurance athletes are calcium, zinc, and iron, which will be covered in more detail below. However, you must also ensure that you're getting adequate levels of both water- and fat-soluble vitamins, which are critical for energy production and metabolism, absorption of essential minerals, and a host of other functions such as blood clotting and creation of red blood cells.

Water-soluble vitamins—which include thiamin (vitamin B_1), riboflavin (vitamin B_2), folic acid, niacin, vitamin B_6, vitamin B_{12}, biotin, pantothenic acid, and vitamin C—are important for metabolism and energy production and can be found in small amounts among all major food groups. Fat-soluble vitamins—which include vitamins A, D, E, and K—can be found in such foods as fruits, vegetables, milk and dairy products, whole grains, and fish oils.

Calcium

Calcium is a particular concern for women who do not consume dairy products. A chronic low calcium intake, especially when combined with an inadequate energy intake, is associated with decreased bone mineral density, leading to elevated risk for stress fractures and osteoporosis. Furthermore, a calcium deficiency may lead to severe cramping during endurance exercise because calcium plays a critical role in normal muscle function. Recommended intake of calcium ranges from 1,000 to 1,500 milligrams depending on the individual. Good sources include calcium-fortified foods, nonfat milk (1 cup = 300 milligrams), nonfat yogurt (1 cup = 450 milligrams), low-fat cottage cheese (1 cup = 140 milligrams), ricotta cheese (1/2 cup = 340 milligrams), calcium-processed tofu (4 ounces = 145 milligrams), almonds (1 ounce = 332 milligrams), legumes (1 cup = 90 milligrams), and collard greens (1/2 cup = 179 milligrams).

Iron

Iron, a trace mineral, is a major component of the body's red blood cells or hemoglobin, whose role is to carry oxygen to various body tissues, including muscle, for use during aerobic activity. An iron deficiency may lead to premature fatigue during exercise due to lack of oxygen transport to working muscles. Although iron is found extensively in several plant foods—such as barley, almonds, soy patties, hummus, and Spanish peanuts—the absorption is reduced by 20 percent when compared to the iron found in animal products such as red meat. Therefore, the risk for iron deficiency is increased in vegetarian athletes even if total iron intake meets the U.S. recommended daily allowance (RDA) of 10 to 15 milligrams. For added absorption of vegetarian iron sources, consume foods rich in vitamin C (such as orange juice, strawberries, and citrus fruits).

Zinc

Because zinc is found only in small amounts within foods, an estimated 50 percent of women athletes have been reported to fall below the recommended daily intake for zinc (12 milligrams per day). Zinc is also lost in small amounts via sweat during heavy training, which makes women athletes more vulnerable to reduced zinc levels. Zinc deficiency will compromise immune function as well as basal metabolic rate and thyroid hormone levels, which can have a major impact on endurance performance and health. Fortunately, a recent study from the U.S. Department of Agriculture (2002) found that zinc levels can be maintained within normal limits with a diet that includes such zinc-rich foods as oysters, chicken breast, beans, milk, yogurt, tofu, and peanut butter.

If dietary intake of any one of these nutrients falls short of recommendations, female athletes should check corresponding blood levels to see if a dietary supplement is warranted. If blood levels fall within the recommended range provided by your physician, it is not necessary to take supplements. In fact, taking additional amounts beyond the recommended daily allowance will not only fail to provide any performance-enhancing benefits, but it can actually be dangerous, especially in athletes with normal blood levels of the nutrient. Furthermore, you should note that supplements are not regulated by the Food and Drug Administration (FDA), which means that supplement manufacturers are not required to prove claimed benefits, to show safety with accurate or chronic administration, to commit to accepted quality assurance practices, or to follow the stringent labeling regulations followed for food products. Therefore, athletes should always be careful when choosing to supplement their diet with additional vitamins and minerals.

Water

Water is perhaps the most common nutrient deficiency among athletes, with an estimated two out of three athletes failing to meet daily fluid needs. Poor fluid intake is dangerous since water makes up three-quarters of a person's total body weight. Furthermore, water plays many essential roles within the body, including the following:

- Generating saliva to help aid digestion
- Lubricating joints
- Cushioning organs
- Transporting nutrients, hormones, and oxygen to working muscles
- Removing waste products such as carbon dioxide and lactic acid
- Maintaining normal blood volume
- Carrying waste products out of the body via urine
- Regulating body temperature during exercise by transporting heat to the skin where it can evaporate (sweat)

Perhaps the biggest mistake endurance athletes make is waiting until they are thirsty to start drinking. Upon the onset of thirst, an athlete is already 3 percent dehydrated, which reduces maximal performance capability by 15 percent. This adds up to be a large chunk of time when looking at such endurance events as marathons, long-course triathlons, and adventure races. In fact, one study discovered a 6 to 7 percent reduction in 5K and 10K running speed in athletes who were 2 percent dehydrated (Gisolfi and Lamb 1990). This would be equivalent to adding 2 minutes 48 seconds to a 40-minute 10K. Dehydration becomes life threatening when 10 to 20 percent of body weight is lost.

To prevent dehydration, it is best to sip on fluids throughout the day until urine flows pale yellow. Daily fluid needs vary depending on the body composition and total weight

© John Segesta

Dehydration is a major performance limiter. It's important to drink whether you feel thirsty or not.

of the athlete. The following equation can be used to estimate daily fluid needs in ounces:

body weight (in pounds) / 2 = daily fluid needs in ounces

For example, a 130-pound athlete requires at least 65 ounces of fluid per day. This figure includes anything that is liquid at room temperature (ice cream, broth, juice, milk) that does not contain caffeine. Caffeine amounts beyond 300 milligrams, or approximately two cups of coffee, tend to increase gastric emptying of fluid. Athletes should not try to "hyperhydrate" or consume more than the recommended fluid intake above. Consuming too much fluid, especially in the form of plain water, can increase the risk of an electrolyte imbalance, which is discussed a little later in this chapter.

Note that fluid needs increase based on exercise levels. Hydration requirements during training and racing are covered later in the chapter.

DETERMINING DAILY ENERGY NEEDS DURING TRAINING

One of the most common nutritional mistakes made by women athletes is restriction of calorie intake, whether intentional for weight loss or an unintentional result of high training demands. Unfortunately, restriction of energy intake can lead to suboptimal storage of muscle glycogen, catabolism of lean body mass, increased risk for muscular injury, feelings of staleness, poor immune function, and loss of bone mass, none of which are conducive to peak triathlon performance. Calorie needs will vary widely among athletes based on metabolic function, training volume and intensity, lean body weight, and age. Table 13.5 provides an estimate of the daily energy demands of women athletes based on duration of training. Note that those athletes desiring weight loss should not restrict calorie intake by more than 1,000 each day. In fact, most women report better energy levels when only restricting daily calories by 500. On long training days, intense training days, or race days, calories should not be restricted.

TABLE 13.5 Calculating Daily Calorie Needs for Maintenance of Lean Body Weight

Daily training schedule	1 hr. or less (training for sprint-distance triathlon)	1-2 hr. (training for Olympic-distance triathlon)	More than 2 hr. (training for half Ironman or Ironman-distance triathlon)
Calories	16-20 per lb. of lean body weight	21-25 per lb. of lean body weight	25-30 per lb. of lean body weight

OPTIMIZING GLYCOGEN STORAGE

Because muscle and liver glycogen makes up the majority of fuel used during high-intensity sprint-type exercise (approximately 95 percent of max heart rate) as well as moderate- to high-intensity endurance exercise (approximately 70 percent or more of max heart rate), the goal is to spare as much of these glycogen reserves as possible and increase your utilization of fat as a fuel source. While your carbohydrate fuel tank is fairly small, your fat fuel tank can store upward of 100,000 calories worth of fuel. If you could just burn those 100,000 calories of fat prior to dipping into your carbohydrate fuel tank, the Ironman triathlon would no longer feel like the physical challenge that it is. Although it's not possible to just switch on your "fat-burning" engine and assume that your body's precious glycogen reserves will be spared, there are strategies you can use to encourage this type of energy consumption.

Proper Fueling Before Training and Racing

Most athletes can get away with not eating before moderate-intensity training bouts lasting less than an hour, but performance tends to decline if food is neglected prior to exercise lasting longer than an hour, especially if the exercise occurs in the morning (after a prolonged fasting state). The food consumed before longer training bouts will restock your liver glycogen stores, helping to stabilize energy levels during the initial stages of training and increase fuel efficiency due to sparing of muscle glycogen. Athletes who fail to fuel prior to long training sessions will start depleting their muscle glycogen stores prematurely and will most likely "hit the wall" or bonk.

> As a general rule, for every hour between eating and exercise, consume about 0.5 gram of low- to moderate-glycemic carbohydrates per pound of lean body weight.

For example, a 110-pound female triathlete with a body composition of 15 percent body fat (85 percent lean) requires approximately 47 grams of carbohydrate, which would be equivalent to consuming a PowerBar one hour before training or racing. Make sure to drink approximately 16 to 24 ounces of fluid in the one to two hours prior to exercise as well to help aid in digestion of the carbohydrate. High-glycemic carbohydrates, which include most sports drinks, are appropriate for consumption within an hour prior to exercise, but they should not make up the majority of a meal eaten more than one hour before starting a workout. Foods rich in fiber (more than 5 grams per serving), protein (more than 15 grams), and fat (more than 3 grams per serving) should be *avoided* in the preworkout meal since these nutrients cause a diversion of blood, oxygen, and water flow to the stomach to aid in digestion, thereby leading to a "dead-legged" feeling and a frantic search for a rest room. You should try several different preworkout meals during training to determine what helps you perform and feel your best. New foods should *NOT* be experimented with during racing.

Proper Fueling During Training and Racing

The goal on longer training days, as well as race day, is to preserve glycogen and use the abundant amount of fat stores you have in your body. Remember, "fats burn in a carbohydrate flame"—that is, fat cannot be burned efficiently without the presence of carbohydrate. Picture carbohydrates as kindling under a fire and fat as the log. Without an adequate amount of kindling, your body fails to burn fat and starts to deplete your precious muscle glycogen stores until your fuel tank is empty.

To increase your fat-burning capabilities, you must start refueling your tanks after about 60 to 90 minutes of moderate- to high-intensity exercise. The following equation can be used to determine your hourly carbohydrate needs based on 60 to 90 minutes of exercise:

0.5 grams of high-glycemic carbohydrate × lean body weight in pounds
= hourly carbohydrate needs

During training, especially for sprint- and Olympic-distance triathlon, you want to have a fast release of carbohydrate into your bloodstream to allow for a quick energy boost. Even triathletes training for longer events, such as the half and full Ironman, should focus on higher glycemic carbohydrates such as glucose, dextrose, and maltodextrin (inclusion of a smaller amount of low-glycemic carbohydrate, as seen in energy bars, may benefit triathletes who struggle with their blood sugars during the later stages of their race or training). Most energy gels and sports drinks solicit a fast release of carbohydrate into the bloodstream.

For optimal digestion and absorption of carbohydrates, make sure to maintain a carbohydrate concentration of approximately 6 to 8 percent (larger athletes may be able to tolerate up to 10 percent); this means that per 8 ounces of fluid, you should not consume more than 20 grams of carbohydrate. All energy gels and solid carbohydrates consumed during training and racing should be accompanied by water. Since most gels contain about 25 grams of carbohydrate, athletes should consume at least 10 ounces of water to avoid potential digestive problems and consequent gastrointestinal distress. To determine the carbohydrate concentration of foods you eat during training, use the following equation:

(grams of carbohydrate consumed per 8 ounces of fluid / 240 milliliters)
× 100 = % carbohydrate concentration

In addition to carbohydrate, consuming smaller amounts of protein during longer training bouts or longer races may also help enhance endurance performance. The most dramatic proof of protein's benefits in a sports drink was shown in a study conducted at the University of Texas (Res et al., in press). Researchers compared the effects of a conventional 7.75 percent carbohydrate sports drink and a carbohydrate-protein sports drink containing the same amount of calories in cyclists during exercise of variable intensity. This was followed by a high-intensity cycling bout to exhaustion. The sports drink containing carbohydrate and protein (in a 4:1 ratio) increased endurance 24 percent over the carbohydrate-only sports drink and 57 percent more than water.

Athletes interested in experimenting with protein should aim at consuming 1/8 gram of protein per pound of lean body weight every hour of activity beyond 60 minutes. Some sports foods containing protein include energy bars, Spiz sports beverage, and Accelerade. In addition, athletes can obtain the ideal 4:1 ratio of carbohydrate to protein by adding 1 tablespoon of protein powder per 25 grams of carbohydrate ingested.

Calculating Calorie Needs on the Bike

Because the bike leg consumes the majority of the time taken to complete a triathlon, especially the long-course triathlon, what you do nutritionally on the bike can either make or break your race. During the bike leg, you should replace 30 to 50 percent of calories burned, with the majority of these calories coming in the form of carbohydrate. Nutrition demands on the bike are dictated by speed, time, and body size. Exercise physiologist James Hagberg, PhD, developed the chart presented in table 13.6 for calculating calorie needs

TABLE 13.6 Calculating Calorie Expenditure During Cycle Workouts

Note: To approximate the number of calories you burn per minute, simply choose your average speed and multiply your body weight by the corresponding coefficient. For example, for a 130-pound female maintaining a pace of 15 mph, the equation is as follows: $130 \times 0.0561 = 7.3$ calories burned per minute.

Average speed (mph)	Coefficient (cal./lb./min.)*
15	0.0561
16	0.0615
17	0.0675
18	0.0740
19	0.0811
20	0.0891
21	0.0975
23	0.1173
25	0.1411

*Additional calories will be burned when climbing.

Note: Athletes only need to replace 30 to 50 percent of calories expended when riding.

when riding. This chart will help you practice your calorie replacement needs during training and ultimately help you create a performance-enhancing nutrition plan (remember, you should replace just 30 to 50 percent of calories burned) for the bike leg of your next triathlon.

Hydration Needs During Training and Racing

Maintaining fluid balance during exercise requires replacement of fluids that are lost via sweat by drinking such hydrating beverages as water and sports drinks. The American College of Sports Medicine recommends drinking 5 to 12 ounces of fluid every 15 to 20 minutes of exercise. If the exercise bout is under an hour, water is an appropriate fluid replacement beverage. Beyond an hour, a sports drink containing a 7 percent concentration of carbohydrates will enhance performance.

To determine a more accurate estimate of your fluid needs, you must first determine your sweat rate. To establish sweat rate, weigh yourself pre- and postexercise on several different occasions. Every pound of body weight lost during exercise is equivalent to approximately 16 ounces of fluid. For example, if you consistently lose 1 pound of body weight during a 30-minute run where you are not drinking anything, your hourly fluid needs are 32 ounces per hour. Use a chart similar to the one in table 13.7 to jot down your hourly fluid needs in different conditions (e.g., hot and humid versus cold and dry; intense intervals versus a long run).

TABLE 13.7   Calculated Fluid Needs

Date				
Preworkout weight (lb.)				
Postworkout weight (lb.)				
Weather conditions				
Calculated fluid needs				

Electrolyte Replacement

In addition to fluid replacement, replacement of electrolytes is critical in endurance bouts lasting longer than one hour, especially when completed in hot and humid conditions. The principal electrolytes include sodium (generally bound to chloride), potassium, magnesium, and calcium. These electrolytes are involved in metabolic activities and are essential to the normal functioning of all cells, including muscle function. An electrolyte imbalance includes symptoms similar to dehydration: nausea, vomiting, muscle weakness, muscle cramping, muscle twitching, overall fatigue, labored breathing, and confusion. Table 13.8 lists the functions of the principal electrolytes, recommended dosing patterns during exercise, and performance daily intake (PDI) recommendations for athletes.

A potentially life-threatening condition can occur if an athlete fails to use an electrolyte replacement drink during exercise bouts lasting longer than an hour. There have been several incidences of "water intoxication" (hyponatremia) in athletes, which causes blood sodium levels to drop dangerously low, causing an electrolyte imbalance and triggering seizures, coma, and even death. Initial symptoms are similar to dehydration and include confusion, disorientation, vomiting, and muscle weakness. So remember, for longer events and training bouts, use a sports drink containing the electrolytes identified in table 13.8.

TABLE 13.8   Electrolytes to Replace During Exercise

Electrolyte	Primary roles	Dose per 8-12 ounces of fluid	Performance daily intake (PDI)
Sodium	Muscle contraction Nerve transmission	150-250 mg.	1,500-4,500 mg.
Chloride	Peak muscle function	45-75 mg.	N/A
Potassium	Muscle contraction Nerve transmission Glycogen formation	50-80 mg.	2,500-4,000 mg.
Magnesium	Muscle relaxation ATP (energy) production	20-30 mg.	400-800 mg.
Calcium	Bone health Nerve transmission Muscle contraction	10-15 mg.	1,200-1,600 mg.

Enhancing Recovery With Nutrition

Triathlon training often requires twice-a-day workouts and long-duration workouts that are performed on consecutive days (e.g., a long ride on Saturday and a long run on Sunday). This type of heavy training depletes glycogen stores, making nutrition an essential component of restoring energy for subsequent workouts. To ensure adequate recovery after high-intensity or long-duration training or racing, follow these three nutritional strategies:

1. Replace lost fluids and electrolytes immediately after the workout. For every pound of body weight lost during exercise, drink between 16 and 24 ounces of a sports drink. Choose a sports drink containing sodium, an electrolyte that helps retain the fluid you drink.

2. Eat a carbohydrate and protein combination within 30 minutes after the workout. Research has shown that athletes who consume a 4:1 ratio of

carbohydrates to protein within 30 minutes after exercise can reduce postexercise muscle damage by 36 percent due to a favorable effect on insulin, which carries carbohydrates into muscles for glycogen (stored carbohydrates) repletion. Note that this 30-minute window is crucial to enhanced recovery. John Ivy, PhD, chair of the department of kinesiology and health education at the University of Texas, has found that muscle cells are highly sensitive to insulin at this time. This means that when carbohydrates are present within 30 minutes postexercise, glycogen replenishment occurs approximately two to three times faster than when carbohydrates are eaten about two hours postexercise. As a general rule, aim for about 1/2 gram of high-glycemic carbohydrate and 1/8 gram of protein per pound of lean body weight within 30 minutes following exercise. Examples of postworkout recovery foods containing a balance of carbohydrates and protein include peanut butter and jelly sandwiches, low-fat chocolate milk, meal replacement shakes such as Ensure or Boost, pineapple and low-fat cottage cheese, Endurox recovery sports drink, smoothies with a protein boost, and rice and beans.

3. Continue eating small meals rich in carbohydrates every two to three hours after exercise. Glycogen stores replenish at a rate of about 5 to 7 percent per hour, which means a full reestablishment of glycogen stores following a glycogen-depleting bout of exercise takes at least 20 hours. Therefore, it is essential to continue to consume approximately 50 to 75 grams of moderate- to high-glycemic carbohydrates every two to three hours until total carbohydrate intake equals about 500 grams (or 3.2 to 4.5 grams per pound of body weight).

Remember that these nutritional strategies are only one aspect of a smart approach to recovery. As highlighted in chapter 6, your training levels must also be balanced with adequate rest to ensure you receive the performance-enhancing benefit of recovery.

Carbo-Loading for Race Day

Most endurance athletes practice some form of carbo-loading prior to races to avoid hitting the wall or bonking. This may involve eating a big plate of pasta the night before a race or even each day leading up to the event. However, a more regimented form of carbohydrate loading will help "supersaturate" your muscle cells with glycogen to levels 50 to 100 percent greater than normal, thereby delaying or eliminating the dreaded bonk.

In the past, carbohydrate-loading protocols prior to an endurance event involved athletes going through a glycogen depletion phase, where they engaged in one long training session a week out from their event followed by three to four days of minimal carbohydrate intake and continued exercise. In the final three days prior to the event, athletes loaded up on carbohydrates and engaged in minimal training. However, athletes who followed this depletion strategy by and large experienced fatigue coupled with illness, injury, and irritability secondary to low blood sugar. New research supports continuous intake of low- to moderate-glycemic carbohydrates during training to maximize muscle and liver glycogen stores in the days leading up to the race.

In fact, a recent study conducted by Australian sports scientists revealed that athletes who increased their carbohydrate intake a mere 24 hours prior to their event after following a traditional high-carbohydrate training diet nearly doubled their glycogen stores without any negative side effects (Bussau et al. 2002). In the study, highly trained cyclists loaded up on approximately 700 grams (2,800 calories), or approximately 5 grams of carbohydrate per pound of lean body weight, for 24 hours following a short (three minutes), high-intensity spin. To supersaturate glycogen stores and potentially boost endurance performance by 2 to 3 percent, triathletes should plan to consume approximately 3 to 5 grams of carbohydrate per pound of lean body weight (approximately 70 percent of total calories) in the 24 hours prior to race day. Because each ounce of glycogen stored requires 3 ounces of water, athletes must follow proper hydration strategies, which entail consuming approximately half their body weight (pounds) in fluid ounces. Refer to table 13.9 for a sample 500-gram carbo-loading protocol.

TABLE 13.9 Sample 500-Gram Carbo-Loading Protocol

Meal	Menu item	Carbohydrates
Breakfast	Strawberry banana smoothie: Blend 1 cup 100% orange juice with 1 cup low-fat vanilla yogurt, 1 frozen banana (sliced), 1 cup frozen strawberries (chopped), and 2 tablespoons protein powder.	105 grams
Snack	1 large (approx. 4 ounces) whole grain bagel spread with 2 tablespoons natural peanut butter. Drink 2 cups 100% fruit juice with snack.	125 grams
Lunch	2 bean and rice burritos served with 16 ounces water.	90 grams
Snack	2 cups mixed fruit. Drink glass of water with snack.	65 grams
Dinner	Pasta dinner: 2 cups cooked pasta with marinara sauce, served with small salad topped with balsamic vinaigrette dressing and 2 slices whole grain bread. Drink plenty of water with meal.	115 grams
TOTAL		500 grams (approx. 70%)

PEAK PERFORMANCE SUMMARY

• ***Achieve energy balance by consuming enough calories to meet training demands.*** The average female triathlete requires anywhere from 16 to 30 calories per pound of lean body weight to meet the high demands of endurance training and prevent catabolism of lean body weight. For fat loss, calories should not be restricted by more than 1,000 calories a day.

Calories should never be restricted on high-intensity or high-volume training days or race days. To meet the high demands of endurance training, consume four to six smaller meals throughout the day rather than one or two larger meals.

- *Maximize muscle glycogen stores by including a variety of healthful carbohydrate sources at each meal.* Depending on their daily training routine, women triathletes require 3 to 6 grams of carbohydrate per pound of lean body weight. Concentration should be on low- to moderate-glycemic carbohydrates such as legumes, low-fat dairy foods, fruits, whole grains, oatmeal, and sweet potatoes. High-glycemic carbohydrates should be consumed with an equal portion of protein to ensure optimal blood sugar control.

- *Prevent muscle catabolism with a diet rich in protein.* Most women athletes require anywhere from 0.5 to 0.8 grams of protein per pound of lean body weight depending on training volume. Pregnant or lactating athletes require an additional 6 to 10 grams to support growth. Vegetarian athletes should consume 110 percent of their recommended protein intake (since plant protein is less easily absorbed than animal protein). Quality protein sources include dairy, eggs, beef, poultry, fish, and soy. Other vegetarian protein sources such as beans and nuts should be combined with whole grains to ensure intake of all essential amino acids.

- *Include healthy fats in your diet.* Fat is as essential as protein and carbohydrate for optimal health and peak triathlon performance. Athletes should consume about half their body weight (pounds) in fat grams or approximately 20 to 30 percent of their total calorie intake. Focus on plant sources of fat such as nuts, seeds, olives, and avocados as well as fatty fish such as salmon and herring.

- *Avoid restriction of major food groups.* Women triathletes often are prone to deficiencies in calcium, zinc, and iron because of inadequate intake of major food groups. Make sure to include a variety of foods at each meal to ensure proper intake of all vitamins and minerals. Supplementation is generally not necessary unless blood levels of a specific nutrient are tested low.

- *Drink up to avoid dehydration.* Shoot for drinking half your body weight (pounds) in fluid ounces, which does not include caffeinated beverages. Intake of fluids beyond this amount, especially if originating from water, increases the risk for electrolyte imbalances. Before exercise, consume 16 ounces of fluid. In order to meet fluid losses during training, aim for 5 to 12 ounces of water (during training bouts less than 1 hour) or sports drink containing electrolytes (during training bouts more than 1 hour) every 15 to 20 minutes. For every pound of weight lost during training, rehydrate with 16 to 24 ounces of a sports drink.

- *Fuel prior to long or high-intensity training and racing.* For every hour prior to exercise, consume approximately 1/2 gram of low- to moderate-glycemic carbohydrate per pound of lean body weight. Avoid excessive fiber, protein, and fat at this meal.

• *Optimize fuel usage during training and racing.* Beyond 60 to 90 minutes of training, consume 1/2 gram of high-glycemic carbohydrate and 1/8 gram of protein per pound of lean body weight.

• *Enhance recovery with proper nutrition.* Within 30 minutes of training or racing, consume 1/2 gram of carbohydrate and 1/8 gram of protein per pound of lean body weight. Sample recovery foods include meal replacement shakes, low-fat chocolate milk, smoothies with a protein boost, a bagel with peanut butter, and recovery sports drinks such as Endurox R4.

• *Practice carbo-loading prior to long training bouts and long-course races.* In the 24 to 48 hours prior to race day, consume 3 to 5 grams of carbohydrate per pound of lean body weight. Do not restrict calories, because this is counterproductive to maximizing muscle glycogen stores and can prevent peak endurance performance.

Managing and Avoiding Injury

Britt Caling, MS

In the past decade and a half, with an increase in triathlon participation as well as a sharp rise in the level of competition, there has been a corresponding increase in the number of triathlon-related injuries. The good news is that sports medicine physicians and exercise scientists understand more about these injuries than ever; the bad news is that triathletes, in general, continue to be ill informed about how training affects their bodies and how to avoid injury in pursuit of peak fitness. The philosophy among many triathletes continues to be "more is better."

This chapter will provide insight into the most common injuries experienced by triathletes, inform you about how to manage specific injuries, offer guidance on maintaining fitness during periods of injury, and recommend strategies to avoid injury.

WHAT WE KNOW ABOUT INJURIES IN TRIATHLETES

Avoiding injury is the most important component that allows an athlete to train consistently, which in turn is essential to improving performance and achieving results. Published research on triathlon-related injuries reveals the following:

- Studies have shown that the incidence of injury during competition phase is greater than during training phase, with the average triathlete experiencing between 2 and 5 injuries per 1,000 hours trained during base phase. During the competition period, this injury rate has been found to increase to between 5 and 17 injuries per 1,000 hours trained.
- The majority of triathlon injuries are overuse injuries. An overuse injury is one that results from repetitive activities and excessive use of a body part such that cumulative microtrauma occurs. An overuse injury may be acute (of recent onset) or chronic (present for a long duration).
- The longer a triathlete has been in the sport, and the greater the number of hours trained per week, the more likely she is to suffer an overuse injury.
- Most injuries are related to running, with a higher number of running miles during precompetition phase increasing the likelihood of injury during competition.
- The most common areas of injury in triathletes are the knee, low back, and shoulder.

COMMON TRIATHLETE INJURIES

Here is a list of the most common injuries seen in triathletes.

Running-related injuries
- Achilles tendinitis and tendinosis
- Shin pain and tibial stress fracture
- Plantar fasciitis
- Iliotibial band (ITB) friction syndrome

Cycling-related injuries
- Patellofemoral knee pain
- Low back pain

Swimming-related injuries
- Shoulder pain related to tightness, instability (weakness), or trauma

Achilles Tendinosis

A tendon is a strong connective tissue structure that joins muscle to bone. The Achilles tendon attaches the calf muscles to the back of the heel bone. Overuse injury to a tendon occurs when the tendon has been repeatedly stressed until it is no longer able to tolerate further loading. If a tendon becomes acutely inflamed due to overload, the injury is labeled a "tendin*itis*." However, if the stress is present for a longer period, the tendon substance becomes degenerative, and the injury progresses to a "tendin*osis*." Achilles tendinosis/tendinitis is recognized as one of the most common overuse injuries resulting from running.

In my experience as an athlete, coach, and sports physiotherapist, I have found that most triathletes will not seek medical help until the injury has progressed to an Achilles tendinosis and symptoms begin to restrict training. Symptoms include pain in the Achilles region that is exacerbated by impact or heel raising. The tendon itself may be thick, swollen, and tender to touch, with stiffness and pain usually most severe when stepping out of bed in the morning.

The cause of Achilles tendinitis may be related to a sudden increase in training load, especially rapid increases in distance, gradient, or speed of running. Improper footwear, poor foot function, or other biomechanical issues (such as poor ankle bend range due to tight calf muscles) may also result in increased stress through the tendon. Because the Achilles tendon has a poor blood supply, it may be slow to heal, and chronic tendinosis may require three to six months of rehabilitation before the athlete is ready to return to full competition.

Initial treatment should involve a combination of regimens including ice, nonsteroidal anti-inflammatory drugs prescribed by a physician, alterations in training levels, and correction of musculoskeletal and biomechanical factors, particularly foot function and calf tension. A specific strengthening program of eccentric exercises directed by an allied health professional is indicated for a tendinosis. Surgery may be considered in the most severe cases.

Shin Pain and Tibial Stress Fracture

There is much debate regarding the exact nature and cause of shin pain; therefore, this section is limited to a discussion of inside, lower leg (tibial) shin pain, often known as "shin splints," and the development of tibial stress fractures. Female runners are particularly susceptible to lower leg overuse injuries, with shin splints accounting for 20 percent of their injuries, compared to 7 percent in male runners.

The traditional notion of shin splints is that pain results from inflammation of the attachment of the deep calf muscles onto the tibia. A second theory relates to increased stress being directly transmitted to the inner border of the tibia. Because the tibia bends slightly during weight bearing, repetitive loading may directly cause bone stress and pain. Factors that predispose an athlete to either of these mechanisms include the following:

- Excess foot pronation that results in increased work of the deep calf muscles and therefore small tissue tears or increased traction on the bony attachment
- Rigid, high-arch feet that are less able to absorb the shock transmitted to the tibia

- Excess body weight, increasing ground reaction stress
- Poor flexibility and muscle function around the foot, knee, or pelvis that may alter the ability of the foot to absorb shock
- Changes to running surfaces or training regimens, particularly insufficient recovery or doing "too much too soon," resulting in the bone breakdown rate being greater than bone formation

An athlete with shin splints will complain of a generalized area of pain and increased tenderness along the inside border of the tibia, commonly extending along the lower one-third of the leg. Pain tends to be most severe during warm-up, easing once warm and recurring after exercise. Pain and stiffness may also be present when getting out of bed in the morning.

Shin splints is generally believed to be a precursor to tibial stress fracture. Stress fractures involve bone damage that results from the inability of new bone to remodel faster than old bone is broken down. Tibial stress fractures usually cause a more localized point of bone tenderness on the shin. Pain does not ease with warm-up, and when the injury is severe, the athlete will have night pain and pain when walking. When a stress fracture is suspected, the athlete should undergo a bone scan as soon as possible to establish the extent of damage, and hence, the period of reduced weight bearing required (note that X rays will not always show the presence of existing stress fractures).

The incidence of stress fracture is higher in women with athletic amenorrhea (i.e., absence of menstruation), probably as a result of the decreased bone mineral density associated with this condition. It is therefore essential that younger female triathletes are monitored for menstrual dysfunction and eating disorders to prevent the loss of bone density and the development of stress fractures.

Treatment of shin splints in the acute phase should involve reducing inflammation by using ice and anti-inflammatory medications and a relative reduction in weight-bearing exercise to allow bone and soft tissue to heal. Issues related to muscle and joint flexibility and strength should be corrected, and an assessment of foot function may be necessary to fix biomechanics. The severity of a stress fracture will dictate management; however, a period of four to eight weeks without running is usually prescribed. Consult a good sports physician for guidance on these conditions.

Prevention of shin pain and stress fracture involves monitoring increases in training load, especially in the first month after beginning running. Orthotics should be used when required, and soft surfaces should be incorporated into your run training. Most shoe manufacturers suggest that a good training shoe will last 300 to 500 miles of running before it loses shock-absorbing capacity, so remember to replace your running shoes regularly.

Plantar Fasciitis

The plantar fascia is a dense fibrous band of connective tissue that passes lengthwise along the bottom of the foot from the heel to the toes. Plantar fasciitis is an inflammation of this fascia, most commonly at the site of attachment on the heel. Although it's possible to tear the fascia, this condition usually involves an overuse injury that develops from repetitive stress on the fascia. Repetitive stress occurs from activities that involve maximal ankle pointing while the toes remain bent backward (i.e., running on the toes). Increased fascia stress also occurs in runners with excessively flat feet, high arches, or stiff feet and runners with reduced range of movement in the toe joints or weak small muscles of the foot.

Plantar fasciitis pain is associated with stiffness under the foot, especially for the first few steps in the morning.

Conservative treatment is usually successful but involves a period of rest from weight-bearing activities. Pain management should focus on establishing full range of movement in the ankle, foot, and toe joints and strengthening the foot muscles. There is limited evidence that foot taping and heel cushions are more effective than custom orthotics; therefore, taping and anti-inflammatory approaches may be used in the acute stages until a full gait analysis and podiatry review has occurred. Good running technique is important, and adequate strength in the calf muscles must be established before trying to run on your toes. If conservative management fails, a cortisone injection or immobilization (night splint or walking boot) may be prescribed, although further research is needed to establish the effectiveness of these forms of treatment.

Stretching, massage, and core training are all tactics that can improve form and guard against injury.

Iliotibial Band Friction Syndrome

Approximately 70 percent of knee injuries occur from running, with iliotibial band friction syndrome (ITBFS) being one of these. The ITB is a fibrous band passing from the front and outside of the hip, down the outside of the thigh and attaching to the lower leg after crossing the knee joint. As the knee is flexed and extended, the ITB passes back and forth over the thighbone and is prone to excess friction at this point, resulting in inflammation, pain, and scarring on the outside of the knee.

ITBFS will cause an ache over the outside aspect of the knee. This ache will be strongest when running (particularly during longer and downhill runs) but may also be aggravated by cycling. If severe, bending the knee (e.g., to get in and out of the car) may cause pain. There may be a small amount of fluid over the irritated part of the band, and it may be tender to the touch.

The cause of ITBFS involves multiple factors. Excess tension and tightness of the ITB will predispose it to friction when running. This excess tightness may be caused by a number of factors, including poor pelvic control, poor foot control or placement in running, increased tension of muscles that attach to the ITB (namely, the gluteals, quadriceps, hamstrings, and tensor fasciae latae), or poor training regimens. Be wary of rapid increases in running distances, too much time spent running hills and banked or cambered surfaces (e.g., beaches or shoulders of the road), or running while fatigued (e.g., always running off the bike).

When ITBFS is acute, treatment includes regular application of ice and anti-inflammatory gels and avoiding activities that cause pain. Conservative measures are usually successful for treating the injury, but eradication of pain may be slow depending on the role of biomechanical and technique factors. A faster reduction in pain will be achieved if treatment includes the use of deep tissue therapy to reduce and prevent abnormal scarring of tissues and to reduce tightness in the muscles that attach to the ITB. Injury management should also include stretching to correct any muscle or band shortening. An analysis of running (or cycling) technique should indicate which biomechanical factors need correction, and strengthening of pelvic and hip stabilizer muscles (especially gluteus medius at the side of the hip) is usually required before training is resumed or increased. If conservative measures fail, a cortisone injection and one to two weeks of rest may be required.

Patellofemoral Pain

Knee pain is the most common overuse injury in cyclists. *Patellofemoral (PF) pain* is a general term used to describe pain at the front of the knee that arises from stress placed on the kneecap (patella) and thighbone (femur). PF pain is most common in growing children and female and novice cyclists, but it can also affect experienced riders in heavy periods of training.

Athletes with PF pain will complain of vague pain at the front of the knee or "behind the kneecap." The pain is aggravated by prolonged sitting or activities that load the quadriceps muscles such as efforts/hills on the bike, walking up and down stairs, and squatting.

The underlying mechanism of the condition is somewhat unclear, but it appears to be related to the way the patella moves (or tracks) during knee flexion and extension. Abnormal patella tracking may result from a number of factors, including poor anatomical alignment of the foot, knee, or pelvis; poor knee position when riding (a likely result of poor bike setup); or the development of muscle imbalances, particularly in the quadriceps muscle groups. Athletes with PF pain have been shown to have a dominance of activity in the outside quadriceps (vastus lateralis) compared to the inside quadriceps (vastus medialis).

To prevent the onset of PF pain, a correct bike position is essential, with emphasis on shoe or cleat alignment, saddle height, and seat fore-aft positioning. In particular, a saddle that is too low will increase quadriceps loading and predispose a rider to knee pain. It has also been found that using cleat/pedal systems with increased "float" reduces knee load without compromising effective force transmission and is therefore recommended for cyclists with knee pain. Other factors to monitor include pedaling technique (pushing harder gears will tend to aggravate knee pain), asymmetry of limbs or mechanics, and progression of training loads.

Prognosis is good with conservative management that involves correction of muscle imbalances, excess muscle or joint tightness, and bike position. Taping of the patella to facilitate correct tracking and a reduction in cycling load may be indicated in the initial stages of management. To prevent recurrence, a progression of vastus medialis quadriceps strength needs to occur and may be achieved using a directed weight-training program.

Low Back (Lumbar Spine) Pain

A study of Japanese triathletes found that 32 percent of athletes had experienced at least one episode of low back pain (LBP) in the previous year, with 54 percent of those episodes lasting fewer than seven days and 19 percent lasting more than three months (Manninen and Kallinen 1996). Cycling has been proposed as a potential cause for the development of LBP in triathletes. Although the forces generated when riding are not believed to be directly dangerous to the lumbar spine, development of pain may be attributed to an imbalance between trunk flexor and back extensor muscles or to muscle length changes that occur from spending prolonged time in a flexed cycling position.

The low back region consists of the sacrum, five lumbar vertebrae (L1 to L5), vertebral discs (a softer structure located between the central body of each vertebra), corresponding small joints called *facet joints* (located on either side of the spine between the side processes of each vertebra), and a large number of muscles that pass between the pelvis, lumbar spine, and trunk. Although it is possible for any one of these elements to be injured, LBP experienced by cyclists tends to be nonspecific and mechanical in nature, meaning it is more likely a result of maintaining relatively static, flexed postures for long periods. Most athletes will experience some degree of low back discomfort or "ache" resulting from fatigue or tightness in trunk and lumbar spine muscles, hip flexors, and hamstrings. Immobile joints may also cause abnormal postures and discomfort.

Correct bike position is the key to minimizing LBP. The pelvis and lumbar spine should remain stable and still in the saddle while pedaling. Bike setup should therefore focus on ensuring that the athlete is not positioned beyond her individual flexibility limits and that she can activate key pelvic and spinal stabilizing muscles (particularly gluteals and abdominals) in this position. Anatomical differences in limb length should also be addressed to enhance the stabilizing capacity of core muscles.

Treatment of acute LBP involves assessing bike position, improving flexibility of spinal musculature, and mobilizing stiff joints. Maintenance of lumbar and thoracic mobility and range of extension, and the inclusion of an individualized core stability program (discussed later in this chapter), are also necessary for the correction and long-term prevention of LBP.

Shoulder Pain

The shoulder consists of a ball-and-socket joint, with the ball of the humerus (upper arm) sitting in the socket formed by the shoulder blade. At the uppermost point of the shoulder, the collarbone forms a joint with the shoulder blade called the acromioclavicular joint (AC joint). An extensive number of muscles interact on and around the shoulder, ranging from the large muscles that act as prime movers of the arm (such as the latissimus dorsi and pectorals) to the muscles that control the position of the shoulder blade on the chest wall, to the smaller, deeper muscles known as the "rotator cuff" that act to stabilize and center the ball in the socket.

Because of the complexity of anatomical, mechanical, and muscle interaction factors around the shoulder region, shoulder pain can be a complicated issue. I have therefore tried to simplify it by defining shoulder pain by cause:

- Excess muscle and joint tightness
- Poor stability or weakness around the shoulder girdle
- Trauma

Shoulder Pain Related to Excess Muscle or Joint Tightness

Overuse injuries of the shoulder are due to repetitive, forceful activities that occur at the extremes of range. Swimming is one such activity, and unfortunately, triathletes are notorious for having poor shoulder and thoracic flexibility, meaning they are at risk for many forms of shoulder overuse pain. If muscles around the shoulder joint have poor flexibility or are overworked and become tight, shoulder range of motion may be restricted, and pain will develop as the athlete attempts to push the joint into a position it cannot achieve. This may cause repeated compression and may "impinge" the soft tissues that pass under the bony arch of the AC joint. In this case, pain will be present on the top of the shoulder and may radiate to the outer aspect of the upper arm. Although the athlete will mostly note pain only when swimming (especially during the catch phase when the arm is starting to press on the water, or under the increased load of paddles), she may also feel discomfort when performing tasks that further impinge the tissues, such as performing activities with the arms overhead.

Treatment should first be directed at reducing the pain and swelling by icing and avoiding painful positions. Good shoulder range of motion and normal mechanics must be restored before returning to swimming. Technique should be monitored, and an athlete with pain during the recovery phase should be assessed for body rotation and upper back stiffness. Fins can be used initially to unload overworked muscles, and pull sets and paddles should be avoided during rehabilitation.

Shoulder Pain Related to Poor Stability or Weakness

Pain resulting from lack of muscle stability or strength is particularly common in young female swimmers and is frequently present in both arms. It may be a result of dysfunction, weakness, or fatigue in the stabilizing muscles of the shoulder. An unstable joint (i.e., one that moves too much) can result in a number of interrelated forms of shoulder pain.

Shoulder pain caused by instability is usually more "vague" and more widespread than impingement pain. Depending on the degree of instability, pain may be present during any or every phase of the swimming stroke and will often persist after activity. If severe, pain will be present during daily activities and may wake the athlete when she's sleeping on the affected side.

Correcting an unstable shoulder is generally more difficult than releasing a tight shoulder. Elimination of pain will usually take longer and require more effort from the athlete and direction from a therapist. Rehabilitation focuses on both achieving a stable shoulder blade to improve the efficiency of the rotator cuff muscles and improving the control and strength of stabilizing muscles. Recovery is highly variable and depends on the current level of muscle control and on the athlete's compliance to the exercise program. An athlete with either poor stability or weakness around the shoulder will benefit from a weight-training program focused on the upper body, which should be continued throughout training.

Shoulder Pain Due to Trauma

Shoulder pain resulting from trauma is most commonly due to the following:

- A bike crash in which the athlete falls directly onto the shoulder. An injury to the AC joint or a fractured collarbone should be suspected. When an athlete falls onto an outstretched hand, the force may be transmitted to the upper arm. Fractures should be excluded in either case via X rays.

- Heavy contact during swimming. In triathletes with underlying shoulder instability, heavy arm contact may result in a partial joint dislocation.

Management of these conditions will vary depending on diagnosis. The best approach is to consult a good sports physician and follow up with an allied health professional, such as a sports physiotherapist, to ensure timely and injury-free return to competition.

GOOD BODY MAINTENANCE TACTICS

There are several measures you can take with regard to body maintenance that will not only go a long way toward ensuring enjoyment and success in the sport, but will also educate you about your biomechanics and help you to stay relaxed and fresh during your training. Practicing some of these injury-preventing tactics may also help make you a more powerful triathlete and lead to improved performance.

Musculoskeletal Screenings

A musculoskeletal screening involves standardized tests of posture, range of motion, flexibility, and strength. The screening is generally administered by a physical therapist and is used to identify previous or existing injury, to detect body regions that are at greater risk for injury, and to highlight areas where flexibility, control, and strength can be improved to maximize performance. A screening is a good way to identify areas that need the most attention in the assisted and self-maintenance strategies discussed below.

A screening should highlight areas of poor flexibility and areas of increased or decreased tissue tone. While *flexibility* refers to muscle length, *tone* relates to the muscle tension or hardness. Muscles with either poor flexibility or abnormal tone can alter technique, reduce efficiency and strength, and change the shock-absorbing capacity of muscles and joints.

A triathlon-specific screening consists of a series of tests that assess the musculoskeletal system. The tests are based on an understanding of the ideal mechanics and musculoskeletal requirements needed for optimal performance in each of the three triathlon disciplines. To ensure optimal performance, the typical triathlete should do the following:

- Improve thoracic (upper back) extension (backward bend) and rotation mobility to aid swim technique and help counteract the prolonged time spent in a flexed position on the bike.

- Improve shoulder internal rotation/elevation range, as well as the combined movement of arm elevation overhead and thoracic extension. Shoulder internal rotation is the movement of the hand toward the floor when the shoulder and elbow are flexed to 90 degrees. Improvement in these areas will allow the athlete to "catch" the water better when swimming and improve streamlined body position.

- Maintain flexibility of the pelvis and lumbar spine (low back) to improve aerodynamic cycling position in the aerobars and minimize low back pain.
- Have good hip extension and ankle dorsiflexion (bending) to improve running efficiency and minimize injury.
- Have exceptional pelvic control and lower abdominal strength to improve performance in all disciplines and help avoid many forms of injury.

Assisted Maintenance Strategies

Assisted maintenance refers to the use of regular massage, physical therapy, osteopathy, or chiropractic to maintain or improve musculoskeletal factors. It is generally accepted by the sports community that massage helps prevent injury, enhance performance, and extend the time an athlete is able to compete in sport. When used correctly, massage has no adverse effects, and I advocate that all triathletes incorporate it as part of their body maintenance routine every one to three weeks depending on training level. Massage can also be used before competition to increase muscle extension and blood flow as part of warm-up. Additionally, according to studies, using 30 to 60 minutes of massage after competition is two to three times more likely to promote recovery than rest is.

I also advocate physical therapy, osteopathy, and chiropractic for body maintenance and preventive therapy. A good therapist should be able to identify and correct areas at risk of injury before they become injured. She should also be able to help optimize and improve performance by targeting areas of weakness or tightness identified by a musculoskeletal screening. You may need to search for a therapist that is skilled at preventive therapy. You should have your goals for competition and training clearly defined so you can discuss them with your therapist. Be aware that it may take a therapist a few sessions to get a feel for how your body responds to treatment.

Partner stretching can also be included in this category and may be in the form of static holding, dynamic movement, or proprioceptive neuromuscular facilitation (PNF) sessions. PNF is a form of stretching that involves taking the muscle group to end range and then contracting the muscle against resistance, with this process continued as many times as necessary to achieve a desirable muscle length. Studies have shown that PNF stretching after exercise may be one of the most effective ways to improve specific muscle flexibility.

Self-Maintenance

There are a number of ways you can improve muscle and joint flexibility and reduce excess muscle or soft tissue tone on your own at home.

Stretching is the primary way of increasing muscle flexibility. Stretching at low load and holding for longer has been found to be more effective in achieving permanent muscle lengthening than short-duration stretching. The key areas triathletes need to stretch are the hip flexor, quadriceps, and calf muscle groups; thoracic spine extension; and shoulder internal rotation/ elevation range.

Muscle "trigger points" are local areas of irritation within a taut band of muscle or surrounding tissue that can cause increased muscle tone with tenderness. It's possible to perform self-trigger-point therapy to settle these areas. For example, self-triggers can be performed by finding a tender spot in a muscle and resting a hard ball (e.g., a golf ball) on the spot until the tenderness decreases. This step is performed along the length of a muscle until the muscle is soft and nontender. Self-triggers can be used regularly to help prevent the development of excessive muscle tone or as a component of home injury management.

Similarly, it is a good habit to perform regular self-massage in areas of muscle tightness. Regular self-massage can be used to help maintain normal muscle tone and will improve your "feel" for how your soft tissues are responding to training. Improved awareness will help you identify potential problem areas before they progress to injury and will allow you to seek early assistance from a health professional.

Weights and Core Stability Sessions

Athletes must realize that stability and strength are separate entities. *Stability* refers to the ability of the body to remain stable and under control while performing movements. In triathletes, *core stability* or *pelvic stability* refers to the ability to keep the trunk and pelvis stable while swimming, cycling, and running, which requires the activation of key muscles in particular activation sequences. These key muscles consist of muscle fibers that are not easily fatigued and are well suited for prolonged low-intensity activity. These muscles include the deepest abdominal layer (transversus abdominis and obliques), the pelvic floor, the gluteals, and select muscles around the shoulder girdle. Good core stability is important because muscles that are anchored to a stable base (e.g., pelvis, spine, or shoulder blades) are able to act more efficiently. Both improved efficiency and increased strength will reduce the amount of energy required to perform a task. This results in higher levels of work maintained for longer periods and therefore improved endurance. Perfect for triathletes!

Core and pelvic control can be improved by undertaking a four- to six-week program of daily stability exercises tailored to your needs (for specific core-strengthening exercises, refer to chapter 7). Once control is satisfactory, a 20-minute advanced program should be incorporated three times per week to maintain improvements.

Strong, flexible muscles are less susceptible to injury and, when working in correct symmetry, will improve joint stability. Due to the repetitive nature of triathlon, with most movements being in the front/back plane, triathletes are particularly susceptible to muscle strength imbalances, postural deviations, and overuse injuries. Weight-training programs should be devised to strengthen underused muscles and promote symmetry. I am a big supporter of the use of strength programs by triathletes to reduce the risk of injury and improve performance. Increased strength may be achieved through a supervised weight-training program or circuit classes two or three times per week, depending on the phase of training. I also advocate using free weight exercises on independent limbs to improve awareness of any strength differences that may exist or develop.

Yoga and Pilates

Yoga and Pilates are becoming increasingly popular forms of body maintenance. They can help improve flexibility, control, and strength—and, most important, enhance body awareness. Yoga is also believed to induce relaxation and stress reduction and may help improve mental performance.

INJURY TREATMENT

Your approach to even a minor injury can make or break your triathlon experience. Neglecting to properly treat an injury could lead to further complications and ultimately sideline you for weeks or months at a time, while also putting you at risk for reinjury once training is resumed. Smart injury treatment should involve establishing a good rehabilitation team, diagnosing and eliminating the cause of injury, and adequately resting the affected area.

The Rehabilitation Team

It's important for any injured athlete to establish a good rehabilitation team. This team may consist of any combination of the following: coach, sports physician, physiotherapist, osteopath, chiropractor, acupuncturist, massage therapist, podiatrist, dietitian, naturopath, sport psychologist, strength and conditioning coach or gym instructor, orthopedic surgeon, or other health professionals. Effective injury management involves each member of the rehabilitation team developing a good rapport with the athlete to promote a speedy return to competition.

Family, friends, and training groups can also play a positive role during periods of injury. They can help you to stay focused on the positives. Friends should become involved in cross-training alternatives to help you stay active and maintain cardiovascular fitness. As a result, you will have a more positive attitude toward injury treatment and will return to competition more quickly. Never be afraid to enlist the help of friends and family when you need it!

Steps of Injury Management

The first step of injury management is having your injury diagnosed. This involves a health professional taking a thorough and accurate history and using musculoskeletal testing or imaging procedures to establish the nature and extent of injury. This diagnosis will dictate the pathway of treatment required and the ideal amount of time before a return to full training or competition. However, you should also establish your goals and priorities, because these may dictate the actual time available before competition. A good rehabilitation team will understand these priorities and acknowledge that injury management does not always follow the ideal pathway. In this case, it is the role of the rehabilitation team to guide and advise you the best way possible.

Once the injury has been identified, management should involve correcting any abnormal musculoskeletal or biomechanical factors associated with the injury. Biomechanics may be corrected through the use of orthotic devices, braces, splints, taping, or other aids such as heel raises or wedges. Joint and muscle flexibility may require specific stretching or mobilizations. Treatment of increased soft tissue tone and tension may involve the use of such techniques as deep massage, fascial or myofascial releases, acupuncture, or dry needling. Poor body, joint, or muscle control or strength may require specific exercises with the long-term aim of progressing to a strength program that incorporates weights or other forms of resistance.

Unfortunately, there are no set guidelines for managing specific injuries. Every injury will require slightly different management depending on severity and duration of injury, previous history of injury, your understanding of and response to treatment, and the skill of the treatment provider.

It is essential that the cause of the injury is identified and eliminated. This may involve reviewing technique or assessing biomechanics and postural factors, joint and muscle flexibility, or muscle control and strength. Failing to perform this step may result in the return of injury and a very unhappy athlete!

Reduced Training Load Versus Complete Rest

It's rare that a triathlon injury requires complete rest from all three disciplines. Usually a reduction in training load (frequency, intensity, or duration) or a change in technique will allow adequate and timely injury management. As a physiotherapist working with elite and age-group triathletes, my first priority is to try to establish a balance between allowing the athlete to continue training so she maintains neuromuscular firing patterns and reducing load to allow healing. You, as an athlete, must understand why and for how long you need a reduced load from set activities. This understanding will improve compliance and injury management.

MAINTAINING FITNESS DURING INJURY

One of the most difficult aspects of injury management is succumbing to a loss of fitness during rehabilitation. However, with the right approach, it's possible for most athletes to maintain a high level of fitness while they rehabilitate an injury. And for triathletes, rehab can serve as an opportunity to strengthen other areas of training. This section describes specific strategies for maintaining fitness during injury.

Cross-Training for Cardiovascular Fitness

One of the greatest benefits of competing in a sport that incorporates three distinct disciplines is that sustaining an injury that limits participation in one discipline usually gives you the opportunity to improve in another. A common example is the triathlete with a tibial stress fracture who is unable to run for six weeks. This period rarely restricts swim training and therefore allows the athlete to incorporate additional swim sessions or other cross-training strategies to maintain cardiovascular fitness *and* improve swim performance.

Cross-training strategies such as water-based training (water running or aqua aerobics), in-line skating, cross-country skiing, or working out with gym equipment such as stair machines and elliptical trainers can all be used to maintain cardiovascular fitness during periods where full weight bearing must be avoided.

Water running is a common training option for injured athletes. It reduces the stress and weight-bearing forces on injured soft tissues, bone, and joints while still allowing maintenance of cardiovascular fitness and some of the neuromuscular patterns used during land running. Water running can be performed in shallow water (less than three feet in depth) or by using a floatation belt in deep water (more than five feet in depth). Proper technique must be maintained while water running. The goal is to replicate dry land running technique to enhance the crossover effect of technique and patterns of muscle use. Both coach and athlete should also recognize that direct transfer of land-based run training is difficult because the physiological responses to water running are lower than those to land-based running. It is generally accepted that target heart rates during deep water running should be prescribed at 12 to 17 beats per minute lower than during land running.

When used correctly, training alternatives such as in-line skating and cross-country skiing can be extremely useful in maintaining fitness and improving core stability. They can provide a fresh alternative to your normal swim, bike, and run routines.

Focusing on Technique, Control, and Strength

Most overuse injuries occur as a result of poor training programs, poor technique, or inadequate control and strength. Periods of reduced training load due to injury or illness provide an ideal opportunity to focus on and improve each of these areas.

Technique drills can be modified according to the injury management conditions. For example, during running an athlete's body experiences a force of four times her body weight through the weight-bearing limb. To reduce this force by half, many drills can be performed in double-leg support positions. Alternatively, for triathletes with shoulder pain, the use of long fins in swimming significantly reduces the amount of force generated by the shoulder muscles and allows the athlete to perform useful water awareness drills. Control exercise programs and weight-training programs can usually be modified at this time to concentrate on areas of weakness.

Periods of injury or relative "downtime" should be used to develop routines and form good habits by implementing the body maintenance strategies discussed earlier in this chapter.

15

Training Through Pregnancy

Bonnie Berk, RN

When women become pregnant, so much of the information they are bombarded with speaks to what they should not be doing during their pregnancy: Don't consume alcohol, don't smoke, limit your caffeine intake, and so on. But what about what you *can* do? And what happens to your training regimen when you're an athlete?

As a triathlete, your lifestyle revolves around being active, putting your body to the test, and training for peak performance. And while there's no doubt that you should not train at the same high intensity during pregnancy that you would while training for a big race, there are ways to incorporate training into a healthy, happy pregnancy that will leave both you and your baby in great shape.

SETTING REALISTIC GOALS DURING PREGNANCY

The first rule is to realize that once you become pregnant, it's time to switch your focus from training for triathlon to training for the event of a lifetime!

As you know, training is sport specific. If you want to be a good runner, you need to run. In pregnancy, you need to start training as soon as you learn you're pregnant. There is some controversy about being able to strengthen an already stretched muscle, so the sooner you work on strengthening muscles that support the pregnancy, the easier it will be for your body once the baby starts growing in size. You'll also need to continually modify your training program to meet the increasing demands of growing a baby.

While moderate exercise intensities have been proven to be beneficial in pregnancy, strenuous exercise during pregnancy has not been well studied. There are concerns that during strenuous workouts (exercise above 80 percent of your max heart rate and more than one hour in duration), the woman is competing for oxygen with her fetus. Exercise causes diversion of blood from the internal organs, including the uterus, to the working muscles. The harder you exercise, the more blood is directed away from the uterus and your baby.

Some researchers believe that physically fit women have more oxygen-carrying capacity on their hemoglobin, which makes up for the decrease in blood flow to the baby. Unfortunately, there is controversy surrounding this issue, so it is best to err on the side of safety. If the risks of exercising strenuously outweigh the benefits, then why take unnecessary risks?

For many women athletes, reducing exercise intensity is a challenge. They fear that changing their training habits will negatively affect the momentum they worked so hard to attain. However, the reverse is true. By adapting training goals to meet the needs of your pregnant body, you will help reduce the risk of injury to both you and your baby, thereby preparing you to continue your training with renewed devotion once your body has recovered from pregnancy.

Other issues concerning strenuous exercise during pregnancy include increased internal body temperature, the effects of the hormone relaxin on the pregnant woman's joints, as well as consuming enough calories to support the growing fetus. However, if you follow the exercise safety tips included in this chapter, you should be able to continue training throughout pregnancy and enjoy a healthy pregnancy and postpartum period.

Before you review the specific exercise guidelines for triathlon, consider the following general exercise guidelines:

- Exercise to feel good, to reduce the common discomforts of pregnancy, and to maintain your fitness level. Do not try to achieve great gains. Regular moderate exercise is preferable to intermittent strenuous activity.

- Communicate with your obstetric health care provider regarding your training goals and have him monitor your baby for adequate growth and development.

- Dress for the weather. If it is hot outside, exercise in the morning or evening, not midday. Layer clothing so you can decrease body temperature as your body temperature rises. If it is cold outside, wear warm clothing. In general, try to avoid exercising in extreme temperatures. On very hot or cold days, exercise indoors.

- Never exercise if you have a fever. High internal body temperatures, especially in early pregnancy, are associated with birth defects. Avoid using hot tubs and saunas.

- Be sure to eat a light, low-fat snack at least one to two hours prior to exercise to avoid low blood sugar. If you typically exercise in the morning before breakfast, drink at least eight ounces of juice before you exercise.

- Never hold your breath! With resistance exercises, be sure to exhale on the effort.

- Drink plenty of noncaffeinated fluids before, during, and after a workout. Be sure to replace fluids even if you choose swimming as an exercise activity. Dehydration is a threat whether exercising in the water or on land.

- Wear sunscreen if you are exercising outdoors. Pregnant women are more susceptible to sunburn.

- Do a low-intensity warm-up for 5 to 10 minutes (e.g., walk slowly, bike slowly, and so forth) prior to performing any exercise.

- Avoid performing any exercises on your back after the first trimester. This can decrease blood flow to the baby.

- Monitor heart rate during peak levels of aerobic activity to ensure that exercise intensity is within a desired range. Pregnant women should keep exercise intensity between 50 and 80 percent of their maximum heart rate. If you don't already know your max heart rate, a general guideline is 220 minus your age. To find your desired range, multiply that number by 50 percent and 80 percent: $(220 - age) \times .50$ and $(220 - age) \times .80$.

- During pregnancy, your heart rate will rise about 10 to 15 beats per minute above your nonpregnant heart rate. So, measuring heart rate is a poor predictor of exercise intensity. In addition to measuring your heart rate, monitor your "perceived exertion." Exercise at an intensity that allows you to maintain a conversation. If you are feeling out of breath, your baby may not be getting adequate oxygen.

- Always cool down for 5 to 10 minutes after exercising by slowly decreasing your pace and performing gentle stretches.

- Never exercise to the point of fatigue.

- Avoid competitive sports throughout your pregnancy. Competing while pregnant may push you beyond your individual tolerance level.

- Eat a nutritious diet and increase caloric intake to offset calories burned during exercise. You will need to consume at least an additional 100 calories for every hour of exercise.

- Listen to your body! Every day, you are changing. What you did yesterday might not be feasible today. Rest when you get tired. Remember, if you are feeling tired and worn out, your baby is probably not getting enough glucose or oxygen.

Warning Signs

The following are symptoms that require you to stop exercising and consult your obstetric health care provider:

- Dizziness or faintness
- Shortness of breath
- Irregular or rapid heart beat (palpitations)
- Chest pain
- Difficulty walking
- Decreased fetal movement
- Vaginal bleeding
- Uterine contractions
- Excess vaginal fluid
- Calf pain or swelling

Symptoms of Overtraining in Both Mom and Baby

Women who are accustomed to training for long periods throughout the day may have a difficult time reducing the amount of training time during pregnancy. The following are symptoms of overtraining during pregnancy:

- Excessive fatigue
- Chronic pain in joints or muscles
- Loss of motivation to exercise
- Increased susceptibility to injury
- Frequent upper respiratory infections

When a pregnant woman overtrains, her baby is affected. If the exercise is interfering with the baby's ability to get enough nutrients or oxygen, the baby may not grow adequately, resulting in a small-for-gestational-age infant. The long-term effects of a baby being smaller than average are not fully understood, but researchers and obstetric health care providers believe small-for-gestational-age infants are associated with emotional and learning disabilities in childhood.

During a rigorous exercise session, the baby may not move as much as usual. Generally, after an exercise session, the baby will move two or three times within the first 30 minutes. If you notice a decrease in movement after exercise, consult your doctor or midwife. Once it's determined that your baby is okay, modify exercise intensity and consider exercising less often.

Disregarding your body's signals to slow down poses risk of injury to yourself and your baby, and it may compromise athletic performance postdelivery. Injury risks include back injury, knee injury, or premature labor that requires bed rest for the remainder of your pregnancy. Too much strenuous exercise could affect fetal growth and development, effects of which may last a lifetime.

Just like a triathlon, pregnancy and childbirth are athletic events. To meet the demands of pregnancy and have a positive birthing experience, you need to switch your training goals. And even though you won't be training as intensely as you did when you were not pregnant, you may find that after you deliver, you have more energy and stamina because of the physical demands that pregnancy places on your body. In fact, in the early part of the 20th century, European athletic trainers encouraged women athletes to get pregnant as a means of strengthening their bodies!

There are many unknowns when it comes to pregnancy, and there are many things you can't control. But by eating nutritiously and exercising at appropriate intensity levels, you know that you're doing what's safest for you and your baby.

© John C. Russell/Team Russell

While competition should be avoided during pregnancy, you needn't lose all your triathlon-specific fitness.

TRIATHLON TRAINING AND PREGNANCY

Although pregnancy is a time to maintain and even improve your health, it is not a time to improve in any of the disciplines of triathlon. Instead, your triathlon training should be used to influence a healthy pregnancy while helping to keep you in touch with the sport you love.

The best way to train while you are pregnant is to focus on shorter, more frequent workouts as opposed to exercising for long periods. For example, on weekdays, plan to swim for 30 minutes to an hour in the mornings, and then either bike or walk/run for 30 minutes to an hour in the afternoons (following the intensity guidelines outlined in this chapter). Then, on the weekends, get some rest and consider emphasizing yoga and core training (which can greatly enhance your delivery).

Mix and match your workouts to suit your specific needs. Listen to your body and adjust your training schedule according to your individual tolerance level (remember, you should feel energized not fatigued). Alternate workouts to avoid overuse injuries.

Following are guidelines for incorporating a triathlon lifestyle into your pregnancy.

Training During Your First Trimester

Your first sign of pregnancy might be unexplained nausea, breast tenderness, or a feeling of being "out of breath" without exerting too much effort. All of these symptoms are related to the increase in hormones that help support a healthy pregnancy.

If you listen to your body, it will tell you to slow down, rest, and eat foods that are healthy for both you and your baby. Just because you don't look pregnant doesn't mean you can continue training at high intensity levels. The minute you find out you're pregnant, it's time to adapt your workouts. Consider the following.

Swimming

Swimming is probably the best exercise you can do during your pregnancy. Particularly during the second and third trimesters, the water is the only place a pregnant woman is "light on her feet," and swimming provides a good strength and aerobic workout. Swimming is also an activity where it is easy to adjust pace according to how you feel.

During your first trimester, swim as often as you like (within the appropriate intensity), but also realize that just like in regular training you should take recovery time between workouts. Four or five swim workouts a week is a healthy target.

Biking

Biking is also a great way to exercise in the early months of pregnancy, provided you follow the prescribed exercise safety guidelines. In the later months of pregnancy, your balance may be compromised, and you should switch to a stationary cycle.

During your first trimester, consider cycling up to four days per week at no more than 80 percent of your max heart rate.

Running

Running within your target heart rate is fine in the early months of pregnancy. Some people mistakenly believe that running might interfere with implantation of the embryo. Usually, though, the egg is firmly embedded before a woman is aware that she's pregnant. Some women are also concerned about running causing a miscarriage. However, research confirms that there are very few lifestyle factors that will lead to miscarriage during early pregnancy, assuming you have no other risk factors.

If you have a solid running base, you can consider running within your target range up to four days a week. Adding a day off from running between each run workout will offer a safer approach that still allows you to stay in great shape and helps you ease into a decreased run program as your pregnancy progresses.

Weight Training and Other Exercises

You can safely continue your weight-training program, but be careful never to hold your breath and to lift no more weight than you can comfortably manage for 12 to 15 repetitions. After each exercise, stretch the muscles you just worked before performing another set.

In addition to your swim, bike, and run regimen, keeping your core muscles strong will help you avoid low back pain, may enhance delivery, and will likely decrease recovery time after delivery. As pregnancy progresses, your balance is also compromised, which may hamper your training. Emphasizing balance and core exercise early in your pregnancy will help you in the later months. Following are some exercises to practice throughout your pregnancy.

KEGEL EXERCISES

The Kegel exercise is the most valuable pregnancy exercise you will practice. Pregnancy and childbirth put stress on the muscles of the pelvic floor that support the expanding uterus, bladder, and bowel. When these muscles are weak, you may experience increased discomfort in the third trimester of pregnancy, urinary incontinence, and decreased sensation during sexual intercourse.

Practicing Kegel exercises will help you do the following:

- Strengthen and tone pelvic floor muscles
- Improve comfort during the later stages of pregnancy
- Prevent or alleviate urinary incontinence
- Speed up the healing process after an episiotomy
- Improve sexual satisfaction

To perform the Kegel exercise, find a comfortable position. Breathe slowly and deeply. As you exhale, gradually (to the count of five) tighten the muscles around your vaginal opening as if to pull it up toward the inside of your belly button (be sure to relax your shoulders, neck, and jaw—only your pelvic floor muscles are tight). Inhale and relax. Perform at least 20 Kegels twice a day.

ROUNDED CAT STRETCH

While on your hands and knees in a tabletop position (i.e., your back is flat), check your low back with your hands to make sure your back is straight. Take a breath. As you exhale, tighten your abdominal muscles, perform a posterior pelvic tilt, and slowly round your back, tucking your chin in (see figure 15.1a).

During inhalation, bring your back to a "hollow cat back" while keeping your abdomen firm (see figure 15.1b). Continue this exercise for 12 breath cycles, and then rest with your buttocks on your heels and your arms stretched above the crown of your head (child's pose). Repeat for another 12 breath cycles.

Figure 15.1   Rounded cat stretch.

BELLY BREATHING

Sit in a comfortable position with good posture (ears over shoulders, and shoulders over hips). As you inhale, relax your belly. As you exhale, pull your belly toward your spine to "hug the baby." Repeat for 20 breath cycles.

BALANCING SUNBIRD

Starting on your hands and knees with your back flat (tabletop position), stretch your right leg behind you. Keeping your back straight, raise the heel to the level of your buttocks or below (see figure 15.2a). Keep your abdominal muscles engaged to support your low back, and hold for three to five breaths. Bring your right leg in and repeat the exercise on the left side. Bring your left leg in and rest in child's pose.

Return to tabletop position and straighten your right leg behind you, raising your heel to the level of your buttocks or below. Shift your weight onto your right hand and straighten your left arm next to your left ear (see figure 15.2b). Balance in this position while you continue to breathe normally for three to five breath cycles. Use the muscles of your abdomen to support your back. Repeat on the opposite side. Rest in child's pose. As pregnancy progresses, try to keep the extended leg at or below hip level to avoid overstressing the low back.

Figure 15.2 **Balancing sunbird.**

Figure 15.3   Hip flexor/monkey stretch.

HIP FLEXOR/MONKEY STRETCH

Start by kneeling on both knees. If this is uncomfortable, roll a towel or blanket under your knees for additional padding. Move your right foot forward, just in front of your right knee. Interlace your fingers on top of your right knee. Inhaling, shift your weight forward and hold for three to five breaths (see figure 15.3). Repeat on other side.

STORK POSE

Stand with good posture with your feet hip-width apart. Shift your weight onto your right leg while bringing your left foot to the inside of your right leg. Keep your palms together in front of your heart center (see figure 15.4). Hold this pose for as long as you can and then switch to your other leg. If you feel balanced, try to raise your arms above your head while maintaining balance.

Figure 15.4   Stork pose.

Keeping Active During Your Second Trimester

By the second trimester, most women will feel more like themselves again. Around the 20th week of pregnancy, hormones start to level off and nausea subsides. You will notice that you are now "showing," and you may even feel your baby moving.

Swimming

Continue your swimming but pace yourself according to your energy level. If you have a hard time with the rhythm of your breath when swimming freestyle, alternate to breast- and backstrokes. You can also consider taking a pregnancy water fitness class or engaging in water jogging.

Swim as many days as you like but remember to allow your body to recover from the movements. No matter how low impact the activity, your muscles will always benefit from time to recover and rebuild.

Biking

Pregnancy increases the curves in your back, making you appear "round shouldered" and predisposing you to low back discomfort. The increased weight of your breasts may also pull your upper body forward. As your baby grows, it might be more difficult for you to pedal in a forward position without hitting your abdomen. This is a good time to switch your biking posture. Instead of leaning forward by rounding your back, try flexing at the hips and keeping your back straight. This can be easily accomplished by switching from a traditional bike to a recumbent bike at the gym.

If you feel up to it, consider cycling three to five days per week during your second trimester.

Running

In the early part of the second trimester, you might still be able to run but at a lesser intensity (shoot for closer to 50 percent of max heart rate than 80 percent) and for shorter periods. Again, listen to your body, and consider alternating between a walk and jog at this point. Splitting up your workout time into two segments might also be helpful. Run or walk up to five days per week at the recommended intensity.

Weight Training and Other Exercises

Now's the time to decrease the weight being lifted and increase the number of repetitions to 20 per set. Weight-training exercises performed while lying on your back should be avoided. To prevent low back discomfort, try lifting free weights while sitting on a physio ball as opposed to a weight bench.

In addition to the core-conditioning exercises discussed earlier, following are some additional exercises to incorporate during your second trimester.

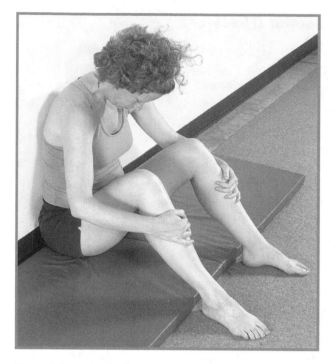

Figure 15.5   Sit-backs.

SIT-BACKS

Sit with your knees apart and your feet flat on the floor. Place your hands on your shins. Exhaling, pull your belly toward your spine and bring your hips forward, rounding your back. Inhale and straighten your spine. Repeat 10 to 12 times. Follow with Monkey Stretch (discussed on page 214).

A good way to be sure you are rounding the low back properly is to perform the exercise against a wall. When you round your back, you should feel your low back touching the wall behind you (see figure 15.5). As you straighten your back, your low back or waist area should move away from the wall.

SIT-BACKS WITH SPINAL TWIST

This exercise involves a modified form of sit-backs. Sit with your knees apart and your feet flat on the floor. Place your hands on your shins. Exhaling, pull your belly toward your spine and round your back while turning your torso to one side. Inhaling, straighten your spine. Repeat on the other side. Alternate sides for a total of 10 to 12 times. Follow with Monkey Stretch.

GARLAND POSE

From a tabletop position, shift your weight onto the balls of your feet. Extend your arms between your knees (see figure 15.6). Hold for three to five breaths.

Figure 15.6   Garland pose.

WALL-SUPPORTED BACK STRETCH

Lean your hips against a wall with your heels about six inches from the wall; your arms are relaxed by your sides and your knees are slightly bent. As you exhale, bring your chin toward your chest and slowly "peel" your back off of the wall (see figure 15.7). Continue to breathe normally, and each time you exhale, try to stretch a little bit further. Do this for three to five breath cycles. Then, as you exhale, tighten your abdomen and slowly bring your upper body back onto the wall starting at the base of your spine and slowly working up toward your head. Repeat this sequence three times.

Figure 15.7   Wall-supported back stretch.

Figure 15.8   Bound angle (butterfly pose).

BOUND ANGLE (BUTTERFLY POSE)

Sit with good posture and with the soles of your feet together. Hold your ankles as your knees press toward the floor. Stretch up through your spine. Lean forward and hold this position for three to five breaths. See figure 15.8.

SQUATTING

From a tabletop position, place your feet wider than your hips and walk your hands toward your knees while shifting your weight onto the balls of your feet and then, if you can, your heels. (Your knees will be off the floor, and you will be in a squatting position.) Bring your palms together in front of your heart with your elbows in front of your shins (if this is difficult, keep your hands on the floor for balance). Hold for three to five breaths. The squatting exercise will help stretch the muscles around the pelvis, making room for the baby and aiding in the labor and delivery process.

Cool-Down

At the end of every exercise session, lie in a comfortable position on your side. Close your eyes and relax your body. Breathe deeply and visualize the tension being released from all the muscles in your body. Imagine your body as being like ice melting in the sun. It is during this rest period that your body is able to restore balance. When you are ready, take a couple of deep breaths and slowly resume a sitting position.

Staying Fit in the Final Stretch

The third trimester may feel like the longest three months of your life! But don't get discouraged; there truly is light at the end of the tunnel.

Women are generally surprised by how tired they feel during the last trimester. But by this time, you will have gained anywhere from 20 to 30 pounds, assuming you have not gained any weight in addition to "baby weight." Go into a supermarket and pick up four five-pound bags of sugar and see how you feel carrying them around for a while. This is what you are carrying every minute of every day.

Be good to yourself. Consider this equation:

$$\text{body mass} \times \text{work of exercise} = \text{exercise intensity}$$

When your body mass increases, the exercise intensity increases even when the work of the exercise session stays the same. So, during the second and third trimesters, as your weight increases, you need to actually reduce the work of exercise to maintain the same intensity.

Swimming

Swimming remains the single best exercise you can do in the third trimester. While keeping in mind the recommendations given for the first and second trimesters, consider swimming as often as you feel up to it.

You can also use the water to create resistance for strength maintenance (e.g., biceps curls, triceps exercises, lunges), which is preferable to using free weights or machines during this period.

Biking

Switch to stationary biking if you haven't already. Decrease resistance so your knees are not working too hard. Remember, your knees are supporting you and your baby all day. And with the addition of the hormone relaxin in your body, you are more at risk for knee injury. Again, bike as often as you feel up to it without pushing yourself.

Walking or Running

Walking or jogging in water is much better for you now than running. Breaking up your walk into two or three segments throughout the day will help to reduce stress on your hips as well as your back.

If you keep the impact low, you can walk as often as you like. You'll find that your body will speak very clearly about what it can and can't do during this final phase of pregnancy.

Rest

Now is a good time to plan to rest at least 30 minutes a day on your side. The best indication of fetal health is fetal movement. While you rest, count the number of times your baby kicks or moves. Ideally, you want to feel at least 10 kicks in a 2-hour time frame. Check with your health care provider regarding fetal movement guidelines.

Postdelivery Training Recommendations

Remember that you are recovering from your biggest endurance test ever, which means it's important to listen to your body and do only what you comfortably can. Start Kegel exercises as soon as possible and continue to practice them as much as possible. Some women start "Kegeling" right on the recovery table! Every time you feed your baby, perform about 20 Kegels. You can also practice the belly breathing that you did during pregnancy to help strengthen the transverse abdominal muscles, which are stretched during pregnancy.

Swimming

You should avoid swimming until any vaginal bleeding stops and your cervix is closed (which usually takes about four to six weeks), but you can continue to stretch and take frequent walks throughout the day. Try low-intensity walking at least 20 minutes in the morning and 20 minutes in the afternoon or evening.

Biking

Biking is also not a good idea until your body has recovered, especially if you had an episiotomy. If you have a stationary recumbent bike, consider starting with 10 to 15 minutes a day as soon as you feel strong enough. To err on the safe side, avoid cycling until at least four weeks after delivery, depending on how you feel. As with any form of exercise, start back slowly and build in duration and intensity gradually.

Walking or Running

Babies love the outdoors, and so will you after being in the house all day. If it's too cold or too hot to take the baby for a walk, see if your spouse or a relative can watch the baby while you take a "relaxing" walk (as soon as you have the energy to do so). Using an indoor treadmill is also a great way to get your fitness back when you have a newborn.

Continue taking walks for the first month after your delivery. Then, depending on how you feel, consider starting your run training again (slowly). Each individual is different, but consider starting with a 20-minute run three days a week, and avoid adding more than 10 percent duration per week.

Don't push yourself too much in the early days postpartum, especially if you had a cesarean delivery. As in pregnancy, listen to your body, eat nutritiously, and give your body some much needed rest.

GETTING BACK INTO RACING SHAPE

Once your health care provider gives you the go-ahead to start training again, you will want to gradually build back up (over a period of 6 to 12 weeks) to where you were before pregnancy. The specific time frame will depend on the type of delivery you had and how well you are feeling postpartum. The key is to listen to your body.

If you are breast-feeding, it is always a good idea to feed your baby prior to training. That way, you won't have the weight of "full" breasts to impede you in any way. If you find you need to feed your baby after a training period, wash your nipples with water and pat them dry before feeding. Babies typically do not like the taste of sweat mixed with mother's milk.

The best way to get back into training is to perform Pilates exercises or work with a stability ball to strengthen your stretched-out core. If you need to exercise with your baby, check out the many jogging strollers that are available.

As you resume your workouts, listen to your body and keep a positive attitude. Remember, you will still be getting up throughout the night, and taking care of a new baby takes lots of energy. If you find that you are getting tired, allow yourself time to rest.

Although there are many sacrifices that come with motherhood, eventually you will find a balance between being a mother and being an athlete. And you'll experience a whole new level of accomplishment that you never imagined.

BIBLIOGRAPHY

Chapter 2

Friel, J. 1998. *The triathlete's training bible*. Boulder, CO: VeloPress.

Goldsmith, W. 2002. *Recovery based training: An alternate method of athlete preparation*. Coaches' Information Service [Online]. Available: http://coachesinfo.com.

McGee, B. 2000. *Magical running: A unique path to running fulfillment*. Boulder, CO: Bobbysez Publishing.

Noakes, T. 2001. *Lore of running*. 4th ed. Cape Town, South Africa: Oxford University Press.

Chapter 4

Australian Sports Commission. Gore, C.J., ed. 2000. *Physiological tests for elite athletes*. Champaign, IL: Human Kinetics.

Baker, A. 1998. *Bicycling medicine*. New York: Simon & Schuster.

Broker, J. 1999 & 2000. Cycling biomechanics. In *USA Triathlon level I & II coaching certification manuals,* ed. J. Jensen and T. MacNamara.

Burke, E. 2002. *Serious cycling*. 2nd ed. Champaign, IL: Human Kinetics.

Burke, E., ed. 1998. *Precision heart rate training*. Champaign, IL: Human Kinetics.

Friel, J. 1996. *The cyclist's training bible*. Boulder, CO: VeloPress.

Friel, J. 1998. *The triathlete's training bible*. Boulder, CO: VeloPress.

Gottschall, J.S., and B.M. Palmer. 2002. The acute effects of prior cycling cadence on running performance and kinematics. *Medicine and Science in Sports and Exercise* 34:1518-1522.

Janssen, P. 1987. *Training lactate pulse-rate*. Oulu, Finland: Polar Electro Oy.

Langley, J. *Bicycling Magazine's complete guide to bicycle maintenance and repair.* 1990. Emmaus, PA: Rodale Press.

Lim, A. 2002. Personal communication.

McArdle, W., F. Katch, and V. Katch. 1996. *Exercise physiology: Energy, nutrition, and human performance*. 3rd ed. Baltimore: Williams & Wilkins.

Noakes, T. 2001. *Lore of running*. 4th ed. Cape Town, South Africa: Oxford University Press.

Phinney, D., and C. Carpenter. 1992. *Training for cycling*. New York: Berkeley Publishing Group.

Pruitt, A. 2001. *Medical guide for cyclists*. Chapel Hill, NC: RBR Publishing Co.

Scott, D. 1986. *Dave Scott's triathlon training*. New York: Simon & Schuster.

Chapter 6

Brukner, P., and K. Khan. 2001. The tired athlete. In *Clinical sports medicine*, 2nd revised ed., 787-797. New York: McGraw Hill.

Budgett, R. 2000. Overtraining and chronic fatigue: The unexplained Underperformance Syndrome (UPS). *International Sports Medicine Journal* 1(3).

Derman, W., M.P. Schwellnus, M.I. Lambert, M. Emms, C. Sinclair-Smith, P. Kirby, and T.D. Noakes. 1997. The 'worn-out athlete': A clinical approach to chronic fatigue in athletes. *Journal of Sports Sciences* 15:341-351.

Gleeson, M. 1998. Overtraining and stress response. *Sports Exercise and Injury* 4:62-68.

Meltzer, S. 2000. Nutritional strategies in the management of chronic fatigue in athletes. *International Sports Medicine Journal* 1(3).

Noakes, T. 2003. *Lore of running*. 4th ed. Champaign, IL: Human Kinetics.

Shephard, R.J. 2001. Chronic fatigue syndrome: An update. *Sports Medicine* 31(3):167-194.

Chapter 11

Humara, M. 1999. The relationship between anxiety and performance: A cognitive-behavior perspective. *Athletic Insight: The Online Journal of Sport Psychology* 1(2).

Marr, A. 2001. In the zone: A biobehavioral theory of the flow experience. *Athletic Insight: The Online Journal of Sport Psychology* 3(1).

Schofield, G., G. Dickson, K. Mummery, and H. Street. 2002. Dysphoria, linking and pre-competitive anxiety in triathletes. *Athletic Insight: The Online Journal of Sport Psychology* 4(2).

Chapter 13

Bussau, V.A., T.J. Fairchild, A. Rao, P. Steele, and P.A. Fournier. 2002. Carbohydrate loading in human muscle: An improved 1-day protocol. *European Journal of Applied Physiology* 87:290-295.

Gisolfi, C.V. and D.R. Lamb. 1990. *Perspectives in Exercise Science and Sports Medicine*, Vol. 3. Carmel, IN: Benchmark Press.

Res, P., Z. Ding, M.O. Witzman, R.C. Sprague, and J. L. Ivy. The effect of carbohydrate-protein supplementation on endurance performance during exercise of varying intensity. *International Journal of Sports Nutrition and Exercise Metabolism*. In press.

Chapter 14

Allingham, C. 1995. The shoulder complex. In *Sports physiotherapy: Applied science and practice,* ed. M. Zuluaga et al., 357-406. Melbourne: Churchill Livingstone.

Brosseau, L., L. Casimiro, S. Milne, V. Robinson, B. Shea, P. Tugwell, and G. Well. 2003. Deep transverse friction massage for treating tendonitis (Cochrane Review). In *The Cochrane Library,* Issue 3. Oxford: Update Software.

Burns, A.S., and T.D. Lauder. 2001. Deep water running: An effective non-weightbearing exercise for the maintenance of land-based running performance. *Military Medicine* 166(3):253-258.

Burns, J., A.M. Keenana, and A.C. Redmond. 2000. The relationship between foot type and lower limb overuse injury in triathletes. Pre-Olympic Congress Sports Medicine and Physical Education International Congress on Sport Science, Australia.

Burns, J., A.M. Keenana, and A.C. Redmond. 2003. Factors associated with triathlon-related overuse injuries. *Journal of Orthopaedic Sports Physical Therapy* 33(4): 177-194.

Carbon, R., P.N. Sambrook, V. Deakin, P. Fricker, J.A. Eisman, K. Maguire, and M.G. Yeates. 1990. Bone density of elite female athletes with stress fractures. *Medical Journal of Australia* 153:373-376.

Cafarelli, E. and F. Flint. 1992. The role of massage in preparation for and recovery from exercise. *Sports Medicine* 11:474-478.

Clements, K., B. Yates, and M. Curran. 1999. The prevalence of chronic knee injury in triathletes. *British Journal of Sports Medicine* 33(3):214-216.

Crampton, J. and J. Fox. 1987. Regeneration vs. burnout: Prevention is better than cure. *Sports Coach* 10(4):7-10.

Crawford, F., and C. Thomson. 2003. Interventions for treating plantar heel pain. In *The Cochrane Library*. Issue 3. Oxford: Update Software.

Curwin, S., and W.D. Stanish. 1984. *Tendonitis: Its aetiology and treatment*. Lexington, MA: Collamore.

Dowxer, C.N., T. Reilly, N.T. Cable, and A. Nevill. 1999. Maximal physiological responses to deep and shallow water running. *Ergonomics* 42(2):275-281.

Egermann, M., D. Brocai, C.A. Lill, and H. Schmitt. 2003. Analysis of injuries in long-distance triathletes. *International Journal of Sports Medicine* 24(4):271-276.

Ellis, J. 1986. Shinsplints: Too much too soon. *Runner's World* 21(3):50-53.

Funk, D.C., A.M. Swank, B.M. Mikla, T.A. Fagan, and B.K. Farr. 2003. Impact of prior exercise on hamstring flexibility: A comparison of proprioceptive neuromuscular facilitation and static stretching. *Journal of Strength and Conditioning Research* 17(3):489-492.

Gregor, R.J., and J.B. Wheeler. 1992. Knee pain: A biomechanical analysis in elite cyclists. Final report to the United States Olympic Committee Sports Science Division. November.

Gregor, R.J., and J.B. Wheeler. 1994. Biomechanical factors associated with shoe/pedal interfaces. *Sports Medicine* 17(2):117-131.

Hamer, P.W., and A.R. Morton. 1990. Water-running: Training effects and specificity of aerobic, anaerobic and muscular parameters following an eight-week interval training programme. *Australian Journal of Science and Medicine in Sport* 22(1):13-22.

Hamer, P.W., and B. Slocombe. 1991. The perceived exertion–heart rate relationship for deep-water running. Annual Scientific Conference in Sports Medicine, Canberra, Australia.

Hamer, P.W., D. Whittington, M. Spittles, and M. Yakovina. 1984. Cinematographical comparison of water running to treadmill running. Unpublished paper.

Holmes, J.C., A.L. Pruitt, and N.J. Whalen. 1991. Cycling knee injuries. *Cycling Science* 3(2): 11-15.

Korkia, P.K., D.S. Tunstall-Pedoe, and N. Maffulli. 1994. An epidemiological investigation of training and injury patterns in British triathletes. *British Journal of Sports Medicine* 28(3):191-196.

Kotke, F.J., D.L. Pauley, and P.A. Ptak. 1966. The rationale for prolonged stretching for the correction of shortening of connective tissue. *Archives of Physical Medicine and Rehabilitation* (June).

Kujala, U.M., K. Osterman, M. Kormano, M. Nelimarka, M. Hurme, and S. Taimela. 1989. Patellofemoral relationships in recurrent patellar dislocations. *Journal of Bone and Joint Surgery* 71B(5):788-792.

Manninen, J.S., and M. Kallinen. 1996. Low back pain and other overuse injuries in a group of Japanese triathletes. *British Journal of Sports Medicine* 30(2):143-149.

McLauchlan, G.J., and H.H. Handol. 2003. Interventions for treating acute and chronic Achilles tendinitis (Cochrane Review). In *The Cochrane Library,* Issue 3. Oxford: Update Software.

Meagher, J., and P. Boughton. 1990. *Sports massage: The classic handbook for every athlete.* New York: Station Hill Press.

Myerson, M.S., and W. McGarvey. 1999. Disorders of the Achilles tendon and Achilles tendinitis. *AAOS Instructional Course Lectures* 48:211-218.

O'Toole, M.L., W.D. Hiller, R.A. Smith, and T.D. Sisk. 1989. Overuse injuries in ultraendurance triathletes. *American Journal of Sports Medicine* 17(4):514-518.

Ramaratnam, S., and K. Sridharan. 2003. Yoga for epilepsy (Cochrane Review). In *The Cochrane Library,* Issue 3. Oxford: Update Software.

Simons, D. 2002. Understanding effective treatments of myofascial trigger points. *Journal of Bodywork and Movement Therapies* 6(2):81-88.

Smart, G.W., J.E. Taunton, and D.B. Clement. 1980. Achilles tendon disorders in runners: A review. *Medicine and Science in Sports and Exercise* 12(4):231-243.

Usabiaga, J., R. Crespo, I. Iza, J. Aramendi, N. Terrados, and J. Poza. 1997. Adaptations of the lumbar spine to different positions in bicycle racing. *Spine* 22(17):1965-1969.

Wilk, B.R., K.L. Fisher, and W. Gutierrez. 2000. Defective running shoes as a contributing factor in plantar fasciitis in a triathlete. *Journal of Orthopaedic and Sports Physical Therapy* 30(1):21-28.

INDEX

Note: The italicized *f* and *t* following page numbers refer to figures and tables, respectively.

ABOUT THE EDITOR

Christina Gandolfo is the editor in chief of *Her Sports* magazine and the former editor in chief of *Triathlete* magazine. She holds a bachelor's degree in journalism from San Diego State University and has more than 14 years of publishing experience.

As a sports journalist, Gandolfo has covered triathlon across four continents. She has also written for several endurance sports publications, including *Outside* magazine, and regularly contributes to www.IronmanLive.com.

An avid triathlete and distance runner, Gandolfo resides in San Diego, California.

Photo by Jennifer Yeast

ABOUT THE CONTRIBUTORS

Lisa Bentley is a professional triathlete, seven-time Ironman champion, and four-time top-10 finisher at the Hawaii Ironman Triathlon World Championship. She lives and trains in Caledon, Ontario, Canada.

Bonnie Berk is a registered nurse, master personal fitness trainer, registered yoga teacher, and founder of the award-winning Motherwell maternity fitness programs, which are offered by prestigious health and fitness facilities in the United States and abroad. She also developed the U.S. Army's physical fitness program for pregnant soldiers. Berk has a degree in health education and is completing a master's degree in health science and wellness. For more information about Motherwell and maternity fitness, visit www.motherwellfitness.com.

Gale Bernhardt served as the 2004 Olympic men's and women's triathlon team coach as well as the 2003 Pan Am Games coach. She is the author of *Training Plans for Multisport Athletes*, *The Female Cyclist: Gearing Up a Level*, and *Workouts in a Binder for Triathletes*. Bernhardt is an elite-certified coach by USA Cycling and USA Triathlon. Learn more about her coaching system at www.galebernhardt.com.

Lori Bowden is a professional Canadian triathlete and a two-time Hawaii Ironman World Triathlon champion with 12 career Ironman victories worldwide. She has finished four Ironman races in under 9 hours.

© John Segesta

Kimberly Brown, MS, RD, is a registered sport dietitian and Ironman triathlete. She is a regular contributor to *Triathlete* magazine and *Her Sports* magazine and a nutritional consultant to athletes worldwide via her Web site, www.kbnutrition.com. Brown lives in San Diego, California.

Linda Buchanan is one of the early figures in women's professional triathlon and a two-time world champion (1983 and 1986). She holds a master's degree in sport psychology.

Libby Burrell served as the U.S. triathlon team leader for the 2004 Olympics and is the director of the USA triathlon national teams program. A native of South Africa, she served as the country's 2000 Olympic triathlon team coach and is the former head of the sport science, physical education, and recreation department at the University of the Western Cape in Bellville, South Africa. Burrell holds a master's degree in sport science.

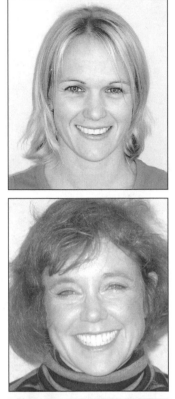

Britt Caling is a full-time physiotherapist who works with Triathlon Australia and their junior elite team for the World Triathlon Championships. She serves as a consulting lecturer for the University of Queensland physiotherapy department. In 2003 she traveled to France as physiotherapist to the Australian Institute of Sport for the European Triathlon Training Camp. Britt lives on the Gold Coast, Australia.

Liz Dobbins is a triathlon coach, director of women's services at the National Triathlon Academy, and a member of USA Triathlon's women's commission. A long-time competitive age-group triathlete, Dobbins holds a silver medal in world championship long-course racing.

Heather Fuhr is a 13-time Ironman champion and the 1997 Ironman Triathlon World Champion. Her Ironman marathon personal record of 2:51, set at the 1998 Ironman Switzerland, is the second fastest in history among women. She also holds the second-fastest run split at the Hawaii Ironman (3:04). Originally from Edmonton, Alberta, Canada, Fuhr now lives and trains in San Diego, California.

Jackie Gallagher began competing in triathlon in 1992 and won the elite Australian National Series in her first season. She spent eight years as a professional triathlete, winning the World Triathlon and Duathlon Championships in 1996 to become the only person ever to win both in the same year. With a master's degree in exercise physiology and cardiac rehabilitation, Gallagher is currently the head coach and program manager of the Australian Institute of Sport Triathlon Program.

Siri Lindley is the 2001 ITU World Champion and winner of the ITU World Cup series in 2001 and 2002. She is currently a triathlon coach and in 2004 coached the USA's Susan Williams to a bronze medal at the Olympics. Lindley also served as a television analyst for the Games in 2004, covering the Olympic triathlon for NBC.

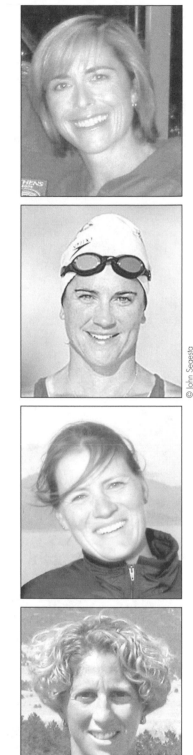

© John Segesta

Barb Lindquist swam competitively for Stanford University before becoming a professional triathlete. A former U.S. national champion, Lindquist has been ranked the top female short-course triathlete in the world multiple times and finished ninth at the 2004 Olympic triathlon in Athens.

Bettina Younge is a USAT-certified triathlon coach, USAC-certified cycling coach, and former professional cyclist. She holds a PhD in chemistry from Stanford University and is director of coaching for Total Trainer (www.totaltrainer.com), an online provider of free software that tracks and analyzes training.

Joanna Zeiger swam competitively for Brown University before becoming a triathlete. She placed fourth at the 2000 Sydney Olympics in triathlon and is a four-time top-10 finisher at the Hawaii Ironman World Triathlon Championships. Zeiger holds a PhD in genetic epidemiology from Johns Hopkins University.